London
Business
School
Series

Business forecasting

London
Business
School
Series EDITED BY M. E. BEESLEY

Business forecasting

A managerial approach

Thomas E. Milne

Longman

LONDON and NEW YORK

51668

LONGMAN GROUP LIMITED
Burnt Mill
Harlow
Essex CM20 2JE

Distributed in the United States of America by Longman Inc., New York

Associated companies, branches and representatives throughout the world

First published, 1975

ISBN 0 582 45052 7

Library of Congress Catalog Card Number: 74–82097

Set in IBM Journal, 10 on 12 point

Printed in Great Britain by
Whitstable Litho Ltd

This is for
Stewart and Alastair
for their future
is in our trust

Acknowledgements

We are grateful to the following for permission to reproduce copyright material: Haymarket Press for an extract from *Management Today*, January 1967, and The Controller of Her Majesty's Stationery Office for two tables and an extract from *Economic Trends*, No. 207, January 1971.

Contents

Preface

One writes a book in the belief that others will find it worth their while to read it. This implies that the author has a conceit that he has something worth saying to someone. Since prefaces are supposed to let the potential reader know whether the author has something worthwhile to say to him or not, and since this is far from being the first book to be written on business forecasting, perhaps I had better explain myself.

I have many friends who are managers, and my work brings me into contact with many more. Universally they recognize the need to form a systematic and coherent view of the future as a basis for making decisions. And yet their views on organized business forecasting frequently go far beyond healthy scepticism to an attitude of outright cynicism. It follows, therefore, that if organized forecasting has something valid to offer the manager, there must have been a communication failure somewhere. In tackling this book I have tried to diagnose the reasons for that failure and to rectify them. I believe there are three things wrong with the traditional presentations of business forecasting, and that these tend to alienate the intelligent manager.

First, existing accounts of forecasting are with few exceptions written for other forecasters in a cryptic and elliptical statistical jargon, which is hard even for the other forecasters to follow, and totally inaccessible to the non-statistically initiated. The few accounts designed for a non-technical (managerial) readership are reduced to a level of simplistic 'appreciation', far removed from any recognizable managerial frame of reference. Either way, it appears as though the mathematically arrogant are trying either to humiliate or to insult the intelligence of those whom they are supposed to be serving.

Second, existing accounts tend to take a partial view of forecasting, claiming that one or other approach is 'rational' or 'scientific' while all the others are 'naive'. The bewildered manager — indeed the bewildered practising forecaster frantically making the best of the data and techniques available to him — must be forgiven if he cries 'A plague on both your houses' and gives up.

Third, existing accounts frequently bear little relationship to the kind of problems which managers recognize as realistic, or to the unifying themes of management and administration, of which forecasting should form an integral part.

In this book I have strenuously sought to avoid those pitfalls. I started out to write a book of the traditional type with the added feature of case applications. As the material evolved and was discussed in courses and seminars with managers it became apparent that this was the wrong approach, not least because the techniques of analysis in the form in which they were usually presented never seemed to bear much relation to the case problems as managers saw them. It was then that I realized that my experience as a forecaster, of exercising a great deal of intuitive make do and mend in each situation, and treating each one on its merits rather than as a textbook job, was not something to apologize for. On the contrary, it was inherent in honest workmanship in serving the managers who had the decisions to make.

With the realization that management is messy, and honest forecasting has to be messy with it, this book began. It evolved into a conducted tour, designed for managers, of a forecaster's workshop: a workshop containing well tried tools, some sharp with regular maintenance and use, and some rusty through neglect: containing, too, elaborate models and inventions some of which work well enough while others are melons: some others are incomplete but might be made to work some day. As well as the tools of the trade, the tour includes some finished products, and some which went wrong. Throughout, the theme of the tour is, 'What will the bit we are looking at now do for regular managers?' Every effort is made to clarify the range of applications and limitations of the tools, the techniques and the perspectives.

Perspective is very important in a forecaster's workshop, just as it is in a manager's office. The perspective adopted for this tour is the manager's point of view. But this is not meant to be a hurried single evening tour. When we examine some aspect of the business we do so thoroughly, explaining how techniques work and what they are meant to achieve, and showing as far as is possible and relevant how the interested executive can operate them himself. As a matter of policy all the explanations are conducted as far as possible in English and arithmetic. Where incursions to a little mathematical notation are unavoidable, the starting assumption is that the reader has had no formal instruction in mathematics since he failed his 'O' levels twenty years ago. His ability to count and reason numerically is however assumed to be in the excellent working order which one would expect of a successful manager.

Much of the material in the book has been worked over in the classroom, in private discussions, and in forecasting assignments, from which it has appeared that the most acceptable order of presentation is one which is less than rigorously formal. As a result, little attempt is made to work from formal definitions and highly specified problems; instead the exposition proceeds from a general discussion of management problems involving futurity forward into the techniques, with technical terminology and rigorous working only being introduced by the time their meaning and purposes are entirely clear from the preceding discussion. We lose a lot of mathematical economy of expression in this way, but we hope to gain in communicability to the non-mathematician and non-economist. Another implication of adopting the viewpoint of the manager is that an attempt is made to bring into the fold all the approaches to forecasting which are in common currency, without attaching nice or nasty labels to any of them, but simply trying to show what sort of a job they will do.

As is by now evident, the book is pragmatic in nature. For problems, a number of real forecasting situations have been incorporated, with all of which I have personally been involved. No attempt is made to set out the whole case, or pretend that pat solutions exist where none are possible. The examples are used not to get answers so much as to illustrate how techniques can be used in real situations in order to contribute to the forecasting process. No attempt is made to duck the shortcomings as well as to expound the possibilities. For that reason, although specific questions are frequently raised (of the sort which students too often raise with me) answers tend to be more generalized. No apology is needed for not being more definitive: that comes when we are dealing with live issues and today's decisions.

Based though it is on pragmatism, I have tried not to produce a disintegrated book. It is integrated around a systems view of management (although knowing how much my manager friends mistrust my professional argot I do not believe that this term reappears until the last sentence of the text proper). If anyone should have the hardihood to read from here to there, they should by then understand what I have been trying to say in this preface.

Finally, it is necessary to acknowledge, with sincere gratitude, a host of contributors to this work, who in the absence of these words, would go totally unthanked. When a book has been in preparation as long as this one, the list of those even quite directly involved becomes so extensive that individual acknowledgement of them all becomes impossible. I would therefore plead the indulgence of those who should have been named, on the ground that the preface would have become inordinately long had I properly thanked everyone. Let me mention them by groups.

Among the most important contributions are the records of various forecasting jobs which the companies have all willingly allowed me to use. I apologize to some for the pseudonyms under which they appear. Then there are the many managers who have attended forecasting and marketing courses, and the Residential Course for Business Managers, in the Universities of Edinburgh and Glasgow. They have been responsible for many changes of direction in producing the book, and it has certainly come out vastly differently by virtue of what I learned from them. This applies even more forcefully for that small group of managers who are my friends and who have given generously of their time in discussing their forecasting problems with me.

Another important source from which I learned was colleagues, fellow students and former teachers in the Universities of Glasgow and Edinburgh and at Harvard Business School. There are many such who could spot some part of the text as being rehearsed with them at some, to them inconvenient, time.

None of those who have been so cavalierly covered by the foregoing blanket acknowledgements will, I believe, feel it unjust if I finish by thanking two people personally. The first is Mrs Maureen Christie. I have very much appreciated her care and skill in turning my hieroglyphics into usable manuscript. The second is my wife, Marion, who has had to suffer the strains of authorship afflicting her husband for an unconscionable time. She has borne this with great patience and goodwill and is in no small measure responsible for the fact that somehow this manuscript attained completion.

Tom Milne
University of Glasgow

August 1973

1 Forecasting and managerial action

1.1 What forecasting is and does

'You don't know what's going to happen tomorrow, next month, or next year any more than I do.' Utterances like this are commonplace in the professional fore-caster's life. They are generally true in fact. Their truth merely proves the obvious. Forecasters are not prophets.

This does not change the fact that managers are forecasters, and they are fore-casting for much of their time. They plan production in expectation of certain levels of sales. They set prices in expectation of certain levels of wages, raw material costs, financial availability, and sales. They build warehouses in expectation of certain levels of stocks and sales. They recruit labour, buy materials, arrange finance, or plan factories in expectation of certain levels of sales and other activity. And so on.

Business activity, and therefore managerial activity, is entirely based on expecta-tions. Management is about the uncertain future. Formal forecasting has a modest place in that grand scheme of things, in so far as it can offer support for well founded, rather than badly founded expectations. Good forecasters aspire less to providing answers than to providing intelligent points of view. They should help sharpen and clarify the intelligence system upon which managerial expectations are founded. Their end product is not facts but opinions: better thought out opinions than would exist in their absence. Their sole justification lies pragmatically in the extent to which the improved opinions lead to better, more efficient, decisions. Formal forecasting then is simply a support service to management.

Many decisions, perhaps most, need not embody explicitly forecasts derived from formal procedures. In many aspects of their activities, managers may be very confident about the future course of the key determinants of possible outcomes. In others, the margin of safety in the implementation of a decision may be so wide that a wide range of outcomes, even embracing all feasible outcomes, would be tolerable. Even here, however, this very confidence may be based on a coherent and intelligently based view of the future. In this context, the role of this book is to discuss the areas in which some sort of formal support may be required.

Forecasting is not, however, solely concerned with formulating a basis for intelligent expectations, its other major concern is with future uncertainty itself, and the consequences of that uncertainty for current decisions. We return to this theme in chapter 9, but let us illustrate it here with an example. Suppose that a toboggan manufacturer knows that his sales depend heavily on substantial snowfall over a reasonable area of Britain by mid-January. Given the notorious unpredictability of British weather, is the production of a sales forecast for any given winter an insoluble problem? In the obvious sense it is. But the production of a sales forecast is never an end in itself; the underlying general objective of any sales or other forecast is to give management a tool for maximizing long-run profits (or to achieve some other objective). The purpose of this section is not to discuss objectives, but only one particular aid to meeting them.

To begin with it is necessary to specify how much snow, over what areas of the country, by what date, lying for what length of time, make a material difference to sales. From the extensive records maintained by the Meteorological Office it would be possible to compute how often the various relevant weather conditions have occurred over past winters. Assuming that such a pattern continued in the future, probabilities of occurrence of heavy, timeous, well placed snowfalls could be worked out. Even with this simple example a lot of simplifying classification would be required, but might result in a table of expectations about conditions in the following form: Ideal, 1 year in 20; good 4 years in 20; moderate 8 years in 20; poor 5 years in 20; bad, 2 years in 20. The classifications ideal, good, moderate, poor, bad, could be associated with probable levels of demand for the toboggans which we suppose would be associated with production levels, if only we knew which outcome would be produced in the coming selling season. Since we do not know this we must now compute from in-company knowledge the likely profits or losses that would result from each of the five production levels at each of the five outcomes. The likely profit or loss must be weighted by the probability of the outcome in question, when each production level will be seen to be associated with a total profit or loss over the twenty years, and the production strategy which maximizes total profits, or avoids unsupportable losses in any one year, can be detected.

Summarizing, forecasting is a service whose purpose is to offer the best available basis for management expectations of the future, and to help management understand the implications for the firm's future of the alternative courses of action available to them at present.

Adequate forecasting involves understanding the wide variety of influences at present at work which will contribute to the shape of the future, large volumes of data processing to put raw information into managerially useful form, intricate knowledge of the working of the individual firm in order to work out the implications of future uncertainties for profitability. In this there is normally room certainly for specialist support, working closely with chief executives, in any organization where really difficult decisions are being made; that is decisions involving substantial risks with large quantities of resources at stake, in a situation of any complexity involving growth, decline or change. It is the fact that business situations today have these elements in an increasingly exigent form that accounts for the growth in formal business forecasting activity attested to by Reichard and others (Reichard, 1966; Butler and Kavesh, 1966).

Managers operate on the basis of information received from many sources, collected formally or absorbed informally. Information whose relevance is for the future is simply one type of the many required by managers. Beyond the fact that its relevance is orientated towards decisions involving futurity, there is nothing to distinguish it from any other information being regularly handled in the firm. From this it follows that the business of applying current knowledge to help get a feel for the future course of relevant things is just one aspect of the general information system employed by management to provide itself with necessary services. The task of designing coherent and interrelated management information systems is one which at the time of writing is still in its infancy in British business. But work is now going ahead in many British and overseas companies to rationalize the heterogeneous inputs to managerial decisions from the accounting and control systems, market research and sales reports, and production and quality control. The reporting of information relative to the future environment and standing of the firm will increasingly become engrossed in the well-managed firm's intelligence, information and control systems. Seen in this light, forecasting can be managed as a coherent activity, part of a larger one, unified not by its sources or methods, but by its purposes, which are to improve intelligence and sharpen control in certain areas where operational methods of working can be evolved (see Kelley, 1968).

Much of this book is based on a view of forecasting as an aspect of the information and control systems of the firm. This is its unifying theme. It is in contrast to earlier views of forecasting as little more than the collection, processing and projection of data in response to occasional specific management information needs. (An 'information systems' view of forecasting raises problems of managing forecasting activities which are dealt with in chapter 10.)

A forecasting system, to be instrumental in contributing to better management decision-making, needs certain conditions. First, it must involve the managers whose decisions are affected; second, individual forecasts and groups of forecasts have to be specifically relevant to the decisions being taken; third, the forecasts must not claim too much validity or authority; fourth, the users must be able to evaluate the shortcomings, which means, again, their involvement in the forecast's creation, and a careful statement of all assumptions, guesses and inadequate data involved in it; fifth, implications of the various probable errors in the predictions for the organizations need to be thoroughly worked through, so that management can evaluate the consequences of the probable range of likely outcomes; finally, management must at least know how badly things could go wrong if all the guesses turned out wrong. All these points apply equally to the creation of a single forecast for a projected capital investment decision, or the construction of a series of thousands of short run projections of the sales position of a warehouse's product line for stock control purposes.

In the current state of the craft, formal forecasting embraces four broad categories of activity. First, attempting to find regularities of economic behaviour which hopefully will carry over into the future; second, trying to relate occurrences relevant to management decisions to others whose occurrence regularly leads the relevant one by a sufficiently long time period that it can be used to predict the relevant one; third, asking people for their opinions or about their expectations relating to the future; and fourth, the creation of models of the interaction of the key variables in the firm (e.g. sales, profits, cash availability) with economic variables, (e.g. growth of gross national product, or changes in birthrate or bankrate), or with things the firm may do (e.g. increase advertising or change prices). The last, indeed, is an elaboration of the second, but one of sufficient magnitude to merit a class by itself. However, for summary purposes we can say that forecasting involves the search for regularities, relationships and responses.

When forecasting activity is viewed as part of the management information system, a number of naive but commonly made observations on the subject turn out to be irrelevant or misleading. There is no clear line of distinction among short-, medium- and long-term forecasts, between subjective and objective forecasts, point or band forecasts. The selection of methodology and techniques, and the mode of presentation of results, depend on the purposes for which the forecasts are required, the nature of available secondary sources, the type of primary material it is economical and possible to collect, the time limits within which the estimates are required, and whether the decisions to be based on the forecast are momentous enough to demand complex and detailed analysis or not.

In practice it is normally found that the application of basic techniques in a simple and commonsense manner is almost invariably adequate for the commonly encountered types of business decision. The number of situations in which esoteric methods are justifiable in terms of their contribution to reduction of uncertainty about a decision is small. Even decisions which may be critical to the long-term health of organizations are unlikely to obtain a more confident basis from development of sophistication in the application of any one technique, for example, regression analysis. A more fruitful approach is generally to *multiply the techniques* and the *number of ways* a technique can be brought to bear on the decision. This way there can be many, albeit unsteady, pointers to the future rather than a rigorous development of one pointer, for any one is inevitably based on the shaky foundations of ignorance.

1.2 The ends of forecasting

Forecasts are required for a number of common purposes. The first general use is for the creation of plans of action. As well as forecasts of sales and prices, use is often made of forecasts of market penetration, competitive activity, cash flows, capital investment, stock changes and other factors affecting future business prosperity. Often, however, the forecast of the individual factor's performance is dependent on a sales forecast in the first place. For example, cash flow is functionally related to sales volume and price. A forecast of these is likely to be the basis for short-run budget setting and control, funds forecasting, profit planning and, through this, longer term planning. In other words, it is impossible to evolve a worthwhile system of business control without one acceptable system of forecasts.

But, it is commonly argued, forecasts are always wrong. The business world is too complex to allow correct forecasting. Right or wrong, however, an agreed forecast is the basis for an agreed plan of action and ultimately becomes incorporated into that plan. Whenever managers plan any course of action, a forecast is implied. The argument of this book is that explicit and well reasoned forecasts are better than those implicitly based on hunch. Once the basis for any forecast has been arrived at, it must be open to discussion and amendment by the relevant executive team who will have to fulfil the plans. *The reasoning behind the forecast, therefore, must be fully spelled out so that there may be a basis for rational disagreement.* Once the forecast is agreed, there is an implication of managerial commitment to it. It is not a specialist's forecast, but management's forecast. In many respects, the reasoning is more important than whatever figures may finally emerge.

The second general use of forecasts is to be found in monitoring the continuing progress of plans based on the forecasts. A long-range corporate plan, for example, in which a critical forecast variable was aggregate national population, would not normally require to be drastically overhauled if the Registrar General's population forecasts were amended. But such an amendment would provide the earliest possible intimation of a need to re-examine the plan or its execution. To that extent forecasts serve rather the function of lighthouses to shipmasters at night, reference points for course and speed requiring action/no-action decisions.

A third function is illustrated by the plan which might be drastically untenable in the light of even, say, a small downward revision in population projections. The fact that the forecast, and hence the plan, was so highly sensitive to one of the determining variables ought to be evident in the course of forecast construction and this type of fact requires to be explicitly stated at the forecast presentation and execution evaluation. The forecast in this case provides a warning system of the critical factors to be monitored regularly because they might drastically affect the performance of the plan. These inter-relations are illustrated in Fig. 1.1.

1.3 Forecasting and capital investment decisions

This aspect of forecasting is dealt with first, because for many firms the first perception of a need for formal forecasting procedures arises in the face of a fixed capital investment decision. It arises when the chief executive asks for firm assurance that the output will be saleable over the life of the investment.

In fact this is a complex forecasting problem because a number of alternative

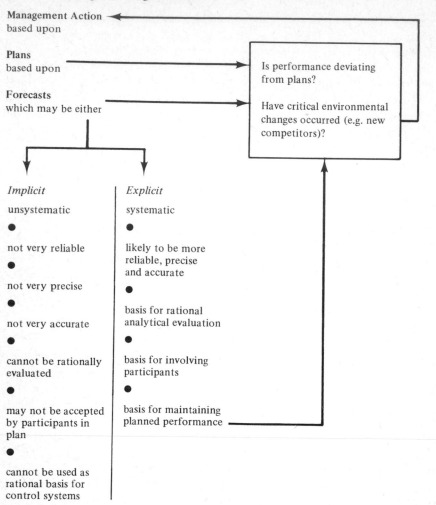

Fig. 1.1 The importance of systematic forecasts as a basis for management action.

possible investments, giving rise to different cost structures and marketing characteristics, are likely to be involved. These in turn give rise to the need to consider the
effects of alternative production run lengths, prices, quality differentials, sales
efforts and distribution systems. Additionally, the forecaster needs to consider the
pattern of sales growth from commissioning to capacity utilization (perhaps with
capacity being intended by the firm to be determined by market saturation levels),
and has the almost impossible task of assessing the likely longevity of the active
sales life of the product in light of determinable and indeterminable technological
innovation in the future.

For example, it is feasible to argue that the age of the internal combustion engine
as applied at present to road transport is coming to an end. It matters very much to

a car maker contemplating a new engine plant to know *when* it will end as a commercial proposition in his new cars. This depends on the rate of technological development of alternative power units on one hand, and their rate of market acceptance on the other (to say nothing of the problem of the future supply and price position of petrol). It requires more than a little courage to put a date on the transition.

This difficulty raises parenthetically the issue of the *planning horizon*. The planning horizon is simply the period over the future to which decisions being made now will be relevant. Thus the planning horizon to which a quarterly sales forecast or annual budget is relevant is contained in its title. The existence of more distant time horizons is relevant to these only in so far as they are explicitly or implicitly evaluated to provide a larger context within which the short period decisions stand self sufficient.

The individual's decision to purchase a packet of cigarettes refers to a relevant planning horizon of one or two days over which they will be consumed. It is a decision quite possibly made in the knowledge of a calculable probability of reduction in life span through contracting disease generally regarded as being induced by cigarette smoking. Once judgment is reached on the larger context it ceases to be relevant to the short-run decision, e.g. to buy a packet now or defer purchase till tomorrow, which is based on knowledge of likely availability of further supplies over the planning period, likely consumption (including an allowance for the chance of exceptional events such as attending a party where consumption may be very high) and availability at present of adequate cash (in light of competing claims).

For any corporate decision there are several relevant planning horizons, the impacts of which on a given decision should normally be considered and eliminated from the decision-making process in order from the furthest to the nearest.

The furthest horizon of all is infinity, and invokes the concept of the firm's survival. No plans will normally be accepted which endanger survival, and forecasts which indicate that survival is in jeopardy have clear implications for long-range policy decisions. Forecasts at this length are a matter of economic, social and technological evaluation on a very complex scale. Such evaluations tend to be very generalized and many have been published (see for example Brech, 1963; Beckerman, 1965).

Forecasts on which capital investment decisions have to be made cannot be constructed in the absence of a clear statement of (*a*) the relevant time scale over which the firm's executives expect the decision to remain operational; (*b*) the alternative decisions which senior executives regard as being feasible; and (*c*) any non-economic, non-technical restraints which the executives would place on the decision; for example, a project involving the evaluation of alternative sites may be constrained by the fact that executives are unwilling to operate in towns X and Y where they find the labour situation uncongenial.

Too often in practice the forecaster spends a great deal of valuable time and the company's money in ignorance of some of such key constraints. In this area, which tends to demand the services of a specialist, albeit perhaps temporarily seconded from another role in the firm, the importance of management giving a *really thorough* briefing to the forecaster cannot be overstressed. This problem can be mitigated by approaching the project in two stages, first a preliminary survey of the field of the relevant decision variables, such as locations, plant suppliers, product characteristics, the competitive situation, and longer term implications of decisions; this should conclude with a clear statement of what are regarded as the alternatives worth detailed study. Enough information is required here to let the executives know what is likely to go forward, and the broad grounds on which these decisions have been reached. The forecaster should then ask for explicit guidance as to directions which it is felt for any reason should not be pursued further, so that attention can be concentrated on the more promising avenues.

The process of selecting the most promising lines of approach is as much organizational as technical. Once the forecaster, or the forecasting team, has clear guidelines on which to work, the technical forecasting exercise can proceed unhampered, without reference back to higher authority, in the knowledge that he is dealing in the relevant areas.

It has already been argued that the selection of forecast methodologies depends on the purpose to which the forecast is to be put. Forecasts on which investment decisions are to be made should be of a nature which allow reliable discounted cash flow calculations to be made,* or to enable such other computations to be conducted as management may deem necessary.

In the face of the complexity of the data required and the importance of its being as reliable as possible, it becomes necessary in this sort of situation to utilize all the forecasting techniques which can be reasonably applied; and in the application of these techniques it is necessary to try to take account in the estimates of all

---

* DCF as a tool of investment planning is beyond the scope of this book: admirable accounts of the methodology and rationale for this technique are to be found in many standard works including ICI's *Assessing Projects* (1970). Essentially, the information required as an input to the DCF calculation is a statement of the cash flows created by the investment, both inward and outward, over the life of the investment. Future cash flows are discounted back to the present whereby a rational comparison can be made between the anticipated performance of alternatives. Since the future cash flows are normally calculated annually, it follows that a complex set of annual forecasts of sales volume and prices are required. As Alfred (1964), points out in his paper 'more time [than with alternative methods of investment planning] may be required to elucidate the assumptions (of future price levels, costs, length of life, etc.) necessary to evaluate the cash inflow; but an appreciation of these basic assumptions should be a prerequisite of any investment decision'. Alternative simpler (but generally inferior) methods of investment analysis include calculations of, for example, rate of return on capital, and the payback period approach (the length of time it takes for an investment to recover its original capital cost), but Alfred's point is that even while the simplest methods require some forecasting for these bases, the DCF method calls for a much more carefully thought out set of 'assumptions'. Those assumptions which form the input to the DCF calculations should properly be the output of the forecasting operation. However elegant the evaluation procedure, it cannot be better than its inputs. If one is contemplating setting at risk sums of money on such a scale that the very survival of the company is at hazard, then it follows that ensuring survival, far less profitability, demands forecasts that are as reliable as human wit and ingenuity can make them.

the complications which the forecaster can visualize. In a very large project, involving millions of pounds, there are so many eventualities and imponderables to consider that the ideal situation may be for a team to construct a series of forecasts, each individual operating a different technique, and then to reconcile their findings. In a recent case where a £5m investment was under consideration, five out of six forecasters found the project to be more than viable. The sixth discovered that the Japanese who had not previously been in the market in question were proposing the installation of massive capacity with a view to dominating the export market. Since a burgeoning export demand was a crucial assumption of all the other techniques these then had to be radically revised downwards, and the investment was not made.

It does not necessarily follow that the forecasts for each alternative in such a project must be pursued in full complexity. The construction process on the forecast itself should be kept under constant observation in light of the technological and organizational requirements of the project. Managers and forecasters should be highly sceptical of proposed projects, and constantly on the lookout for the key discrepancy which will automatically result in a 'No-Go' decision. One of the key tools in the rapid elimination of possible projects is breakeven analysis. Given a knowledge of the fixed and variable cost structure of the total project (including administrative and selling overheads) and feasible price levels, it is simple to calculate the volume of sales needed in order for the project to breakeven. (Breakeven is discussed more fully in chapter 9.) A well constructed forecast should be able to indicate the likelihood of such breakeven levels being achieved, the factors which will contribute to or detract from its achievement, and so give management something specific to decide upon. Very often the clear implication will be not to proceed.

It has to be borne in mind that the way in which many firms conduct their investment decision processes is such that senior management will only pass for formal evaluation a limited number of possible projects, and often these will be ones in which there has been built up a substantial amount of personal involvement among senior personnel (see Williams and Scott, 1965).

Not infrequently formal evaluation is intended to mean justification. On Williams and Scott's evidence there is little reason to suppose that the pre-sorting of projects has been particularly rational or that it will give rise to proposals which have any better chance of being viable than proposals selected more randomly. It is possible to have rational pre-selection processes, but frequently these are not used (Alexander *et al.*, 1969, pp. 197—205). One reason for this is that they tend to require resources beyond the scope of those available in small companies.

In this situation a very large proportion of proposals under formal investigation *should normally be eliminated*. The forecaster may be in an invidious situation. Speedy and decisive elimination is, however, often easy to achieve and politically most straightforward.

In summary, then, it is in investment planning, of all parts of the decision-making structure, that forecasting needs most to be regarded as an integrated and all-embracing activity, involving interrelationship with senior executive team and involving the contribution of an entire range of forecasting techniques. Shortcuts to elimination of projects should be sought wherever possible. The output requires to be usable for a variety of complex financial sums: it needs to cover estimates of sales and prices at points of time (normally annual) over the projected lives of the alternative projects, it requires to embrace the technical characteristics (involving their marketability) of the alternative outputs, it has to invoke competitive considerations, and for each proposal it will probably involve a number of different forecast estimates based, perhaps, on different forecasting techniques and, certainly, on different sets of assumptions about future market forces, giving rise to estimates of varying probability of attainment including the point where a project is thought to change from viable to non-viable. By manipulating break-even analysis it is possible for a wide range of outcomes to be examined.

An alternative simple approach to the problem of tying forecasts to decision margins is as follows:

Assume a project requires a minimum sales level of X to be viable at a specific point in time t, and an appropriate level of sales growth to ensure maintained viability. Figure 1.2 shows one possible relationship between the projected outcomes and the required outcome. As well as charting through time, however, a more complete snapshot of the probability distribution at time t can also be created, representing a normal curve, or a curve of such other shape as the forecasters feel is appropriate.

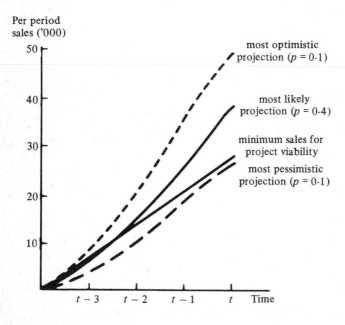

Fig. 1.2 Assessment of optimistic, most probable and pessimistic outcomes through time.

The point at which the minimum cutoff cuts the probability distribution ($p = 0.01$) means that there is thought to be one chance in a hundred that the required sales level will not be met. This is the risk involved in the project. Rarely if ever will a project be mooted in which there is no risk. It is the senior executive's job to decide what is an acceptable risk. Of 100 such projects as the one discussed, one will probably fail. '$p = 0.1$' for the minimum level of sales to enable the project to proceed would mean that there is thought to be one chance in ten that the required sales level will not be met. Of ten such projects as the one discussed, one would probably fail. Will the other nine generate sufficient profits to pay for the failure? Are there sufficient resources to contemplate another project? One of the most valuable services that a forecaster, whether manager or specialist, can perform for his board is to face them with the finite quantitative realities of risk acceptance. In this case say the forecasters think there is only one chance in four of their 'most probable' estimate materializing. Is this a good enough offer to ensure acceptance? These are the quintessentials of management decision-making.

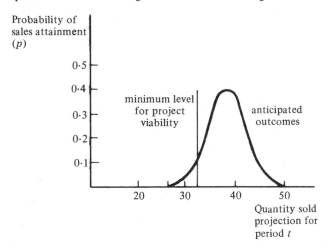

Fig. 1.3 Probabilities of different outcomes of a decision taken at time $t - 4$ occurring in time t.

This essential type of reasoning is also necessary to make DCF calculations entirely rational and a reliable managerial tool. At the moment DCF generally suffers from the drawback of working from one 'bench mark' estimate with little knowledge of how likely it is to be wrong, or by what magnitudes, and even less knowledge of the implications for the decision of these factors. Good forecasting can never be definitive, but it should be able to provide the inputs for the evaluation process in such a form that management can obtain a realistic feeling for what it is letting itself in for. Once a set of realistic probabilities of outcome has been decided, management can operate the simple and powerful technique of decision tree analysis to evaluate the payoffs likely from implementing the decision. This type of analysis is described in chapter 9.

1.4 Strategic planning

Much of what was said under investment decision-making applies with equal force to forecasts constructed as a basis for strategic company plans. Here the principal change of emphasis is that the issues for which forecasts are required are even more complex and comprehensive. In strategic planning forecasting the forecaster no longer has a fixed and short list of projects to investigate. Instead his attention is diffused into a much wider range of possibilities, for what he is trying to determine is the location of possible economic and commercial 'soft spots', at least as far as his company is concerned, which appear to offer the highest probability of commercially viable payoff over what may be very extensive planning horizons, up to several decades. (This type of thinking has led some companies to the position of being highly diversified conglomerates, where the necessity for reliable forecasts becomes all the more apparent.) The whole range of problems becomes much larger, because any type of market opportunity, real or imagined, is a candidate for examination, whether or not the company is heading at present in the particular direction suggested by the opportunity. The fundamental problem is to ensure that the projects are coherent and that they integrate with the overall strategic plans in the process of formulation. This is an organizational communication problem of great magnitude.

Where the whole problem of market entry and exit is involved, as in the strategic planning area, the penalties for wrong decisions are particularly severe: not only is a piece of plant at risk, but so is a whole organization. Some years ago the leisure business, so called, came into fashion as an object of British business analysts' attention. Many colourful predictions were made of the extent to which this would be one of the boom areas throughout the latter parts of the century. So, to an extent, it has proved. Consumers' expenditure on leisure, including especially motoring, has been rising at an increasing rate and seems likely to continue to do so. But many decisions to enter this market went wrong for a number of reasons which boil down to bad forecasting. In the first place, the rate of growth of this market was often wildly overestimated. Secondly, inadequate allowance was normally made for the extent to which the disposable income increase which was supposed to be spent on leisure would actually find its way into other markets – convenience foods, motoring, travel, overseas holidays and clothes being important ones. Finally, the rate of entry of competitors into the market was underestimated even at the rates of growth which have materialized, frequently less than the growth rates which were being predicted. It is incredible that executives who thought they were getting in on a gold mine should have imagined that many others were not equally enthusiastic about the opportunities.

The sums, then, must be done more critically, objectively, sceptically and comprehensively than all too often in the past.

Forecasting for long range planning involves feasibility testing and opportunity identification over a very wide range of market situations. Because of sheer numbers the initial estimates have to be made in rapid form, in the hope of eliminating perhaps 95 per cent of the original propositions in no more than a few hours' work each in a large department, a few minutes' for a small one. The field is so complex that the data base is inevitably inadequate.*

Problems of forecasting from inadequate data tend to force the forecaster back into deductions derived from general economic data. It becomes difficult in these circumstances to derive a coherent programme of forecasts and to ensure that the work being undertaken is sufficiently specific and relevant to the overall strategic planning operation. Forecasters should, therefore, have well identified connections with the strategic planning teams, their objectives should be clearly specified and their work should proceed in a series of steps starting with 'soft spot' identification, referred back to the strategic planning team, followed by preliminary forecasting to eliminate non-starters, based on the most convenient methodologies, before proceeding to the detailed forecasts of areas in which major company direction changes may be involved, or major financial commitments, having ensured that there is no objection in principle by management to accepting these commitments. A full discussion of strategic planning is beyond the scope of this work but insufficient attention has been paid in the literature of that subject to the problem of obtaining a viable forecast basis for planning (see Ansoff, 1968).

The business of forecasting by elimination is best handled by screening through the setting up of a comprehensive set of key parameters for acceptance of an idea even at the stage of detailed project investigation. If very many ideas need to be considered, then two such screens can be used, one coarse and one fine. The coarse screen can be operated on a very routine basis, though the fine screen may involve parameters requiring more investigation (Alexander *et al.*).

1.5 Forecasting for product and market planning

It has been stressed that much of the effort put into forecasting for long-term planning purposes is where the primary objective is elimination of the infeasible, the undesirable or the unprofitable. The wheat which remains when the great mass of chaff has been eliminated becomes the raw material for a fixed investment forecast. The search for viable product and market opportunities in the short as well as the long run is of the same class. The lode-bearing ore is effectively invisible under the valueless overburden. The task is to dispose of the overburden as expeditiously as possible, and only when the ore is isolated to assay it thoroughly.

Product and/or market planning may be more or less long-run. It is differentiated from strategic planning in that it generally does not involve strategic investment or organizational criteria. It is more likely to be concerned with such problems as filling idle capacity on production lines or expansion into markets related to existing fields, with only relatively minor investment or organizational issues at stake, even over long periods. But there is no hard and fast dividing line between

---

* The *data base* refers to the quantity and quality of data available, in terms of relevance to the problem, available detail, adequacy of time period covered, and authority of source. These and other deficiencies invariably constrain the quality of the forecast which can be produced.

the two types of activity, at least before the completion of the relevant forecasting projects. Thus the search for a strategic opportunity may well throw up opportunities for line-filling and vice versa, and the opportunities in these opposite directions should never be overlooked.

Another principal differentiating feature is that the forecasting objective is likely to be much more precisely specifiable at the outset of the project than for strategic planning application. Management may indeed specify the project too narrowly and in too specific a manner to allow themselves to derive maximum benefit from it. Thus it may be that imbalance in productive resources (idle capacity in one part of the plant) may lead to an investigation into suitable byproduct or other markets which will utilize this capacity, where the relevant specification might be to investigate a total product field involving major investment extensions and directions for corporate diversification which would simultaneously take up productive or organizational slack. We are close here to realms of advanced economic and management theory. (For a full discussion of the problem of organizational slack, see Cyert and March, 1963.)

The principal complication related to forecasts for product or market planning purposes is that the nature of the projects may be very diverse. Under the same umbrella title can be grouped a large number of forecasting tasks: sales for new products; sales of existing products in unknown markets; sales of existing products in existing markets, including forecasts to determine whether a product or market should be discontinued; potential for products slightly differentiated from existing lines; extensions or additional segmentation of an existing market position. The second complicating element is that this type of forecast normally takes account of effects induced by the alternative product or opportunity on sales of related products or in related markets, either complementary to or competitive with the project under investigation.

Normally the most productive type of forecast in this situation is the construction of some form of simple model relating sales and prices to the variable under investigation. For example, if management feels that sales are a function of, say, a number of outlets and their size, the effect of widening distribution may be readily assessed in terms of the potential of the new outlets. There are many other variables of this type which may determine sales in any given situation, for example, range of product line, price, product quality, advertising volume, media type used, number or quality of salesmen, 'below the line' promotional effort, or the activities of competitors in the marketplace.

A product or market planning decision normally implies varying some of these elements of the firm's marketing mix in response to changes in buying habits, competitive behaviour, or managerial objectives. Highly specified mathematical models are fantastically difficult to create in this very complex situation, and analysts are normally content with a model relating one or two of these independent variables to the dependent variables of sales, profits, etc. The snag with simple models is that they may overlook vital parts of the relationship. Here again the critical point to stress is the importance of combining the precise, if over-simplified, models of the analysts meaningfully with the complex, if muddy ill-defined models of the managers.

1.6 Forecasts for sales and production planning and stock control

The area of sales and production planning and stock control utilizes principally the techniques of time series analysis. Generally what is required here is a set of forecasts covering a short time span which can be produced cheaply and frequently, and in time to be of value for short-term planning applications. This is the great problem in producing this kind of forecast. Assuming that the purchasing director requires to know today how much of a critical raw material he should order, we may consider the following situation. Lead time between order and delivery may be four weeks. To minimise stockholding costs he wants the purchases to begin to go into production within a week of delivery. Processing time, let us say is two weeks, with an average time in finished stock of two further weeks before delivery. The purchasing director therefore wants to know what will be the quantity of despatches nine weeks from now. If the length of order book is four to five weeks this offers inadequate help, and in many situations the way in which the order book fills up through time varies in a random manner, so there will often be little ground for supposing that, for example, nine weeks before closing the order book is typically, say, 18 per cent full, so that one could extrapolate the final state from the present state. The error margin will be too great for this kind of information to be usable.

The problem of forecasting sales eight to twelve weeks away, and, indeed, up to about a year, is further complicated by a number of factors. First, the data on which the forecast is to be based may not become available for a matter of perhaps a week, in the case of the individual firm, and a month or more in the case of a group of firms or an industry. The data base is therefore inevitably (and sometimes perhaps critically) out of date.

Second, short-term forecasts usually ask for sales over a very short period, for example, in the week starting ten weeks from now. To get reasonably on the mark for such a short period is difficult wherever there is much random variation in sales. Thus if a line is constantly working at capacity the sales forecast is easy, it is capacity output for the week in question; but if the year's sales, after netting out seasonal and other regular variations exhibits a highly variable quality from week to week, then the production of this type of forecast is virtually impossible. This sort of problem is likely to arise when, for example, arranging in advance for contractor-owned transport to deliver the finished products.* It is less likely to be critical in production planning where buffer stocks are normally varied to help to even out the production flow, and at the raw material purchase stage with any luck the problem may become negligible due to the series of buffers between the raw material arrival and the final goods despatch. When asked for this type of forecast,

* Haulage contractors live by their ability to produce transport at short notice to meet varying demands for their services — probably a function of just this phenomenon of difficulty in predicting what these needs will be.

therefore, the forecaster is well advised to inquire into the purpose for which the forecast is to be used, to establish whether a trend estimate through the period in question would not in fact be adequate. Failing this solution, he then has to investigate the movements till then regarded as random, to see whether there is some predictable pattern in them. This is likely to involve teasing through the ordering behaviour of the individual customers one by one and perhaps investigating the underlying rationale for each, an expensive and time-consuming process which will only be worthwhile where the pay off in profit increase through better planning is likely to exceed the costs of the exercise.

The third major complication in this type of forecasting arises from the present state of the art of general economic management current in most of the developed Western economies. In Britain it has been typified as 'stop—go' control. What this type of economic management means to the business forecaster is that looming over his short run forecasts is always the danger of credit squeeze or incomes freeze, or their removal.

The obvious-looking answer to this is, of course, 'can't we try to predict the incidence of these eventualities, at least over the short periods we are considering?' Even the 'yes and no' answer to this reasonable question is unfortunately fraught with qualifications. What the 'yes and no' answer means is that yes, we can often foretell that some event is going to occur. When it will happen, however, is critical in the short-run context and this is likely to be hedged round with all sorts of political factors which can easily elude even the careful reader of the better quality Press. The second qualification is that our economic managers are constantly exercising great ingenuity in varying the recipes of restriction and expansion, and each new recipe has different incidences on the sales of different industries. Thirdly, specially if some aspect of the economy is reputed to be going through some kind of crisis, and even more so if the action to be taken is thought by any of the influential political power groupings to be somewhat unacceptable, then it may not be 'the done thing' even to admit that the eventuality in question is likely to come about. It was most instructive on the day after the 1967 devaluation of sterling to discover how many commentators claimed to have been predicting that it would happen over a period of months or even years. Scrutiny of their published views before the event hardly bears out many of their exaggerated claims to predictive skill. At best, the most direct of all their contributions to the debate was highly qualified by their uncertainty until a few days before, when the fact that the decision had been taken was in any case leaking out of Whitehall like water out of a sieve. A number of senior executives with extensive international interests, to whom devaluation eventually meant large differences in their profits and loss accounts, were saying both privately and publicly only weeks before the event that devaluation was not something that they expected to happen.

In *Management Today* for January 1967 the following appeared:

Henry Furness, Hoover's chief fortune-teller, is not dismayed by a plus or minus 40 per cent error for some products on these short term (three months) forecasts. Over longer periods, using more basic and familiar techniques, Furness expects greater accuracy — a 5 per cent to 10 per cent margin of error. . . . Throughout the industry the complaint is less of the unpredictability of the consumer than the Government.

Forecasters in the appliance industry, one of those most directly affected, went on record with the following comments: 'We could see the economy cracking back in August 1965 but the Government chose to paper over the cracks. And what were we expected to do? Cut back production although order books were as long as ever?' And, 'The actual timing of any measures is a purely political decision.' On the other hand, Henry Furness of Hoover pointed out that by watching the general economic indicators some forewarning could be achieved. 'I could have given you the Prime Minister's July speech three months earlier,' he was reported as having said.

Accepting that there are particularly intractable problems involved in forecasting the short run, at least for some firms and industries, there has been a tendency to adopt one of two ways out of the problem. The first is to fall back entirely on objective if somewhat naive methods of time series analysis and extrapolation, principally using moving averages as a method of analysis, the simple moving average method now being almost entirely superseded by the technique of exponential smoothing (see chapter 5). The alternative approach is to attempt to keep a running check on likely economic movements through gauging the temperature of the economy from published economic indicators and to maintain a file of observed effects on the firm attributable to previous economic shocks, held preferably in a quantitative way and ideally in the form of a model. Even if this counsel of perfection were to be adopted, however, interpretation of the situation by an economist is still necessary, for economic history is unlikely to repeat itself precisely. As managers know only too bitterly, economists invariably are two-handed: 'On the one hand . . . and on the other hand.'

One well-known forecaster adopts the following two ground rules for short-run economic evaluation in Britain, and on a basis of somewhat inadequate data they appear to have provided so far some operational decision rules. The first is that there will be buoyancy in the economy and a run up in consumer spending in advance of a general election, and the second, that there will be economic stringency for the first two years of a new administration.

1.7 Forecasting for budgetary control and financial planning

Reliable sales forecasts are the *sine qua non* of a reliable budgetary control system. The period covered is normally a year, with a second year sketched out, prepared three to six months ahead of the start of the first year. This is normally a fairly straightforward kind of forecasting period, incorporating expected seasonal fluctuations, and most companies seem to cope comfortably on the basis of time series predictions supplemented by economic forecasts, production and marketing feasibility data and executives' evaluations of likely competitive activity. In such an approach forecasting and short-run planning are inextricably intertwined, and since the forecasts are amended for internal consistency as the dialogue between the forecast expectation and the planning intention proceeds, this type of forecast tends to be self-fulfilling. Hence it is particularly awkward to try to evaluate its reliability at the end of the planning period, because in the absence of any major unanticipated shock it will be made to have come true.

Although this area of forecasting is among the best understood, it contains some of the trickiest managerial problems. The typical way of proceeding is to derive sales forecasts from two main sources, cost and capacity forecasts from production sources, which is normally a fairly straightforward operation, and to combine these into projected profit and loss accounts and funds forecasts.

The areas which have to be carefully watched are (*a*) derivation of sales forecasts; (*b*) derivation of cost estimates; and (*c*) allocation of overheads.

There are two principal sources for sales forecasts: professional forecasts derived from past sales and current economic data, and sales force estimates. The first is likely to be a basis for projecting broad product category deliveries, while the second will be the basis for regional and area breakdowns. There then follows a complex process of reconciliation which, from the sales force point of view, is very complicated. For a start, the size of the sales force is likely to be much larger than that of the professional forecasting group, so that in the final negotiation top sales management will be negotiating on the basis of information originally prepared at grass roots level, and thereafter modified and reconciled at area, region and general sales management levels; the professional forecaster who did the academic estimates will probably be at the meeting in person. But the plot is thicker still. It is highly likely that the sales force and management have a performance element in their remuneration, an element which is based on exceeding a quota. The basis for the quota may well be the forecast, so that throughout the forecast construction exercise from the sales force side, each man and manager will be conscious that the figures he is contributing will have a direct bearing on his earnings in the ensuing year.

The managerial problem is to devise a system of remuneration not based directly on the salesmen's inputs to the forecasting system. This is no mean problem and a number of managements have devised very complex systems for creating quotas which are in no way based on the forecasts: there is a lack of logic in this procedure and a strong element of the tail wagging the dog. But where profitability is closely determined by accurate short-range planning the force of this process is understandable.

A closely related problem may arise on the production side, where managerial bonuses may also be tied to accurate performance in relation to predictions. The problem is likely to be much less acute, however, as the fundamental issue of sales volume generation is not at stake.

The problem with overhead allocations is that these materially affect either the price of each component in the product line (hence the sales volume likely to be attained) or the profit recorded from the line, which may relate again to the issue of managerial bonuses from sales performance. At this point we are on the brink of the vast and complex area of motivation and control, an issue which goes far beyond our scope: it is raised here to illustrate one crucial area where the forecast creation process significantly interacts with the total control system of the company.

1.8 Forecasting for competitive position planning

One objective firms frequently state is to obtain a given penetration for each of their products in specific markets. To measure whether such an objective is being achieved involves measuring the total market size to compare with the firm's sales. To *plan* to achieve such an objective involves forecasting the total market size. This is sometimes easy, sometimes difficult, and sometimes wellnigh impossible, depending on the nature and availability of market data. It is not always a relevant exercise, and experience indicates that it is in those markets in which the data are hardest to acquire that the exercise is least important.

There is, for example, ample data on the sales and output of the fuel and power, metals, cars, shipbuilding, appliance, food and textiles industries in which many markets tend to be dominated by a smallish number of massive concerns whose market share is vital to them. In engineering, electronics and electrical goods, and other industries where there are large numbers of small, specialized companies, often not competing directly with each other, or where rapid product innovation is occurring, total market sizes may be hard to obtain, but hardly need to be obtained very often, for sales level is likely to be a function of technical ingenuity or marketing and selling skills, rather than total market size.

In the category of stable, well-documented industries, a common forecasting technique is to assume that market size is growing (or static or declining) simply as a function of time, and therefore to be fairly readily predictable, at least in the medium term. Given a market share objective, the sales forecast is totally defined. This kind of arithmetic is not applicable to the situation where, say, a small vigorous new market entrant with a novel product is carving out a corner of the market. It does not become relevant until its growing market share is noticed by the principal competitors and retaliation begins.

As will be argued in chapter 2, no sales or business forecast should be constructed without placing it in a wider context. This context will probably, though not necessarily, be that of the market or industry group which, from available sources, may contain many non-relevant activities.

In such a set of activities a better procedure is usually to try to work from the segment of discretionary incomes available to the potential buyers of the product, and to aim for a share of this income. For example, the market facing a firm introducing a new line of highly priced toys — say Go-Karts — is hardly definable in terms of the toy market generally but is more likely, in the 1970s, to involve competition with deep freezers, dishwashers and colour televisions, even air-conditioning and swimming pools. The trick then is to figure out the origins of the money being spent on these highly priced items and to forecast this segment of discretionary income as a sales forecast basis for competitive position planning. Here again, line management is likely to have as much to contribute to the definition of the problem as has the professional forecaster.

1.9 Summary

The objective of this book is to enable managers and management students to obtain a thorough grounding in what business forecasting is, and what professional forecasters do. As well as helping them to understand the work of others, it is hoped it may enhance their own abilities in forecasting, a task central to the manager's job, whether or not explicitly recognized.

Forecasting is concerned with two main tasks: first, the formulation of the best basis available for the formation of intelligent managerial expectations; second, the handling of uncertainty about the future, so that the implications of decisions become explicit.

Forecasting activity should be viewed as an integral part of the firm's intelligence system for gathering, analysing and reporting necessary data to management. It also impinges on the control system.

Management is at the heart of the forecasting system, and professional forecasters are only there as a service to management.

There are four methods available to forecasters: the search for an extrapolation of economic regularities; the relation of events and changes in behaviour to some set of indicators which may be easier to predict or may even have happened; questioning people whose answers may be worth having; mathematical model building (a special case of the second group).

The improvement of forecast quality in practice tends to come not so much from elaborating the sophistication of any one technique as from employing a battery of techniques, heavily stabilized by managerial common sense.

The selection of method depends primarily on the purposes for which the forecasting exercise is being done, the decisions to which it has to contribute. Just as important as results is the reasoning underlying them, and management's commitment to the rationale of the whole exercise. Forecasts intelligently used may serve the function of both lighthouse and compass.

Forecasts are commonly applied to capital investment decisions, strategic planning, product and market planning, production planning and stock control, budgetary control and financial planning and competitive position planning.

In general, good methodology involves the creation not only of point forecasts, but also of predictions of the probability of a range of feasible outcomes, stressing especially those outcomes which are critical of the decision-makers, for example, the breakeven point on a project, or the point where cash resources fall to zero.

REFERENCES

Alexander, R. S., Cross, J. S. and Hill, R. M. *Industrial Marketing*, 3rd edn, Irwin, 1969.

Alfred, A. M. *Discounted Cash Flow and Corporate Planning*, Woolwich Economic Papers, No. 3, 1964.

Ansoff, H. Igor *Corporate Strategy*, Pelican, 1968.

Beckerman, W. *The British Economy in 1975*, Cambridge University Press, 1965.

Brech, Ronald *Britain in 1984*, Darton, Longman & Todd, 1963.

Butler, W. F. and Kavesh, R. A., eds. *How Business Economists Forecast*, Prentice-Hall, 1966.

Cyert, R. M. and March, J. G. *An Organizational Theory of the Firm*, Prentice-Hall, 1963.

Imperial Chemical Industries, *Assessing Projects: a programme for learning*, 2nd edn, Methuen for ICI, 1970.

Kelley, W. T. *Marketing Intelligence: management of marketing information*, Staples Press, 1968.

Reichard, R. S. *Practical Techniques and Sales Forecasting*, McGraw-Hill, 1966.

Williams, B. R. and Scott, W. R. *Investment Proposals and Decisions*, Allen & Unwin, 1965.

2 The firm and the economy

2.1 The interrelationship of forecasts

Forecasting is among other things the interpretation of changes in factors in the economy and in society in such a way that meaningful projections may be made of likely future changes in these or other relevant variables. The sources from which information is drawn for interpretation are very varied. The most important is knowledge of current affairs, business and economic trends. The more widespread the base from which knowledge is drawn, the more effective a forecaster will be in practice. One source is provided by forecasts already produced by relevant agencies. This is one reason why forecasting cannot meaningfully be confined to a specialist group labelled 'forecasters': they are likely to have a more limited knowledge of current business events than operational managers.

Just as widespread information and knowledge of all sorts are essential for effective forecasting, so is the application of appropriate analytical techniques to the information, and analytical techniques may be as diverse in character as the information to which they will be applied. It is unlikely that the non-specialist will have the necessary time or skill to be able to operate the full range of possible analytical techniques fully competently. This is not necessarily a major drawback to, say, the individual manager, even though he may be unsupported by specialist statistical or economic services. Many problems are satisfactorily soluble using the techniques of analysis in only a rudimentary, easily mastered and easily operated form. Full-blooded sophistication of technical methodology is rarely required in practice. When it is required it is usually available for hire.

Much the most difficult aspect of forecasting lies in exercising judgment on such matters as the selection of basic data, the amount of confidence to be placed in the continuance of past trends compared with assessing the chances that things will be different in the future, the selection of objectives for the forecasting process that will be relevant to the decisions to be based on the predictions, and other managerial, as distinct from computational, problems.

We must listen with respect when a statistician of the eminence of M. J. Moroney comments on statistical forecasting techniques:

> It is a vile superstition beyond anything imaginable in the middle ages. . . . This is the sort of thing that any competent ice-cream manufacturer does in a flash without statistics. Only where the effect is very marked is it worth doing. In that case it is so obvious that there is no need to do it statistically. . . . What hokum it all is.

Much economic, as distinct from business, forecasting also frankly falls into the category of 'vile superstition'.

What then, if anything, is the role of economics and statistics in business forecasting? Their principal function is to provide easily understood pictures and models of what has gone before, in order to help the process of intelligent interpretation of events designed to cast a coherent image of the future on the screen of the manager's mind. Economists and statisticians tend to draw different kinds of pictures, and both may often be relevant and helpful. But they must be integrated into the type of picture managers need before the whole can be presented as a forecast.

Economists' pictures are usually concerned with patterns of economic relationships — if one sector has more to spend, what does this mean for another, and another, through to the meaning for our firm or our industry. Statistician's pictures are concerned with precision in the interrelationships of data — the trend of points on a graph, or the correlation of variables one with another. Statistics offer sharp clarity, often sharper and clearer than is needed for managerial purposes. Adequate pictures can often be got without recourse to the highly refined processing machine. The danger inherent in statistical analysis is that it is so powerful and precise that it may dazzle the user and blind him to deficiencies in his data, or to the fact that statistics is inanimate and cannot judge the likelihood of future happenings.

Forecasting, then, is an interpretative process, founded on the most relevant and widely based knowledge obtainable and utilizing any analytical techniques able to produce clearer images of what has happened in the past, and the interrelationships inherent in economic behaviour. It must be emphasized that these 'techniques' are not a substitute for judgment, but merely aids to the process of logical and systematic evaluation. A straight line through a set of points showing sales through time extended into the future is not a forecast: it is but the first approach through one possible picture of how things might be, and its nature does not change if, instead of drawing the line by eye, its position is computed by rigorous regression techniques. It may be little better as a guideline, for all the statistical rigour it would then embody.

A   World population–United Nations
B   Aluminium production
C   Max. post-World-War II trend
D   Min. post-World-War II trend
E   Mean post-World-War II trend
F   Mean use index
G   Forecast–mean trend

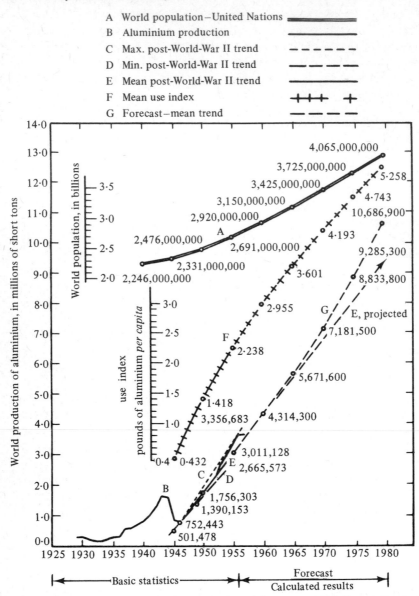

Fig. 2.1 World aluminium production 1929–57 and forecast to 1980. Source: *Purchasing World*, 13 July 1959.

A splendid example of a number of such statistical projections computed with utmost care for a number of interrelated variables is reproduced in Fig. 2.1. But does this impressive array of projected regression estimates contribute materially to solving the problem of planning the installation of aluminium production capacity? With such massive decisions at stake, clearly it is right to try to obtain a picture on this scale, but every one of these projections must be recognized as highly arbitrary. Most business forecasting starts from, and is principally concerned with, forecasting the sales of an individual firm. The firm is a member of an industry, defined here as a group of firms having the objective of earning their profits by satisfying customers' purchasing needs in a mutually related field.*

The industries, thus classified, are participants, with their buyers, in markets. The buyers in these marketplaces are classifiable in many ways, which may or may not always be relevant for forecasting. Industrial buyers are likely to require to be examined separately from final consumer buyers: among consumers, sex, age, and socioeconomic groupings are all frequently relevant distinctions as are, for example, stage of family life cycle or discretionary income. Geographical location is frequently relevant for both groups and buyer behaviour will certainly have to be examined separately in different national markets if international operations are being considered.

Market behaviour, embracing both the activity of firms and the purchasing pressure of their customers is powerfully influenced by the behaviour of the national economy in which they participate, and, through the national economy, the world economy. Beyond the national economy also lies the total structure of national and world society, embracing cultural attitudes, historical institutional development, freedom or restriction of consumer and business behaviour, legal systems, social security systems, forms of government, patterns of national aspiration and many even less tangible aspects of organized living. (It might be instructive for a reader who is sceptical of the validity of such factors to consider each of the above list in turn and the ways in which their different applications have led quite directly to different patterns of consumption, buying and business behaviour in different countries.)

Throughout the hierarchy of human organization — the firm, industry, market, domestic economy, international economy, domestic society, international society — there exists mutual interdependence and consistency. Few interpretations of past economic events at the level of the firm (e.g. Joe Smith & Sons' sales pattern over the past five years) can afford to ignore at least some of the broader currents of which these events form a part.

Given this interdependence, there must be consistency among the various levels. It follows that forecasts produced by a firm should exhibit consistency with acceptable forecasts for the industry, through it the economy, and so on. For any practical forecasting (with the exception of short-run exponential smoothing techniques) the interlinks with industry and general economic behaviour have to be explicitly examined in two contexts. The first is the use of general economic/industry behaviour as a predictor of (say) sales. In other words, the economy or the

* By this sort of definition the steel industry, so called, is not one industry but several, satisfying many sets of related customer needs. If one comes to forecast anything in the steel industry one quickly discovers that precisely this sort of approach to the definition of 'an industry' is required, and the demand for refrigerator cabinets is a different forecasting process from that for sheet for car bodies, boiler plate, structural beams, or stainless cutlery steels.

industry may where relevant be taken as an independent variable. Secondly, the forecasts results should be checked for consistency with any economic forecasts available. This applies with increasing force the 'bigger' the forecast becomes, that is to say, the further projections move into the future and the more important the decisions to be based on them.

2.2. Forecasting the industry or the firm?

Should the individual company forecaster concentrate his attention on forecasting the sales of his own firm, or adopt the industry as his principal line of approach, and rely on management's judgment (abetted by his own educated guesses) of what market share is to be the target? This is a question of simplification of method which is frequently undertaken. In stable, often basic industries, dominated by a few large suppliers, typified by existence of extensive industry and marketwide sales data, normally supplied through a trade association and possessing little room for dramatic switches in market share without evoking sharp competitive response, there is much to be said for forecasting the company's behaviour as a proportion of the industry. The only objection to this process, and that a somewhat academic one, is that it is one more influence helping to institutionalize the moderation and regulation of competition implied by such a system.

Where reliable data are less freely available on an industrywide basis, or where the competitive structure is subject to rapid change, where innovation is frequent and there are ample opportunities for developing market penetration through superior technology or marketing skills, the only real value in predicting industry trends lies in making available industry or market trends. Against this the market share implied by the firm's forecast of its own activities may be evaluated in light of management's views of what an appropriate market penetration might be for them: this may be wildly different in different situations. One firm may not wish to participate at less than one-third market share in a big market, because its managers seek market power; another may not wish more than 5 per cent of a market because its managers value independence in a smaller business and do not wish to attract the competitive or acquisitive attentions of the behemoths.

2.3 Using forecasts produced outside the firm

The company forecaster will use forecasts of associated factors in two contexts. First, he wishes to take advantage of the existence of forecasts of aggregate levels of economic activity, or changes in society, as a basis for his own projections, second, he wishes to evaluate his projections against the wider projections produced by himself and others. Not infrequently sales forecasts produced by British firms are neither derived from economic forecasts nor tested for consistency against them. In American experience by contrast the exercise of general economic forecasting, both at national and state level, frequently dominates the individual firm's forecasting activities. American literature on the subject of business forecasting tends to be dominated by trade cycle and other economic forecasting ideas. (See for example Bratt, 1968, and Butler and Kavesh, 1966.) This may be partly accounted for by the greater American belief in the predictability of the trade cycle.

Some types of sales forecast can be produced in isolation from general economic trends, for example, short-term forecasts based on exponential smoothing. Forecasts of medium-term duration, can be produced with much less confidence that simple extrapolations will take into account changes in the underlying economic trends. This problem becomes increasingly severe as the time horizon of the forecast extends into the future. For example, a twenty-year forecast will certainly require social, technological and economic analysis and prediction to provide a context in which the sales or business activity forecast may be set. Such broad context forecasting is generally beyond the scope of all but the largest business and if it is to be performed at all, is for most medium and small size companies best carried out by an industry trade association.

Increasing numbers of large businesses are beginning to adopt a technique known as 'technological forecasting' in order to attempt to identify the technological environment in which they expect to be operating in twenty years or more. Very specialized techniques are involved in this type of forecasting and it is referred to specifically in chapter 7.

Between the two extremes of the very short and very long forecasts there remains the need to spell out the general economic context within which the ordinarily short-, medium- and long-term predictions of the firm's activity and its sales will be put.

Any firm in Britain has two, three or four sources for published forecasts available to it, depending principally on the sort of industry within which it is operating. The first and in some respects least useful is the government, in the shape of a number of different agencies. The Bank of England produces regular economic reviews, and various 'indicative planning' documents have been published from time to time dealing with a longer-term context (see References, Further Reading). The quality of these documents has improved since the original forecasts which were predicated on an unreasonable projection of the growth rate of the total economy. Having had its fingers burned by the production of an unattainable plan based on poorly conceived forecasts, the government has tended to retreat into what is in many respects the most intractable of all economic forecasting areas, the three months to one year types of projection.

The classic confusion of role between forecasting and planning seems to be particularly obvious in the field of short-term government forecasting. Governments are sometimes careless about specifying whether forecasts are based on absence of government action or on government activities having been initiated to secure a particular course of economic development.

Anyone attempting to use such forecasts as a basis for business forecasting and policy should bear in mind that the purpose for which Treasury and Bank of England predictions are prepared is the control of the country's short-run financial situation. Essentially they are national financial planning forecasts and therefore deal in aggregate economic variables such as fixed capital investment, consumption, government expenditure, imports and exports. They are also deeply involved with detailed activities in the purely financial sector of the economy, such as the banking system. The principal sort of lesson to be learnt from them is an indication of the general monetary and credit situation likely to prevail and to influence business conditions over a period up to about a year hence. They are, however, unlikely to indicate in any detail the specific areas in which financial or credit stringency or relaxation will occur, the form that this would take, and hence the likely specific impact on markets.

The second set of external documents available to forecasters is subject to similar qualifications. These are privately generated economic forecasts, and have only limited usefulness as a means of determining in any sort of detail the likely immediate trend of that segment of business activity in which the company forecaster is particularly interested. There are two readily available sources of such forecasts in Britain, *Quarterly Economic Review* published by the National Institute of Economic and Social Research, and the 'Quarterly forecast of the British economy' produced on the basis of an econometric model operated in the London Graduate School of Business Studies and published in the *Sunday Times* newspaper (Ball and Burns, 1968). Both these forecasts tend to be predictions of economic aggregates rather than individual industrial or commercial sectors. Their value to the business forecaster lies particularly in the fact that the assumptions on which the forecasts are based are systematically presented. Thus it is possible for the forecaster to modify such assumptions to any extent that seems fit to him, rework the conclusions if necessary, and use them as a basis for his own short-run economic predictions, on which in turn his individual sector forecasts can be based. In practice it is found that alternative forecasts frequently come up with conflicting conclusions. It therefore behoves the forecaster in business to form his independent judgment of these conclusions and if necessary to adopt yet another alternative. However, the degree of detailed groundwork which goes into the production of these forecasts is on such a level that it would be largely wasteful to replicate them in the individual firm, and since they are widely available the focus of forecasting attention within the firm ought to be the development of their conclusions for specific application.

A third source of 'deep-lying' forecasts is often to be found in trade association forecasts of total industry activity. At the trade association level it is normally possible to devote sufficient resources to forecasting production and sales to enable long-term and general economic and industrial forecasting to proceed, and to do an adequate job of interpretation of independently produced forecasts. Generally speaking, trade association forecasting is not a short-term activity. The forecasts tend to have very general sorts of objectives; for example, planning production capacity requirements on a wide scale. As a result trade associations are normally confined to medium- and long-term forecasts of an industry's activity, but since this is an area in which there is a lack of nationally produced forecasts of economic activity, this type of forecasting fills an extremely important gap. One of its principal objectives is the rationalization of long-term strategic and capital investment planning throughout the industry and the results are therefore often unhelpful as a basis for competitive planning. The industries which conduct such forecasts are generally characterized as being mature, in that demand growth is proceeding at a rate roughly proportionate to the growth of GNP.

Especially for the small company serving industrial markets forecasts of the activities of their consumers, when available, provide one of the important sources. These may be either in the form of forecasts of a particular segment of the consumer market (e.g. of the changes in incomes over certain minimum value), or, in the case of industrial producers, forecasts of the activity generated through the sales forecasts of the industries of *their* consumers. A commercial vehicle producer, for example, would be most concerned to forecast the likely growth in needs for transportation involving the type of vehicles in which he was interested. In precisely the same way the production of a forecast for demand for or deliveries of sheet steel can hardly be undertaken without reference to the likely demand for road vehicles, among other determinants.

In making use of this type of forecast when it is available, precisely the same consideration must be taken into account as in using published economic forecasts, namely that the adoption of the published forecast is intended to be a short cut for the company's forecasters. The degree of confidence which they can place in their own forecasts will be determined entirely by the degree of confidence which they place in the forecasts produced by their consumers. As before, therefore, it is necessary to check such forecasts and agree them to be acceptable before incorporating them. If they do not exist it may be necessary to prepare them; if done in an industry at one remove from the industry being forecast, this suffers from major hazards concerning the reliability of the data input and from the lack of expert knowledge about the specific conditions regarding supply as well as the state of demand of the consuming industry for which the forecast was prepared.

In summary, what we are saying is that no forecast can be accepted as valid until it has been tested with reference to the broader industrial and economic context in which it is set. Such testing forms an integral part of the forecast construction operation and the incorporation of the firm's forecast into the industrial or economic situation involves simultaneously developing the forecast and testing its validity.

2.4 Economic and industrial indicators

Throughout the preceding section it was stressed that even where the forecaster is willing fairly wholeheartedly to adopt existing forecasts relating to areas of the economy which will determine his own results, he should be able to run a rule over such forecasts to evaluate their reliability in his context. This exercise can usually be most effectively carried out in the first place with reference to the general set of economic indicators available. These are the same indicators as are required in constructing one's own firm's forecasts and they form the basic data store required for efficient forecasting. Many of them are published by the government and some by private agencies and trade associations. Many are freely reproduced in newspapers and business journals. Lists are provided in the Appendix, but we might note here that the three principal sources for British economic demographic, social, industrial trends are the publications of HM Stationery Office; the *Annual Abstract of Statistics*, the *Monthly Digest of Statistics*, and *Economic Trends*. Most countries have comparable centralized reference works.

Indicators of this sort are used for four principal purposes. First, as outlined above, they provide a basis for forecasting economic changes in their own right. Second, individual indicators are frequently selected as being associated directly or indirectly with the behaviour of the variable which it is hoped to forecast; given a statistically significant coefficient of correlation between the two and given an acceptable forecast of the leading indicator, then it is possible to form reliable forecasts for the variable under investigation. Even in the absence of valid correlation coefficients, it is often found that a basic economic indicator leads the behaviour of another economic variable, for example, our economy's sales, by a fairly fixed time interval, in some cases up to six months or even a year. Provided current data on the performance of the variable taken as the independent one becomes available in sufficient time, this can often form the basis for a particularly reliable forecast in the short term of the likely behaviour of the dependent variable after the appropriate timelag has elapsed. The third use of this type of data, related to the above technique, relates to cyclical turning points in economic behaviour. The forecasting of turning points is one of the trickiest exercises facing the forecaster, particularly in respect of the specific time at which the forecast variable will turn. Often the fact of the turning point in a cycle is of greater commercial importance than the magnitude of the rise or fall. If a consistent lead exists between it and some other variable for which some other data become available much more quickly, then without being able necessarily to measure the amplitude of changes, the forecaster may confidently be able to predict the likelihood of a turning point. Finally, any forecast of one variable's behaviour ought to be tested for consistency against accepted forecasts of the likely behaviour of related variables.

2.5 Input-output analysis

The search for consistency among different levels of economic activity has led to the creation of a particular grouping of economic information in the form of input-output tables. These are now available in most of the developed countries and form a powerful tool for forecasting at the aggregate industry level, once an acceptable projection of gross national product changes, or changes in some other major economic indicator, has been attained. These tables are normally produced for purposes of national income accounting. Although national income statistics provide classifications by kind of income and by industry of origin, they do not normally show inter-industry transactions. Input-output tables show the extent to which one industry is dependent on another for the sale of its output and the purchases of its input, and how far each industry's sales are dependent on consumption, investment and export (that is on each of the various forms of final expenditure).

A number of countries have produced annual series of input-output tables. For Britain the Central Statistical Office produced a provisional set relating to the year 1968, following publications for 1963 and 1954. These figures may not be applicable to more recent years. What the input-output tables ultimately show is the extent to which in the years covered by the tables, each of Britain's industries was dependent upon each of the others for both the purchases and sales which were ultimately made. The theory of and problems involved in producing input-output analyses go very far beyond the scope of this text. The interested reader is referred to the basic literature on input-output (Leontieff, 1966; Chenery and Clark, 1959).

The *input-output coefficient* is the figure which measures the extent of this dependence. If we had more frequent tables than have been produced in Britain in the past it might be possible to measure changes over time in these coefficients and to suggest the way in which such changes might continue into the future. As it is we have only three point estimates so it is difficult to calculate any drift in the coefficients. In addition, technicalities of updating and changes in the system of industrial classification in 1968 make it impossible to compare the most recent tables directly with the earlier ones.

There are two ways in which input-output tables may be used as an aid to forecasting. Both depend on the assumption that the input-output coefficients have not changed over time since the tables which are being used were produced. To the extent that the analyst feels that such an assumption might be unwarranted the onus is on him to introduce to the calculation such changes in the coefficient as he believes to be justified. This is likely to prove in practice to be such an inherently arbitrary operation that no advice in attempting the exercise is offered here. All one can do is to emphasize the statement made in the introduction to the 1954 British input-output tables: 'It must be recognized that the average relationships given in the tables for the year 1954 may not be applicable to a more recent year or be the same as the *marginal relationships which would apply for changes in output and expenditure*' (my italics). The significance of the italicized phrase is this. If the tables show a change between one period and another, such a change has occurred in the *average* relationship between two industries. For example, a substitution of aluminium for iron castings in some applications in engineering would show up as a very small change in the coefficients relating the two 'primary' industries to engineering. This is the *average* relationship. In the applications where the change is occurring, however, the coefficients will have changed very substantially; the marginal change (or change in marginal operations *where the change is occurring*) could conceivably be as large as a transfer from all iron usage (coefficient 1) to no iron usage (coefficient 0).

There are two ways of using these tables. First, they may be used to relate

projections of other industries to the output of our own industry or projections
of the change in gross national product or consumers' expenditure, for example, to
changes in any one commodity sector or industry sector. That is to say that since
the input-output tables give us a fully mutually consistent 'balance sheet' of all
economic transactions in the economy, the sort of exercise which becomes possible
is to make a number of assumptions about, say, the level of GNP for the year 1980.
Thereafter, given the assumption that the input-output coefficients remain constant
throughout the period, it is possible by use of a reasonably straightforward computer programme to obtain a complete picture of the likely change in activities of
all industries in the economy in the same year. In other words, an extrapolation of
the very deep-lying economic determinant whose growth is taken to be very stable,
may be associated with a long-term development of demand in one or more
industry groups for the commodities of the industry group in which the analyst is
interested.

The second use of these tables is in testing forecasts for consistency. In the same
way that an accountant can produce projected balance sheets for a number of years
ahead in order to trace the full set of implications of a proposed course of action,
and point out for example the danger that cash may become in a dangerously short
supply at some stage in the project, so input-output analysis can be used, for
example, to show to a manufacturer of transmission lines that the implications for
supply of raw copper of an existing rate of growth in power line installations are
such that before very many years there will not be sufficient copper available in the
world to meet the demand for this one end use alone. This situation did arise a
number of years ago in input-output projections constructed by the Westinghouse
Corporation when discovery of the likely shortfall of copper supply led to their
recognizing the need to develop an alternative technology for electric power transmission. So aluminium transmission lines were brought into existence.

Table 2.1 shows an excerpt from the British summary industry by industry flow
matrix for 1968 and the following comments refer to it. The total output of each
industry group is the aggregate value of goods made and other work done by the
establishments within the industry group. It is equal to the value of the industry
group sales plus any increase and less any decrease in the value of its stocks of
finished products and work in progress. It is measured free from duplication in the
sense that the output of establishments sold to other establishments within the
same industry group is excluded. The output figures for each industry group also
include the secondary products produced by firms within the industry groups. All
transactions in goods and services are valued at seller's prices, that is the net amount
received by the seller as distinct from purchaser's prices, the net amount paid by
the purchaser. The difference between the two represents transport, distribution
and service charges paid by the purchaser but not included in the seller's price.
Imports of merchandise are valued cif, that is including carriage, insurance and
freight. Transactions relate to purchases of goods and services and to their actual
usage, the difference between the two being equal to the value of change in the
physical volume of stocks of materials and fuel held.

2.6 Reading input-output tables

If we examine Table 2.1 we find the headings along the top of the first section (columns 1 to 36 inclusive) relate to purchases by the individual industry group in each column. Lines 1 to 37 relate to sales by industry groups. Thus the first figure in column 5, 896.7 shows that the food industry in 1968 purchased £896.7m worth of goods and services from agriculture, and we find that other major sources of supply for the food industry were, line 9, chemicals £37.6m, line 19, other metal goods, £58.1m, line 25, paper and printing, £100.5m, line 31, transport, £123.2m, line 34, miscellaneous services, £140.6m, and line 36, imported goods and services, £722m. Total purchases of goods and services are shown on line 38 at £2 331.8m. In addition to purchases of materials, the industry made payments for other 'services' shown in lines 39, 40 and 41 as follows: taxes £55.6m, income from employment, £638.2m, and gross profits, £321.8m, providing for depreciation or stock appreciation. Everything consumed in production of the output of the food industry therefore cost £3 347.4m, the total input shown on line 42. Reading along row 5, we can see what the food industry earned by selling this output to others. Just as it was a major customer of the agriculture, forestry and fishing industries, so the food industry is a major supplier to that industry. Column 1 of row 5 shows that the agriculture industry bought £438.3m worth of goods and services from food and, indeed, of all the industries which might have consumed from the food industry this was by far the largest. The total output sold on current account to other industries was £619.2m shown in column 36. Reading further along, however, we see in column 37, not unexpectedly, that a very much greater value of output was sold direct to consumers namely £2 451m. Public authorities (38) took a further £833m while stocks were increased by £47.3m without taking into account any changes in the value of any individual unit of such stocks. It might be noted in passing that column 39 shows that the food, drink and tobacco industry contributed nothing to the fixed domestic capital formation of any other industries (i.e. it did not supply any capital goods to industry). This is, of course, perfectly understandable and may be compared with line 36, column 39 in which we see that the contribution of imported goods and services to gross fixed domestic capital formation was £583.3m.

The value of output of the food industry going into exports was a further £146.6m (41), making a total for the final output going through uses represented in columns 37 to 41 of £2 728.2m making a total output for the food, drink and tobacco industry of £3 347.4m, that is the total of the intermediate output going to other industries and the final output going to end uses. The total inputs paid for including gross profits must, of course, equal the income derived from the total outputs of the industry, hence the earlier description of input-output tables as a sort of balance sheet.

Column 36 line 38 gives the total value of transactions between all the component parts of British industry in 1968, including purchases of imports at £26 615.6m. This table shows transactions between industries together with the transactions of final buyers and can be integrated into the framework of the

Table 2.1 *Summary industry by industry flow matrix 1968 (extract)*

Sales by \ Purchases by	Agriculture 1	Food 5	Chemicals, etc. 9	Total intermediate output 36	Current expenditure — Consumers 37	Current expenditure — Public authorities 38	Gross domestic capital formation — Fixed 39	Gross domestic capital formation — Stocks 40	Exports 41	Total final output 42	Final output 43
1. Agriculture	—	896.7	4.0	978.8	838.5	43.2	18.1	−4.9	70.4	965.3	1 944.1
5. Food	438.3	—	86.9	619.2	2 451.0	83.3	—	47.3	146.6	2 728.2	3 347.4
9. Chemicals, etc.	121.0	37.6	—	155.4	364.5	206.3	19.6	41.1	645.2	1 276.7	2 463.4
19. Other metal goods	15.0	58.1	67.1	1 271.3	3 170.1	12.3	68.3	11.2	293.9	555.8	1 827.1
25. Paper and printing	4.2	100.5	75.0	1 235.8	343.5	114.3	1.7	12.9	179.9	652.3	1 888.1
31. Transport	22.2	123.2	86.6	1 614.6	805.6	94.5	34.6	1.0	1 179.2	2 114.9	3 729.7
34. Miscellaneous services	55.3	140.6	230.4	2 276.2	3 602.6	906.6	238.5	—	626.5	5 374.2	7 650.4
36. Imports of goods and services	108.0	722.0	377.6	5 464.8	2 021.8	433.4	583.3	79.0	465.7	3 583.2	9 048.0
37. Sales by final buyers	1.5	−1.6	6.4	258.1	513.8	−566.3	−333.5	—	127.9	−258.1	—
38. Total goods and services (1 to 37)	1 123.3	2 331.8	1 449.9	26 615.6	23 129.1	7 373.3	7 718.3	210.0	8 723.4	47 154.1	73 769.7
39. Taxes on expenditure less subsidies	−199.2	55.6	47.2	1 604.1	3 983.9	331.7	170.7	—	−36.4	4 449.9	6 054.0
40. Income from employment	326.0	638.2	560.4	25 334.0	—	—	—	—	—	—	25 334.0
41. Gross profits and other trading incomes	694.0	321.8	405.9	11 168.0	—	—	—	—	—	—	11 168.0
42. Total input (38 to 41)	1 944.1	3 347.4	2 463.4	64 721.7	27 113.0	7 705.0	7 889.0	210.0	8 687.0	51 604.0	116 325.7

national income accounts as a whole. To obtain gross domestic income at factor cost, it is necessary to add lines 40 and 41 of column 43, namely £25 334m + £11 168m = £36 502m.

Apart, however, from presenting an interesting snapshot of the economy in 1968, the summary industry by industry flow matrix has been converted into a more useful analytical tool, an extract of which is shown in Table 2.2. (In addition, much more extensive analytical detail is available for 1963 and will in due course no doubt be published for 1968, but our Table 2.2 is the key one for general purposes.)

From the figures in each column of the gross industry purchase tables it is possible to see the direct and indirect inputs required on average by each industry to produce £1 000 of output. Thus, while mechanical engineering requires £51 of input from non-ferrous metals to produce £1 000 of final output (column 12 row 11) non-ferrous metals require £21 of input from chemicals to produce £1 000 of its final product. The total set of relationships of this sort in the economy can be derived from a matrix of 'direct requirements' by a process known as 'inverting the matrix'. This is a complex mathematical process whose technicalities need not concern us here.

One change which the reader will notice in Table 2.2 compared with Table 2.1 is that, whereas in the latter the figures in each entry of the leading diagonal (i.e. column 1 row 1, column 5 row 5, etc.) were zero, these are now shown as a figure of approximately 1 000. This difference is something of a technicality and may be taken to represent the fact that the entry in row 3 column 3, say, represents the gross output of the industry coal mining which is required to produce £1 000 tons of output by the industry coal mining. What may seem at first sight to be a little more puzzling is the fact that almost all the entries in fact come to somewhat more than the exact £1 000. This represents the fact that we are here dealing with the total set of indirect relationships in the industrial sector of the economy, so that when one industry sells some of its products to another, those products find their way into further commodities, a proportion of which is in turn repurchased by the original industry; for example, the iron and steel industry will sell products to the engineering industry and will in turn repurchase some of its own iron and steel when it buys the products of the engineering industry.

The figures entered in Table 2.2 represent the 'input-output coefficients' of the various industries concerned. As was said at the outset, attempts to use input-output tables for forecasting purposes depends on an assumption that the coefficients remain reasonably stable over time or, alternatively, that we have a sufficiently comprehensive series of tables to be able to track the movement of coefficients.

Comparisons made on the average input-output relationships by the Central Statistical Office between tables for broad industry groups suggest that, with few exceptions, the input-output coefficients tend to remain reasonably static. This sort of stability probably depends upon a number of factors. First, a very high level of aggregation is used in creating the input-output tables and it is clear that the more

Table 2.2 Total requirements per £1 000 of final industrial output in terms of gross output, 1968 (extract)

	Agriculture 1	Forestry and fishing 2	Coal mining 3	Other mining and quarrying 4	Non-ferrous metals 11	Mechanical engineering 12	Transport 31	Communication 32	Distributive trades 33	Miscellaneous services 34
1. Agriculture	1 065	1	—	3	—	—	2	—	—	2
2. Forestry and fishing	2	1 000	—	—	—	—	—	—	—	—
3. Coal mining	8	3	1 012	12	9	13	3	3	5	5
4. Other mining and quarrying	6	1	2	1 002	20	3	—	1	—	1
11. Non-ferrous metals	6	5	8	9	1 008	51	4	3	2	7
12. Mechanical engineering	10	11	57	50	23	1 013	8	3	5	6
31. Transport	42	70	35	187	40	36	1 009	46	71	16
32. Communication	10	8	4	11	5	11	4	1 001	30	33
33. Distributive trades	107	32	24	34	46	43	16	7	1 005	12
34. Miscellaneous services	65	78	18	116	44	67	29	16	74	1 016

finely various industries are disaggregated the greater is likely to be the tendency towards instability in the coefficient. Secondly, although average coefficients may remain stable, it does not follow that marginal coefficients will do the same (see p. 31 above). It may take a number of years before the quantity of output to which the new coefficient applies becomes sufficiently large in relation to the whole for the new coefficient to have a substantial effect on the average coefficient. Nevertheless, it should be borne in mind that for forecasting purposes we are particularly interested in marginal coefficients. A further difficulty is that the average input-output relationship for an industry would probably be different for that part of the industry's output added to stocks and work in progress than for that part which is actually sold. This is a special sort of case of coefficients of marginal output. It seems highly probable that the coefficient of marginal output will be very different in the 1970s for many industrial processes as compared with earlier years.

If we are predicting years through 1980 or 1990 and beyond by such a process, and on the assumption that the marginal coefficients have remained stable since the 1960s, we are undertaking an extremely hazardous exercise, but knowledge of specific applications involved may permit intelligent judgments to be made about the drift. Bear in mind, for example, that by 1990 practically all the equipment in use in the 1960s will have gone out of existence and a totally new set of industrial capital will be in operation. When we sound these warnings about the application of input-output to long-term projection of the economy, taken in terms of industries aggregated to thirty-four groupings for which we believe it is relevant to suppose that there is a fairly high degree of stability of the coefficients, consider how very much more hazardous it would be to attempt this sort of exercise for more highly disaggregated industrial groups which we have every reason to believe inherently very much less stable. Readers proposing to pursue the applications of input-output analysis further will find in *Economic Trends* for January 1971, how to obtain a seventy-industry matrix for 1968.

2.7 Shortcomings of macro-economic input-output tables for company forecasting

For company forecasting the published input-output tables suffer from a number of severe shortcomings: (1) lack of frequency of publication of tables; (2) level of aggregation of industry groups in the tables which makes them suitable only for very large firms which are involved over a wide range of the activities subsumed under any one industry heading; (3) lack of indication as to the marginal input-output coefficients for lack of consistency as between tables which have been produced at different points in time. For example, between 1954 and 1968 the number of industries has changed from forty-six to thirty-four or seventy and of these only a small handful are directly comparable. While the broad orders of magnitude of the coefficients remain the same, the impression that perhaps things have not changed very much is almost certainly misleading.

2.8 Construction of specialised input-output tables

There have been large numbers of do-it-yourself attempts at input-output table construction for various purposes. Two approaches are outlined here.

1. *A company with a few large customers.* Where the fortunes of a company are particularly strongly associated with that of one or a few large customers it is not uncommon for company analysts to attempt to create the input-output table relating the company in question to those customers in order to show the input to the consuming companies of the products of the company which is supplying them for every £1 000 of the output of the consuming companies. Thus, for example, a small company whose major customer is, say, a nationalised industry such as the National Coal Board and which could not afford sophisticated forecasting techniques of its own, might ride on the back of the sophisticated forecasts made of activity by such large industries as the one he is dealing with and by computing the input-output coefficient between the two be able to measure the implications for him of plans which the consuming industry has made for expansion or contraction. On a much more sophisticated level it is possible to work out marginal input-output coefficients, that is to say the value of finished output of our firm which will be required in order to implement changes implied by plans being made by the consuming company or industry. Since marginal relationships of this sort are of the essence of the economics of decision-making, potentially the technique of input-output analysis is a more powerful tool for decision-making than any other forecasting technique.

2. *Vertically integrated firms* offer considerable potential for the application of input-output analysis to company planning. One desirable feature of such planning is to be able to investigate rapidly the mix of different end products of sales on the requirements of raw materials, machine time, stocks base and labour inputs at various departments which are mutually interrelated. By setting up the input-output relationship for product output or, indeed, for the input of our products to consuming industries as against the outputs of our various departments, it is possible to use a computer to simulate quickly and accurately the likely effect of a very wide variety of possible changes in our make mix on the requirements on various elements of capacity in the firm. Potential bottlenecks can then be readily spotted as well as making it possible to compute such things as labour requirements, management requirement and so on. Once again it must be stressed that the principal value of input-output in this sort of application as well as in economic forecast application lies in the ability of input-output to highlight inconsistencies in forecasts or in plans. These inconsistencies may represent one or two possibilities. The first is that an irrational element has been built into the forecasting mechanism and that an error therefore has been committed which ought to be rectified. The second is that a previously unforeseen circumstance has been brought to light, thereby pinpointing an area for managerial action.

There are, of course, many types of companies to whom this tool of forecasting will not be applicable. For example, small companies which do not have access to a computer to the extent which would be required to make use of such complex simulations of economic activity as are implied in full utilization of the input-output technique. Second, companies whose prosperity is tied not so much to one large stable sector of the economy as to their skill as entrepreneurs in developing new products technologically or in mounting clever marketing campaigns for their product. (One application in the former case, however, is, of course, the ability of input-output to detect spots where technological innovation will be required.) Another is the closely integrated company in which interdepartmental or divisional transactions are not particularly an important feature of life.

A word about the use of computers may be in order at this point. The problem facing most companies in this direction is not access to computing, but access to the skills needed to utilize computing facilities which are now within reach of any organization. Most of the standard mathematical techniques employed by fore-casters can be computed using standard programs available through computer bureaux, of which there are many in large towns. There are standard programs for regression, multiple regression, correlation and exponential smoothing, as well as matrix manipulations required for input-output analysis which can be operated in any of the commercially available systems. The trick today is not to make programs work — they are all pretty thoroughly tested — but to select the most appropriate system, program, program variant, and data inputs to arrive at a meaningful problem solution.

In these directions, as in many areas of forecasting activity, the problems are managerial rather than mathematical. In general, the state of the forecasting art is such that mathematical and technical development is well in advance of most firms' capacities to exploit these developments thoroughly in pursuit of managerial ends. This is another area which will be dealt with more fully in chapter 9; at this point it is sufficient to signal that the technical resources are within reach of any company.

2.9 Input-output and technological forecasting

Some firms pursue technological change for its own sake, hoping that by being in the forefront of technological innovation they may be guaranteeing a profitable future for themselves. One problem inherent in this strategy is that of creating technological breakthrough for which there is no viable economic market for the firm which has produced the breakthrough. To be profitable for the firm which is involved with technological innovation it is important that the innovation be related to economic opportunity. This gives rise to a need for an objective and consistent way to identify and measure the economic consequences of techno-logical change and the technological consequences of economic opportunity. The economic consequences of innovation can be assessed from the marginal coeffi-cients of input-output which may be derived from a series of input-output tables over the years or, alternatively, investigated directly by comparing the input-output coefficient of the new process with that which it has replaced. The identification of technological opportunity on the other hand can be derived from the average coefficients of the input-output tables by projecting different alternative levels for gross national product at differing time periods, and, having assigned to them the expected probabilities of occurrence, noting the effects of the various alternative outcomes upon existing technological capacity.

Where in light of the knowledge of the technologists and managers in the firm it is held that existing technological capacity will be under severe strain, this clearly points to the areas in which research and development effort should be devoted and in which there is liable to be the greatest economic payoff from innovation.

Published studies of this type of material have generally been based on aggregate economic input-output tables published nationally. As a result they have highlighted those factors of economic development which are already fairly well understood: for example, the growing importance in economic development of such factors as power, transport and communication, business services, finance and property. In this way such studies tend to point up areas of relatively declining significance. Single kinds of material such as metals, quarry products, wood, natural fibres, rubber, leather and so on in each kind of production give way to increasing diversification of the material consumed by each industry. In other words, investigation confirms that the proliferation of new materials and new methods increases the variety of input to each economic sector. With greater variety, the input columns in the tables show more elements in common and the diversification of materials breaks down the primary identity of the major industrial sectors. That this sort of exercise is feasible on the more specific scale of the markets appropriate to the individual company is beyond question. It is, however, an area in which virtually no findings have been published.

Use of input-output analysis in this application is, therefore, the prerogative of the sophisticated company where the level of detailed knowledge and skill will be far beyond the compass of an introductory discussion such as the present. The services of a graduate economist or equivalent are required to exploit the possibilities of input-output, and interested readers are referred to the specialist literature for further reading.

2.10 Summary

In the world economy and society, the fortunes of any one firm or industry are heavily conditioned by a host of environmental factors, operating through the markets in which they participate. Whether it is appropriate to forecast for a whole economy or industry, or for an individual product depends on the reasons for which the forecast is made and on the relationship of the product or firm with the industry or economy. It is not possible to conduct any meaningful forecasting operation beyond short-run mechanical forecasting (if that) in absence of a sufficiently clear perception of the environmental factors affecting the variables under scrutiny.

At its lowest level this may mean simply using published secondary information as a basis for producing forecasts, and checking their consistency with published general economic or broad industry forecasts. At its most sophisticated, it may involve the sort of activity which some firms indulge in of trying to obtain a complete picture of the economies in which they operate, at some appropriate points in future time. In particular, one shortcut method used in producing forecasts is to keep track of appropriate industrial or economic indicators, whose behaviour is found consistently to lead the sort of economic data which we are trying to predict.

One method of examining economic and industrial interrelationships comprehensively is to use published input-output tables, which give a complete snapshot of inter-industry relationships in an economy periodically, and which can be related to the overall level of activity in the economy. Assuming constant input-output coefficients, or assuming that coefficients change to some value predicted from knowledge of economic trends, it is possible to simulate on a computer the overall input-output position of industry at various levels of gross domestic income, taxation, imports and exports.

As an analytical technique for business forecasting purposes, however, input-output is still in a very crude state, and to develop it fully company analysts would require to do much work, especially on marginal coefficients.

REFERENCES

Ball, R. J. and Burns, T. 'An economic approach to short run analysis of the UK economy, 1955–66', *Operational Research Quarterly*, September 1968.

Bratt, E. C. *Business Forecasting*, McGraw-Hill, 1968.

Butler, W. F. and Kavesh, R. A., eds., *How Business Economists Forecast*, Prentice-Hall, 1966.

Central Statistical Office. *Input-Output Tables for the United Kingdom, 1954*, HMSO, 1961; *Input-Output Tables for the United Kingdom, 1963*, Studies in Official Statistics, No. 16, HMSO, 1970; 'Provisional Input-Output Tables for 1968', *Economic Trends* No. 207, HMSO, January 1971.

Chenery, H. B. and Clark, P. G. *Interindustry Economics*, Wiley, 1959.

Leontieff, Wassily *Input-Output Economics*, Oxford University Press, 1966.

3 Forecasts based on mathematical trends

A trend is a trend is a trend. The question is, when will it bend? Will it climb higher and higher, or eventually expire, and come to an untimely end?

A. K. Cairncross

3.1. Pictures and models of economic activity

The central purpose of business forecasting, it has already been argued, is to improve the quality of management decisions by systematically organizing and analysing existing knowledge so as to measure and, it may be hoped, reduce the field of uncertainty about the future, and to trace the consequences of uncertain events on the possible outcomes of present decisions. The central problem is how most effectively to mobilize the data and information currently available to the firm in order to provide a set of readings about the future which has a positive commercial value.

The stages in solving such a problem are as follows: first, the identification of the commercial problem in whose solution the forecasting activity is to be used; second, provision of data and information relevant to the problem; third, adoption of analytical processes which will sharpen the utility of the existing data; fourth, the interpretation of findings and their integration into the decision-taking process.

We have already spent considerable time on the areas of problem identification, with some suggestions as to the types of forecasting techniques which might be appropriate in specific contexts. So far as data provision is concerned, it is difficult to suggest much formally: however, careful reading at any stage of the text indicates clearly the author's misgivings about the quality of data which is commonly available to the forecaster. It cannot be stressed too strongly that no business analysis can be better than the data fed into it, and that the information system in many firms is today inadequate to support more than crude and primitive evaluation techniques. Adequate to good information for decision-making involving implications in the future is a very expensive commodity. Getting the best information for the forecasting task in time for it to be relevant involves a considerable recordable out of pocket cost, whereas the costs of not having relevant timely information go unrecorded but the competition faced by almost any firm today will dictate a severe penalty where management does not really know what is going on.

In this and the next two chapters the focus of our concern will be statistical analysis of quantitative data available within the firm. The emphasis is, however, very much less upon the statistics than on the purposes of the analyses under discussion. The techniques we shall be examining are those designed to analyse time series by means of least squares regression, classical methods and exponential smoothing, and those designed to specify simple models of the interaction of economic and business trends, correlation and multiple regression. Only enough description of the techniques is offered to enable a completely non-mathematical manager to see what they can do for him, and to judge whether he wants to use them or not. The descriptions should also be adequate to enable the manager in a small company to approach a straightforward regression or time series problem manually, and to obtain a slight appreciation of the power of modern computing to turn these techniques into really valuable tools to aid decision-making. It is hoped that references to the standard works will compensate for deficiencies in the technical presentations, viewed from the standpoint of the specialist.

There is an essential unity underlying these three chapters, in that all the suggestions offered are designed to enhance the understanding which a manager may have of the determinants of a set of economic data. For example, assume that we have records of some economic phenomenon — bank rate, gross national product, profits, prices, output and so on — normally through time. All that the whole elaborate process of forecasting is about is trying to understand why the phenomenon behaved as it did, with a view to sharpening our insight as to how it is likely to behave in the future. We can frequently tell a lot simply by examining the figures. Generally we can tell much more by looking at the figures in conjunction with knowledge about related events. Sometimes it is possible to tie one set of figures closely in with another. In other words, we attempt to move from the stage of producing a picture of the events in which we are interested, to producing a working model interrelating one set of events with another.

This is not necessarily the order of precedence which occurs in real life. For example, in a simple situation such as the introduction of a new service by a small entrepreneurially run firm, the entrepreneur will begin with an intellectual model relating what he believes to be the current state of some aspects of technology and society's behaviour to the existence of an economic demand for his service. The model may be an adequate basis for the innovation, without the construction of more than the most impressionistic sort of through-time picture of the social or technological trends involved. In other words, the process of picture-forming and model-building tends to be interactive and iterative in real thinking, as we modify our pictures when the model fails to perform adequately and our model as we get better descriptions of its component parts. No forecasting system may ever, therefore, be regarded as final. The perfect model will never be produced so long as society and technology is evolving.

3.2 Towards the first sketch

Let us start thinking about a very simple case. Suppose we have the sales data for one product line, magnetized torque wrenches, made by the firm of the same name. MTW (for short) first produced this line many years ago, and it is still a central feature of the company's activity. It has wide applications throughout engineering. Recently production has been near capacity of the existing plant, and the question is, should the production facilities be expanded?

The Sales Department can readily produce figures for monthly orders and shipments for a period of ten years and offer to get figures back a further ten years or more at considerable cost in search if we really want them. These figures and some others are contained in Table 3.1. For the moment they are worth only a glance to pick up the basis of the following discussion. Table 3.1 gives us a quarterly presentation of the raw data immediately available in the company's information system. Although the numbers tend to get bigger through time, this tells us nothing we do

Table 3.1 *Magnetized Torque Wrenches Ltd. Sales statistics, 1961–70*

Quarterly data		Deliveries (£'000)	Orders (£'000)	Quarterly data		Deliveries (£'000)	Orders (£'000)
1961	I	2 596	2 781	1966	I	4 124	5 120
	II	3 023	2 809		II	5 176	5 225
	III	2 817	2 712		III	5 232	5 352
	IV	2 592	3 008		IV	2 236	4 811
1962	I	3 574	3 475	1967	I	6 180	5 536
	II	3 712	3 590		II	6 305	5 827
	III	3 595	3 628		III	6 026	6 212
	IV	3 638	3 324		IV	5 976	6 563
1963	I	2 848	2 433	1968	I	6 824	6 622
	II	2 137	2 407		II	7 045	7 073
	III	2 240	2 461		III	7 138	6 946
	IV	2 608	3 382		IV	7 275	7 448
1964	I	3 235	3 543	1969	I	7 508	7 337
	II	3 728	3 467		II	7 412	7 606
	III	3 403	3 491		III	7 724	7 718
	IV	3 469	4 098		IV	8 036	7 603
1965	I	4 402	4 281	1970	I	7 628	7 478
	II	4 589	5 018		II	7 502	7 563
	III	4 333	4 234		III	7 286	7 505
	IV	4 213	4 198		IV	7 588	7 647

not already know. How does management use such figures to help form a judgment on the sort of path they will follow in the future? The answer to this question depends on the answers to a number of questions about the data; these are the business of the remainder of this section.

Some simple data questions are (1) have we a long enough data base relative to the forecast horizon, (2) how relevant are the oldest data, (3) how accurate are the figures (which depends on sources and methods of collection), and (4) how much do we know about the contingent events (strikes, holidays, product changes, etc.) that would materially affect the series?

Then there are a number of questions about what the data are recording and what they tell us.

1. Do the deliveries series show numbers of units or income from sales? If numbers, could these be affected by, for example, a growth in complexity of equipment leading to a much greater value content? If income, how much price inflation is built in over the period? What has been the change in unit value after correcting for inflation? Numbers or weight might be relevant for (say) decisions involving transportation, while value may be relevant for labour supply and income may be relevant to cash flow planning. Which are more relevant for an expansion of capacity decision? It can be argued cogently that in a context of a decision whether or not to extend manufacturing capacity we are interested in three versions of the output measurement variable; physical units produced, value in current terms, and value at constant prices.

The first, physical units, is relevant to problems of materials flow and handling, as well as stockholding capacity. Value in current pounds is relevant to the financial analysis of the project, while value in real terms may be an important measure of the growth in technical complexity of the equipment, when compared with the numbers of units produced. This indicator may be important in planning, for example, for the provision of sophisticated or specialized machinery, in its turn perhaps materially more expensive than conventional equipment and having repercussions on the financial outcome of the project.

Comparison of sales value normally based on invoice summation, and physical units produced, normally from production records, should be reconciled through stock changes. In practice it is never possible to obtain a perfect reconciliation, and an important area for managerial decision lies in judging when the reconciliation has proceeded sufficiently far to ensure that both the sales and production series are acceptably accurate, and the stock changes, if they are to be used as a basis for planning storage capacity, are well accounted for.

If the foregoing comparison and reconciliation is a time-consuming and frequently frustrating task, the problem of extracting constant value sales estimates is positively hazardous. For practical purposes, what usually happens is for product line components which have remained materially unchanged in specification over the period of the analysis to be used for the creation of an inflation index, which is then applied arbitrarily to the whole line. Once the inflationary factor has been discounted, any remaining value increase per unit of output is assumed to measure the net effect of increasing sophistication on one hand and greater production or commercial economies on the other. To disentangle these last two would be enormously complicated and rarely justified.

2. Having satisfied ourselves that the figures are the relevant ones for our purpose, and that compensation has been made for changes in, for example, material intensity or inflation, the next question is whether these data measure what we want measured. In many cases we first have deliveries, i.e. the value of goods actually leaving the warehouse as measured by sales invoices. What we want is customer demand. There are many ways in which our shipments might diverge from customer demand, for example, through production having been delayed by raw material shortages, labour troubles, lack of capacity or transport difficulties. So we must examine whether any deliveries recorded in a given period ought to have been attributed to previous or later periods. This can only be done by recalling the history of the period, through both management's recollections and contemporary records. Any adjustments may have to be made arbitrarily.

3. To what extent do the figures reflect changes in their basis through time? The deliveries series shows what the firm was prepared to deliver, but not necessarily what customers were asking for. In response to demand changes, however, the product line covered by the series might have widened very materially and the recorded sales expansion may reflect merely this single phenomenon. Analysis would be required in this case to distinguish the deepening of sales from the widening of the range, and this would be applied to the decision problem in terms of the proportion of expanded sales which could be expected from existing products as compared with the proportion from a wider product line.

4. Yet another divergence of shipments from demand could arise if our sales growth were to reflect chronic shortage of capacity in a preferred supplier's plant, i.e. customers whose intended orders are choked off through lack of production facilities elsewhere come to us as a second string. If the preferred supplier then lays down additional capacity at the same time as we do, this would be very serious for us. There are two clues, which emerge clearly from market share graphs, which indicate that this might be the case; first, when over the period of the business cycle, our market share goes up in boom times and down in recession times we may be sure we are a second string supplier: second, when in a period of tight general capacity our volume of orders or inquiries is rising at an increasing rate we should be exceedingly suspicious of the extent to which this reflects a true demand increase. It is much more likely to reflect multiple ordering and inquiry.

5. To what extent does the series reflect primary demand changes for the total market offering of these products, and to what extent does it measure a selective demand for our own product line? This may be a question of considerable importance, since the area of general market forces is much more amenable to demand extrapolation than is one company's activities.

Over the area of a whole industry, continuity of activity and gradual change is generally not an unwarranted assumption, whereas for the individual firm changes can be affected abruptly and decisively by managerial intervention.

The stock answer to this problem is to say that the forecaster assumes no new managerial initiatives (though the time series on which his projections are based are themselves the result of managerial initiatives) to create products and variants or to discontinue brands, to advertise or stop advertising, to promote heavily or withdraw support, to seek wider distribution or drop distributors. Even the assumption of a continuation of 'the mix as before' is fraught with uncertainty; a better assumption is the existence of a learning curve for management – that they become more efficient and effective at creating, selling and delivering a product line as time passes.

In summary, we should proceed with the analysis only when we are fully satis-fied that the figures we have either represent or are an accurate proxy for the variable we wish to forecast, that the underlying changes in the structure of the figures are of a sort which is going to continue through the forecast period (other-wise the changes should be disaggregated so that the effects of each can be separ-ately assessed) and that special influences have not been at work to cause artificial depression or escalation of figures, or rephasing of figures from one time period to another. Beware, also, hidden changes in the basis of figures, especially published or total market series. In using secondary sources it is necessary always to read the small print surrounding the data.

3.3 The first sketch

The MTW sales and orders data are recorded in Table 3.1, expressed as time series graphs in Fig. 3.1. The picture is to most minds much clearer in diagrammatic form. Let us ask of these data the questions discussed in the previous section. Further information is sketched in Fig. 3.2.

1. Is the data base long enough? In this case, since extended capacity is relatively simple to install, we are looking to a forecast horizon of one to five years ahead: a ten-year basis should normally be adequate. Also there is a tendency for the trend of the data to inflect upwards during years three and four and to flatten out about year nine, giving rise to the most commonly encountered trend shape in a situation surrounding a real decision, namely a flat S-shaped curve. With two changes of direction of this sort, it is pretty clear that the economic phenomena at the end of the period will have little in common with those at the beginning.

2. Are the earliest data relevant? Probably, in this case, yes. They help to illustrate the existence of seasonal and cyclical swings in the sales pattern which have been somewhat obscured by the powerful trend rise of years five to eight and the effects of the strike in year six. Also they help us locate the beginning of the strong trend rise. Since sales have risen by a factor of three to four times in six to eight years, and the product has been marketed for thirty to forty, a growth trend of the sort shown here cannot have been sustained for long. Already we can therefore tie down our projection problem: knowing that the path of sales has been of a 'lazy S' shape∫, to which statisticians can fit curves, has this also been the pattern of demand, or has

£'000

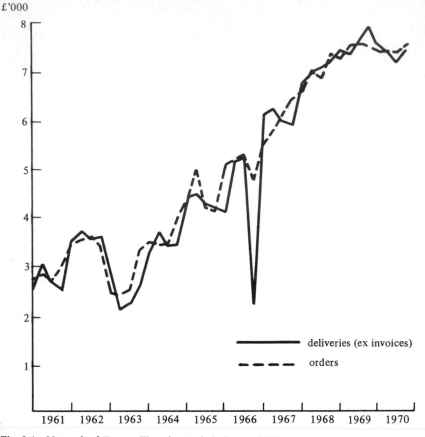

Fig. 3.1. Magnetized Torque Wrenches Ltd. Orders and deliveries: raw quarterly data 1961–70.

demand been suppressed by our lack of capacity and so should therefore be represented by a curve of this shape╱ ?

3. Data accuracy. In this case, since the basic sources are highly reliable analysis of
invoices collected on a continuing basis collected individually for the product group
under forecast, we have no anxieties. However, the timing of payment for goods
received by customers may be out of phase with the deliveries series, with important repercussions for cash-flow forecasting which may need to be taken into
account. This series does not net out any goods subsequently returned as defective,
etc. (around 0.5 to 1 per cent) and to that extent may overstate sales. Throughput
in thousands of units, extracted from works records, is unreliable, as recording may
be delayed by operatives so as to maximize their production bonuses one month
with another, a practice tolerated by management within limits.

4. There was a severe strike in year six with a marked effect on third quarter output. The extent to which business was totally lost, and to which sales were post-
poned, is hopelessly obscured by the powerfully rising market. Product range has

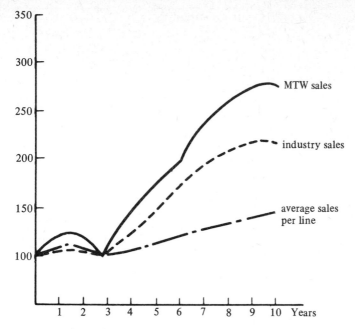

Fig. 3.2. Magnetized Torque Wrenches Ltd: Sales, industry sales and MTW sales per average line
In this rough sketch the data are reduced to an index number basis for ease of graphical comparison.

also widened in the period, from eighteen items at the beginning to a current thirty-two with six being added at the end of year four and three during year seven, the remainder at a rate of one or two in any year.

5. Products added to the line have generally been more sophisticated in concept, but the company has pursued a policy of simplifying design. In particular much attention was being paid to value analysis* in years seven, eight and nine.

6. Despite this, five line components remained unchanged throughout the ten years, and a composite of their price changes has been used to deflate the 'current price' graph to one based on notional constant prices.

7. The reconciliation between deliveries and production through stock changes was too imprecise to be worth recording in the present context because of a bizarre warehouse stock recording system. (The job in fact was never completed.)

8. Both products in the line from the outset and recent introductions have sales growth patterns which vary in an unstructured manner. Although a few products grow consistently fast and a few consistently slowly, these are divided without pattern among old and new products. It is therefore possible to say that the average rate of growth of individual lines seems to be unaffected by line widening. (Details

---

* Value analysis — a technique for reducing costs by comprehensive design reassessment based upon the purpose of a tool or component in use.

of this analysis are not presented here though it is easy to see how it would be done, by creating a weighted average sales per product for each period, divided between the different categories which it was desired to differentiate. From this, any material distinctions in growth rate will emerge clearly. It is a long messy process of trial and error investigation.)

9. On analysis of MTW's sales by comparison with those of the industry group as a whole, given deficiencies in the industry's data, there was no evidence of MTW's being a 'second string' supplier. On the contrary, with the largest market share in the industry and a slightly faster growth rate than the industry as a whole, there is considerable evidence for suggesting that they are one of the most preferred suppliers, and their fortunes are dependent on those of their consumers generally, supplemented by somewhat superior management. The result of this is that selective demand for MTW's lines generally tends to be stronger than primary demand.

Having come so far in preliminary analysis of the available data, the question now is, what basis do they provide for extrapolation? What extrapolations is it intelligent to pursue, and what are the best ways to do them?

3.4 Judgment on time trends

Answering these questions calls for judgment, not only on the shapes of the curves, but also on the extent to which these shapes may have been affected by economic or technological forces of the type identified and discussed above, in other words, the first approach to a rudimentary model explaining our observations. There are three views which the forecaster could intelligently take on the observations in Fig. 3.1.

First, that the data essentially conform to a steadily accelerating growth trend model (*exponential*) which has been unnaturally restricted in the last two years by shortage of capacity (i.e. using the first eight years' data).

Second, that the trend of the last eight years has been essentially linear and the observations of years one and two are now barely relevant. In this case it might be argued that some of the trends are more linear than others, notably the constant value trend, and it would be necessary to argue that the flattening of the last eight quarters was a result of capacity constraints, cyclical downturn, or both.

Third, that using all ten years' figures, the observations provide a classic flattened S-shape growth curve, conforming to our *a priori* expectations of market growth and saturation. Sooner or later the growth curve must flatten out for the long term, whether the flattening we have here is attributable to this or to short term, temporary factors is, on the basis of information presently available, an open question.

Clearly, before deciding which picture we prefer as a basis for projection, we must collect further information. Life is such that, unfortunately, the quick and dirty route to a forecast, namely to try all three projections on a basis of what we currently have, is intellectually satisfying to professional trend men, and would involve them in doing interesting things with computers. Digging out further information, on the other hand, is tedious and frustrating. It does not involve mathematical elegance and rigour. One needs to be strongminded.

Fortunately, one piece of information is readily to hand, the average sales of each member of the product line. This is obtained by aggregating the sales of each component in the product line and dividing the total by the number of such components, thereby netting out the effects of the line widening.

Another statistic which can be produced fairly readily is an estimate of total industry sales, a proxy for total customer demand.

A third possibility would be to extend our sales series back in time to try to get a firmer reading on the S-shaped growth curve hypothesis.

At this point the analyst is confronted with a mass of computation, usually of a basic arithmetic type designed to clean up the data so as to clarify the following readings.

1. The long-term growth pattern of our sales.
2. Any regular fluctuations in this pattern (e.g. cyclical fluctuations which would affect our judgment as to whether the current flattening is cyclical); methods for doing this are discussed in chapter 4.
3. Long-term changes and regular fluctuations in market growth.

The objective of this exercise is to obtain readings which will direct the analyst's attention to likely causal relationships — sales changes associated with demand changes, general economic changes, competitive position changes and any other hypothesis which may seem a likely starter.

Some results of this type of computation are carried in Fig. 3.2, which is one of many alternative pictures the analyst will consider at this point. At this stage the trend lines have been mostly sketched in by eye, running a smooth curve through the actual data. Even this crude version of a complex picture suggests a number of valuable ideas.*

First there is a strong consistency of shape among the three trends, total industry sales, MTW sales, and individual line component sales. This suggests that MTW is broadly typical of the industry (as would be expected in a market leader), but also that industry sales can be used to obtain a sense of the extent to which MTW's last eight quarters' history can be attributed to capacity shortage.

Second, we see from the industry trend that it has been somewhat S-shaped. An alternative to trying to fit a curve for prediction might be to try a linear fit for years one to five, hypothesize that six, seven and eight were exceptional growth years, and that the industry growth in the last eight quarters has been consistent with the old linear long term trend at a slightly higher plateau.

---

* There are considerable and very valid objections to the business of running trend lines by eye, particularly where the data are highly scattered. However, many business time series do confirm to smooth patterns, and no great effort of imagination is required to obtain a quick fit, or even a band of possible fits, which may be quite adequate for preliminary speculative surveys. At this stage we are more interested in quick, speculative sketches than in fully elaborated analyses.

We might infer that since MTW's growth rate *per line* has been lower than the industry average, and total growth greater, the principal reason for the faster growth rate has been a more ambitious innovation policy than average.

The general inference is that MTW's growth in sales at constant value is partly dependent on industry growth rates, and partly a function of differential advantage in product policy. The first of these is amenable to statistical projection, the second to other forms of managerial analysis and investigation.

In this particular case, therefore, one suggests that the most reasonable approach to further analysis is on a basis of a model which calls for MTW growth to be related to industry growth (statistically projectible) modified by important non-statistical elements. Such a model would clearly be Heath-Robinson and would not gladden the heart of the statistical purist. The only managerial criterion is, will it work? (In practice, it did.) We can now turn our attention to statistical projection of the relevant trends, for relevant ends.

3.5 Trend projection

Trend projection is easier to do than to explain; the easiest manually is the straight line, though computer programs are available which will handle a number of complex curve shapes as well as the simple ones. Such programs are simple to operate, but the user must be shown how. The most appropriate place to learn this is in the context of a computing system to which the user has regular access, hence little is said about this aspect here.

What all projection methods aspire to do more or less accurately is to produce a *least squares regression estimate*; this means that the line produced represents the best average slope and position which can be devised for one straight line to represent all the points on the chart. In the present case, the regression of sales on time, it means that the sum of all the vertical distances from each of the actual points is as small as possible; any other line would produce a larger sum of these vertical distances. The expression 'least squares' is used because some of the differences will be positive (points above the line) and some negative (points below the line). The act of squaring these quantities makes all the differences positive, and the best fitting trend line is the one which minimizes the sum of these squares, hence 'least squares' (Fig. 3.3).

Graphical method 1 (approximate). There are many ways of producing a least squares regression of one set of data on another. The simplest is to judge by eye, and where the points cluster closely round a straight line, this will be the simplest one to adopt: simply take a ruler through the points. Where, as is usually the case, the points do not lie neatly on a straight line other quick approximations are possible.

Graphical method 2 (approximate). It is a property of a regression line that it passes

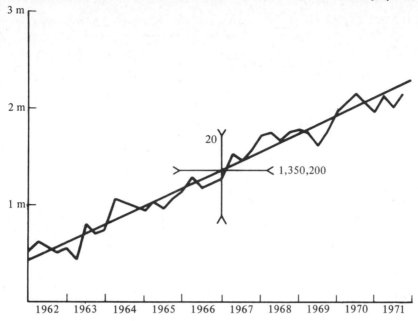

Fig. 3.3. The Specialized Steel Company Shipments (quarterly series) 1962—71.

This series has been chosen to illustrate simple linear regression chiefly because, unlike most economic time series and unlike the Magnetized Torque Wrench series, the data are extremely linear, and therefore a number of simple curve-fitting techniques can be adopted which will enable the analyst to obtain rapid and fairly accurate pictures. These techniques are not confined only to strictly linear series. One hypothesis on the MTW series is that it is made up of three sections in each of which a linear series is the most appropriate form. If this is so, and the economics of the real situation need to be examined in order to establish the validity of the hypothesis, it would be possible to fit curves to the third part of the series using the techniques outlined in this section.

The point 20; 1 350 200 represents the mean of both variables and it can be shown that the estimating line must pass through this point. Thereafter one of the simplest graphical curve-fitting techniques is to draw a line such that it passes through the two means and otherwise has about half the data above and half below the estimating line. In those situations, as here, where the data fall very close to a straight line this technique gives the analyst speedy and cheap pictures which are fairly accurate — most valuable when engaged in a long search process, with lots of possible alternatives to be evaluated.

The best-fitting straight line which can be drawn through the data is one which has the property that the sum of the vertical distances from each point above the line to the line, minus the sum of the vertical distances of each point below the line to the line, is as near zero as can be achieved. In practice, the squares of the vertical distances are used to obviate the problem of computing negative values, hence the description of this line as the *least squares estimator*.

through the average (arithmetic mean) of the points measured on the x axis and on the y axis. The average of the x's on Fig. 3.3 is 20 and the average of the y's for the shipments data is approximately 1 350 200, therefore one point on our regression line is 20, 1 350 200 shown in Fig. 3.3. Another feature of regression lines is that approximately half the points will lie above them and half below, so with one firm point we can make a tolerable stab at the slope, and hence the complete line. The regression line in Fig. 3.3 has seventeen points above, seventeen below and four on the line.

Computer-based method (virtually precise). On-line and batch processing computer systems generally have a capacity to operate regression programs with immense power, simplicity and time economy. For the company which regards itself as too small to have direct access to a large computer, the answer is provided by computer bureaux which are located in every industrial centre. The power of these installations is so enormous that the use of desk calculators to compute regressions must now be regarded as obsolete. All that is required is for the forecaster to enter on a sheet of paper, or type on a terminal, the values of the dependent variable (e.g. sales value) and the independent variables (in this case time) and await the output giving the values of the coefficients of the independent variables which, for visual purposes, are easily transformed to lines on graph paper.

In practice we frequently encounter technical problems such as non-linear relationships and heteroscedasticity variables, which we shall discuss shortly, as well as the managerial problems out-lined earlier in this chapter. Therefore trial and error is involved in using regression, in identifying the most appropriate variables, and model to describe them. For this purpose an on-line terminal associated with a time-sharing computer system is probably the most appropriate. Generally such systems have standard library programs for computing complex regression analyses.

Although the desk-calculator method has been described as obsolete, some understanding of it is probably the clearest way to get into some of the issues raised in using regression for more elaborate and useful purposes than merely fitting the best possible straight line to data.

Algebraic method (precise). Like any other straight line, the linear regression estimate has an algebraic form of the type

$$S = mt + c$$

where S represents sales

and t represents the time period in which these sales were recorded

m and c are constants still to be determined, which will give the best linear fit to any set of data. It must be stressed that the discovery of this best-fitting line is an entirely mechanical process, and whether it is even remotely sensible to try to fit a straight line is a matter for the judgment of the analyst. What the formula above means is that sales will change through time by a constant value m; starting from a value at time $t = 0$ of c. This is illustrated in Fig. 3.4.

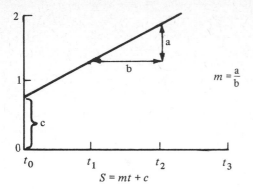

Fig. 3.4 A straight line is determined by an equation containing a term for slope, relating it to changes in the independent variable (*mt*) and a term for location with respect to the ordinate (*c*).

The values of m and c are given by the following formulae:

$$m = \frac{\Sigma\, tS - \dfrac{(\Sigma\, t)\,(\Sigma\, S)}{N}}{\Sigma\, t^2 - \dfrac{(\Sigma\, t)^2}{N}}$$

and $$c = \frac{(\Sigma\, t)\,(\Sigma\, tS) - (\Sigma\, S \,\Sigma\, t^2)}{(\Sigma\, t)^2 - N(\Sigma\, t^2)}$$

where t is the time period

   S is sales

and N is the number of observations

   Σ is the mathematical 'symbol for 'the sum of all the terms'

While it is perfectly possible to apply these formulae direct to the data to find the least squares regression equation, it is better to simplify the calculation in order to avoid the problem of having to handle numbers that are inordinately large.

This is illustrated by calculating the regression equation for annual industry shipments from years one to ten on Fig. 3.3. Use of annual data provides the first simplification, enabling us to use ten rather than forty observations. The second simplification is to deal in round thousands of pounds: any loss of accuracy here is negligible relative to the job which we want the regression to do for us. These raw data are entered in columns (1) and (2) of Table 3.3.

Before proceeding, another simplification is invoked. Columns (3) and (4) of Table 3.3 contain the data of columns (1) and (2) in a *transformed* form. In column

Table 3.2 *Specialised Steel Company*

		Quarterly deliveries (£)			Quarterly deliveries (£)
1962	I	508 220	1967	I	1 289 331
	II	613 480		II	1 536 483
	III	584 271		III	1 462 506
	IV	503 796		IV	1 572 620
		2 209 767			5 860 920
1963	I	547 497	1968	I	1 763 481
	II	432 216		II	1 748 253
	III	801 200		III	1 689 269
	IV	705 623		IV	1 748 221
		2 486 536			6 949 224
1964	I	738 417	1969	I	1 793 089
	II	1 087 235		II	1 776 615
	III	1 026 191		III	1 628 204
	IV	1 004 786		IV	1 752 830
		3 856 729			6 950 738
1965	I	947 232	1970	I	1 986 471
	II	1 020 717		II	2 093 947
	III	929 048		III	2 175 020
	IV	1 031 640		IV	2 086 408
		3 938 637			8 341 846
1966	I	1 144 009	1971	I	1 989 763
	II	1 300 026		II	2 121 343
	III	1 198 784		III	2 019 761
	IV	1 204 062		IV	2 163 202
		4 846 881			8 367 069

(3) the data of column (1) have had 5 subtracted from them, and those of column (4) are column (2) with 5 500 subtracted. These transformations have the effect of producing column sums close to (but not equal to) 0, which is very convenient when we have to square or multiply these column sums, as it avoids our having to work with enormous numbers.

From the last line of Table 3.3 we can read directly values which are required in the formulae to determine m and c. The only things we have to remember are that the resulting value for c is the one appropriate to time period 5, rather than time period 0, and the value we get will be too small by a factor of 1 000 (representing the curtailing of our figures) plus 5 500 representing our transformation. Before obtaining our final solution, our answer needs to be rectified to take these points into account.

Table 3.3

(1) time (*t*)	(2) Shipments (*S*) (to nearest '000)	(3) *t'* (*t*−5)	(4) *S'* (*S*−5.5)	(5) *t'*^{2}	(6) *t'S'*
1	2 210	−4	−3 290	16	13 160
2	2 487	−3	−3 013	9	9 039
3	3 857	−2	−1 643	4	3 286
4	3 939	−1	−1 561	1	1 561
5	4 847	0	−653	0	0
6	5 861	1	+361	1	361
7	6 949	2	+1 449	4	2 898
8	6 951	3	+1 451	9	4 353
9	8 342	4	+2 842	16	9 368
10	8 367	5	+2 867	25	14 335
		Σ *t'*	Σ *S'*	Σ *t'*^{2}	Σ *t'S'*
		5	1 190	85	58 361

The data in this table are derived from the annual figures given in Table 3.2. They illustrate a standard manner of laying out data in order to derive a linear regression equation for a single dependent variable.

The calculations are very simple, however: by substitution from Table 3.2 into the formulae,

$$m = \frac{58\ 361 - \dfrac{5 \times (-1\ 190)}{10}}{85 - \dfrac{25}{10}}$$

$$= 714.6\ (\times 1\ 000) = 714\ 600$$

$$c = \frac{5 \times 58\ 361 - (-1\ 190 \times 85)}{25 - 10 \times 85}$$

$$= -473.2\ (\times 1\ 000)\ (+5\ 500\ 000)$$

$$= 5\ 026\ 800\ (\text{at year 5})$$

or $5\ 026\ 800 - 5 \times 714\ 600$ at year 0

$$= 1\ 453\ 800$$

The required regression equation for annual industry shipments through time, therefore, is

$S = 714\ 600t + 1\ 435\ 800$,

i.e. from a base of £1 435 800 in year 0 the normal sales increase for years 1 through 10 of our time series is £714 600.

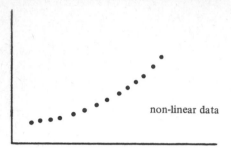

Fig. 3.5 Economic data are usually non-linear

The equation is statistically correct for the period over which it was derived. Does it, however, meet tests of reasonableness in any attempt to extrapolate it? Before extrapolating forward, consider what happens if it is extrapolated backward. Figure 3.3 tells the same story visually.

3.6 Errors in regression estimates and projections

Linear regression fitting is entirely a 'sausage machine' process. Put data in at one end, and the best-fitting single straight line will normally emerge at the other. There are two main sources of statistical error to beware of, conditions under which the resulting straight line will not merely be unhelpful, but positively misleading.

The first is where the data are, as is normally the case, non-linear (Fig. 3.5). If the trend of the observations follows a curve, the linear regression will still fit the best straight line to the data, but any projection will be nonsense. There is a little which we can do with non-linearity graphically, and computers handle non-linear forms as routinely as linear. This is discussed in the next section.

The second problem which vitiates meaningful regression fitting is that of *heteroscedasticity*, that is, where the amplitude of the variances of the actual data points

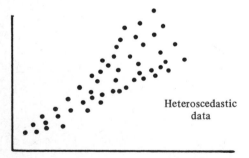

Fig. 3.6 The common problem of data which are not homoscedastic

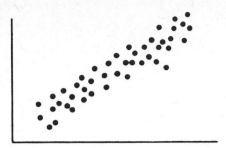

Fig. 3.7 Data invented from a statistician's dream world: perfectly linear and homoscedastic. The real managerial issue comes in deciding, when data are in a form a long way from this ideal, whether getting involved in more time and expense in forcing the data into a form with which regression can cope is worth the effort in relation to the nature of the problem.

on either side of the regression line show a systematic, or consistent tendency to grow or decline as the average value of the observations increases. This is normally evident from a graph of the data and the fitted regression, and computer programs can test for this phenomenon. It is probably enough here to sound a warning to beware of trying to fit regressions where the amplitude of the residual variances increases or decreases steadily as the data values increase or decrease, not an uncommon situation (Fig. 3.6).

This problem may be materially alleviated by the selection of appropriate time periods for analysis. For example, a regular seasonal or cyclical fluctuation may be a constant proportion of the average value, for example, the third quarter's, or month of July's sales, may be roughly a fixed percentage of the annual sales, thus introducing heteroscedasticity given a rising sales trend. Acceptable regressions can still be fitted in this sort of case either by selecting time periods (quarters rather than months, years rather than quarters) which obviate this effect, or by conducting the analysis on deseasonalized data (see chapter 4).

Here we raise a further issue in general, namely the problem of selecting time periods for analysis.

3.7 Selection of time intervals

As we have just noted, aggregating months to quarters or quarters to years tends to dampen the effect of random, seasonal or cyclical variations about the trend. However, there are a number of other considerations to be considered.

To begin with, is any one period particularly relevant to the decision under investigation? For example, if we need to compute the maximum weekly rate of throughput without any opportunity of displacing throughput in the busiest week to adjacent weeks, then we would have to employ weekly data. Such decisions might apply to airport passenger processing facilities, provision of a stock of coaches or of loading bay facilities and so on. In the same way, provision of a city bus service or of electricity supplies might, in the case of some decisions, call for hourly data to determine capacity required to meet peak hourly loads.

Unless a fairly persuasive case can be made for using the shorter periods it is probably better to select longer ones, that is, monthly rather than weekly, quarterly rather than monthly, and in principle, though often not in practice, annually rather than quarterly. In practice most selections come down to monthly or quarterly data.

Longer intervals are preferable in principle because they tend to eliminate random fluctuations and so be more use for 'average' purposes. There comes a point, however, when the time period is so long that to have enough periods in the calculation to offer an acceptable level of confidence that the regression goes in the direction it purports to involves using periods so far back in history that one has no confidence in their practical relevance. We are likely to be unhappy statistically with data from a period of less than twelve to sixteen years: we can be much happier with over twenty. We are generally going to be unhappy in practice using data sixteen or more years old as a basis for decisions affecting as long a period into the future. Hence a common compromise is quarterly data, which gives us a handy number of periods for calculation, twenty to forty, over a reasonably relevant looking time period, five to ten years. At the same time, quarterly data gives us a chance to observe whether there are likely to be seasonal factors which will particularly inflate the need for facilities at particular times of the year.

The other commonly adopted alternative, monthly data, comes into its own, first when the available data base is too short to allow statistical confidence with quarterly data (though if the monthly data are highly variable we may not fare much better with them); secondly, where detailed seasonal fluctuations are required, and thirdly, when capacity to meet peak month loading needs to be computed.

3.8 The standard error and measures of dispersion

Bearing in mind that a regression estimate represents a sort of 'average' we do not expect any of the actual values necessarily to lie on this 'average' line, any more than we should be surprised that the arithmetic mean, 5, of the four numbers 2, 3, 7 and 8, is not one of the members of that particular set of data. We may then, however, be interested in the question, how far off the average, on average, do we expect observations to be?

Given that the residual variances of the observations from the regression are truly random (enforcing rigidly the conditions of linearity and homostedasticity in the data) we can derive useful conclusions on these 'standard' deviations which will be helpful in framing an error band about our projections.

The statistic that does this useful job is the standard error of estimate whose formula is:

$$S = \sqrt{\frac{\Sigma(Y - \bar{Y})^2}{n - 2}}$$

where S is the standard error of estimate

Y is the actual values of the dependent variable (in our case shipments)

$\bar{Y}$ is the values of the dependent variable given by the regression equation corresponding to each Y

and n is the number of observations.

The reason for computing the value of S is that given the conditions expressed above, we know that approximately 68 per cent of all observations (and by inference of all forecast observations) will fall within the band of outcomes measured by S above or below the regression estimate; 95 per cent of all observations will fall within two standard errors either side, and 99 per cent within $3S$ either side. The smaller value of S, the more reliable we may feel the regression to be.

However, where n (as in our steel industry shipments annual data) is a small number, $n-2$ will be materially smaller, and the resultant S materially larger than we might like, which offers one reason for preferring large n's.

The computation is somewhat cumbersome, as we must fit $\bar{Y}$ (the regression estimate of the Y value corresponding to each X) e.g. the estimated shipments value for each time period t) using the regression equation we have just found. (At this point we return to the standard X, Y notation in order to release S, hitherto used for sales or shipments, for its proper function in this context, the label for standard error of estimate.) The working is set out in Table 3.4.

Table 3.4 *Calculation of the standard error of estimate (Data as in Table 3.3)*

x	y	y'	$y - y'$	$(y - y')^2$
1	2 210	2 151	59	3 481
2	2 487	2 866	−379	143 641
3	3 857	3 581	276	76 176
4	3 939	4 296	−357	127 449
5	4 847	5 011	−164	26 896
6	5 861	5 726	135	18 225
7	6 949	6 441	508	258 064
8	6 951	7 156	−207	42 849
9	8 342	7 871	471	221 841
10	8 367	8 586	−119	14 061

where $y' = 715x + 1\ 436$ 932 683

$$S = \sqrt{\frac{932\ 683}{10 - 2}} = \sqrt{116\ 585}$$

or, approximately 340 (thousand pounds)

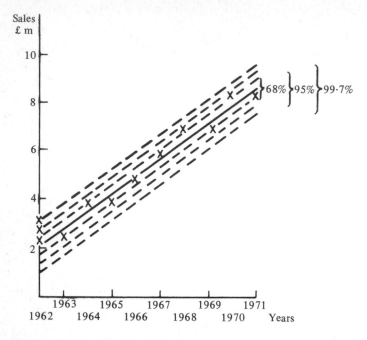

Fig. 3.8 The Specialized Steel Company
Annual delivery data together with the regression estimate and the bands of probability of occurrence derived from the standard error of estimate.

Applying the formula to the results of that table, we obtain a standard error of estimate of approximately £340 000.

The 68 per cent, 95 per cent and 99.7 per cent error bands are shown in Fig. 3.8.

This information is of limited usefulness in a practical forecasting context: it gives the analyst one particular answer to the question, how wide is the band of errors about the estimate? This may not, however, be the most appropriate question for decision purposes. What the decision-maker is more likely to want to know is the probability of any individual outcome being over or under a certain level, or to put it another way, how many of the possible outcomes are likely to give unacceptable commercial results.

The simplest way to approximate this type of information is to divide the observations into bands, such that each band contains an equal number of observations. The usual number of bands for this purpose is ten, each band known as a *decile*: deciles are not of the same width, they each contain one-tenth of the observations.

The procedure is to use the $y-y'$ column of figures (Table 3.4) and arrange the results of this column in rank order, highest to lowest or lowest to highest. The ten groups, each of equal membership are then easily divided, and each group can be distinguished either by an upper and lower boundary, or by a group average. Armed with this information the analyst is in a position to answer questions relating to the best, or worst outcomes, expressed as multiples of one-tenth of the total outcomes.

Another question for which answers are generally needed is, what is the chance of being over a stipulated percentage, or amount, above or below the trend estimate? The answer is easily obtained on demand from the ranked column of variances, on which the required cutoff point has to be distinguished, when it becomes easy to compute the number of observations beyond that point.

It is easy to calculate standard error, deciles, and a ranked column of variances, and cautiously used these can be of great help in bridging the gap between the forecast system and the decision system discussed in chapter 9.

But the cautionary notes can hardly be overstressed. All the foregoing depends on random dispersion of the residuals about the trend, implying linearity and homoscedasticity of the data. There is an implication that the analyst really believes it makes sound managerial sense to project the trend and the bands around it. Finally, there has to be enough data to make the standard error and decile calculations meaningful. One can barely get a meaningful standard error from ten data points unless they are very close to a straight line: clearly it is absurd to try to obtain decile ranges for less than perhaps sixty or seventy observations.

For small numbers of observations it is easy enough to do all the calculations manually. For large numbers this becomes tedious, and computer programs are available which will produce instant standard errors and decile measurements and project them into infinity if required. The danger in that situation is that the power of the computer to produce the answers may be mistaken for operational validity of the method.

Incidentally, regression forecasting programs normally offer the analyst tests for linearity and homoscedasticity, and also possibilities of data transformations which will help to linearize non-linear data and introduce homoscedasticity into heteroscedastic data.

3.9 Non-linear time series

Most economic time series are non-linear in form, and even when linear may be expected eventually to curve towards some sort of saturation point. Already considerable time in this chapter has been devoted to a consideration of non-statistical issues surrounding this aspect of forecasting in the case of Magnetized Torque Wrenches. The purpose of that discussion was to illustrate how tricky trend curves are to handle in a practical context. A second warning which must be sounded now is that although it is possible to fit such curves to data statistically, the exercise calls for considerable statistical as well as managerial judgment, in the selection of the time period to be fitted and in selecting the type of curve to fit.

There is a small number of shapes underlying time series data which recur very frequently. Once they have been accurately described, it is a straightforward enough matter to extrapolate them into the future as far as the analyst has confidence that the underlying causes which produced the historical shape will continue to prevail.

The 'stock' shapes are as follows:

Straight line	$D = a + bt$
Parabola	$D = a + bt + ct^2$
Simple exponential	$\log D = a + bt$
Logarithmic parabola	$\log D = a + bt + ct^2$
Simple modified exponential	$D = a - br^t$
Gompertz	$\log D = a - br^t$
Logistic	$D = \dfrac{1}{a + br^t}$

In all of the general algebraic expressions describing these shapes D stands for Demand in time period t, and a, b, and r, are positive constants (r being less than 1) whose value is to be decided from statistical analysis of the figures for past data. Once values have been determined for a, b, and r, these are set into the formulae, and the net effect in each case is to say that D depends in a more or less complex manner upon t, that is, that the only factor which is being taken as significant in the determination of demand is the passing of time.

The shapes of these curves are sketched in Fig. 3.9 from which it can be seen that some vary only very subtly from others.

The methods of fitting these curves, and the pitfalls inherent in attempting to do so, are admirably set out in ICI Monograph No. 1, to which the interested reader is referred. The authors (Gregg *et al.*) of that work set out their methodology with great clarity, and express it in terms amenable to hand computation. Intending users should, however, ask themselves whether the precision offered by complex curve fitting warrants the time and effort involved in an exercise whose outcomes are subject to quite extreme uncertainties.

An alternative approach to the method suggested in the ICI Monograph which offers greatest promise for the future is to process such curves by standard programs on an on-line computer terminal. The rapid feedback of results to the user makes possible a large number of trial-and-error approaches to the problem of curve selection, through residuals examination, in order to get a good approach to the best fit. Such methodology is, however, very uneconomic of computing capacity, and only justified in situations where considerable uncertainty has to be dealt with.

3.10 Managers and time series

Fitting and extrapolating trend curves on series of data is a tricky business. It is time-consuming and laborious, offers a spurious and seductive sense of precision, and may be very misleading if a poor curve is selected to represent the data, or if trends should change, as they generally do.

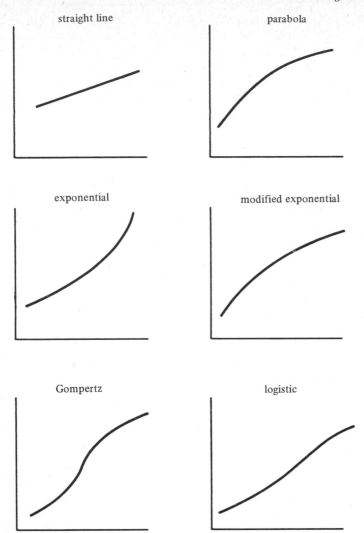

straight line

parabola

exponential

modified exponential

Gompertz

logistic

Fig. 3.9 Some of the more commonly encountered curve shapes

In a forecasting situation, should management attempt trend extrapolation, or encourage others to create and project trends for them? Probably in most cases in which management is seeking sophisticated assistance in forecasting, the answer is 'yes' for a number of reasons. First of all, management will be turning to these forecasting aids because their own uncertainties are considerable, and as we saw with Magnetized Torque Wrenches, this type of exercise can frequently offer very much enhanced clarity of perspective through time. Secondly, the creation of a number of trends of related data may offer the origins of an explanatory model, albeit in imprecise terms, which may help managers to understand the extent to which the dependent variable is in the grip of economic and technical forces, and how far it is under the control of their own actions. Thirdly, when trends emerge in which management feels some confidence (and usually some do) they offer basic benchmarks into the future, around which management may be able to consider the likely outcomes of their activities or of events inspired from outwith the firm. Finally, and of some importance in a context of making decisions based on benchmark (or modified benchmark) estimates, the existence of error bands about the benchmark may be of greatest assistance in helping to discover the payoffs from possible likely outcomes, weighted by their probability of occurrence.

3.11 Summary

This chapter has considered the use of, and problems inherent in, attempting to use mathematical trends of economic or business activity data as an aid to forecasting.

Such trends are preliminary pictures designed to help enhance perspective and clarity in assessment of what had happened in the past, and as a basis for possible tentative, if non-quantitative, explanatory models.

To use such trends meaningfully, it is necessary first, carefully to define the problems to which they are thought to be relevant, second to find an adequate base of relevant data and, third, to find or devise some worthwhile analytical techniques.

Even a very simple case of real data provokes many difficult questions of judgment both about the figures and the use to which they are to be put.

The possibilities of computing linear and non-linear trends were discussed, as compared with the sloppy but not wholly unsatisfactory method of measuring and projecting by eye (which has the great merit that the analyst knows that his method contains no statistical precision, and is therefore unlikely to be beguiled by it). Brief references were offered on the use of the standard error of estimate.

Finally an attempt was offered at evaluating trend analysis as a forecasting aid, with the conclusion that it offers substantial specific rewards, notwithstanding that it is a dangerous tool to work with.

REFERENCE

Gregg, J. V., Horsell, C. H. and Richardson, J. T. *Mathematical Trend Curves: an aid to forecasting*, ICI Monograph No. 1, Oliver & Boyd, 1964.

4 Further analysis of time series

4.1 The problem

We saw in the last chapter how to examine a group of related time trends with a view to obtaining a preliminary impression of the underlying forces acting on them, and some ways were suggested of dealing with the scatter of the actual observations about the trends to help to obtain benchmark estimates of where future observations might fall.

We left unresolved the problem of errors which were not truly randomly distributed about the trend, that is to say, situations in which there might have been a regular component of fluctuation about the trend induced for example by regular seasonal variations. Such variations might have arisen because of some form of economic cycle, or might have been steady changes in the rate of growth or decline of the trend itself.

While such problems are of limited importance when the forecaster's purpose is to obtain rough benchmarks as a basis for an explanatory model of a business situation, there are many circumstances in which more precisely specified estimates may be required, taking into account such regular fluctuations.

For example, the production capacity planning problem dealt with in the last chapter might call for an estimate of likely peak or trough demands and the circumstances under which these may occur. This could occur when management wished to obtain an estimate of optimal production plus storage capacity, together with a plan for stockholding. It is not necessary to provide production plant and warehouse simultaneously, nor is it necessary to be able to meet peak demand if this is likely to occur infrequently.

Another constraint on such a decision might be availability of working capital to finance stocks, work in progress, and accounts receivable at periods of peak activity. Here the model is complicated by the form in which the individual company chooses to maintain its working capital (e.g. cash ratio), its general policy on liquidity, and availability of sources of short-term credit.

In 'exceptional' business conditions such as peaks or troughs of sales activity, management needs to have contingency plans available. It needs to know in such contexts whether envisaged contingencies are likely to occur, and to require advance planning; if so the likely frequency of their occurrence and in particular when the first occurrence might take place; finally, the likely severity of contingencies for which they are being asked to plan.

Management have many options in this area: they may choose to sacrifice growth and development in favour of very secure liquidity. They may choose to run very lean in the hope that liquidity crises will not occur soon enough, or severely enough, to have a crippling effect, and in this they may be lucky; they may choose to be in a position to meet any imagined contingency without strain, or they may choose to take calculated risks. The last of these options involves calculating the risks and preparing plans to deal with the outcomes so that blind misfortune at least loses the advantage of surprise.

Fortunately techniques which enable analysts to produce operationally valid estimates of the likely occurrence, timing and severity of exceptional contingencies are well developed, subject though they may be to certain theoretical objections. They start from probability estimates of sales under different conditions, for example, a point where the underlying trend of demand has been rising strongly, coupled with the peak of the trade cycle and the seasonal peak of sales occurring simultaneously. Such estimates can then be translated into storage plus production capacity requirements, working capital requirements and cash flow forecasts. From operating experience, management in practice usually finds it straightforward to translate the hypothetical situation into terms of likely tactical requirements of sales allocation, rephasing, or promotion and effects on price or discount structures.

To obtain an understanding of the path of a set of sales data in sufficient detail to enable management to answer such questions is a laborious process, involving a number of steps each of which is individually very simple. The cautions observed in the last chapter concerning relevance of data to the task continue to apply, but assuming misgivings have been met at least to an operationally satisfactory level, then the outline procedure has the following rational basis.

The actual history of observations of sales through time is a composite of a number of influences such as which may be sufficiently regular, or be associated with known external events, that we can somehow discount them — explain them away, in order to be in a position to aggregate them back at some later stage in an order that will enable the analyst to present the manager with information in the form he needs it for decision-making purposes.

Classical time series analysis attempts to isolate four components of sales change: the trend, cyclical, seasonal and random components. Properly speaking a fifth category should be added: irregular and unsystematic components which may be attributed to known external factors, such as price changes attributable to tax changes, changes in promotional activity, and so on.

Before proceeding, it is necessary to obtain a clearer idea of what each of these components amounts to, and how they fit into a logical forecasting system, otherwise we are reduced to the application of a blind statistical sausage machine technique devoid of purpose other than to distinguish trend, cycle, seasonal and random, a methodology which has been consistently vilified by responsible statisticians. Yet its elements continue to be widely used by business forecasters — not normally as an end in themselves, at least in responsible hands, but as a means to the end of creating probability-based models in a form useful for decision-making.

In the preceding chapter we discussed the creation of trend pictures, as a first approach to forecasting in some detail. We saw how to fit a linear trend, that more complex curve shapes could also be fitted, and how the scatter band about the trend might be handled. Strictly speaking, the method we employed, regression estimate fitting, implies that what we were saying was that the passage of time is the reason why the 'trend' was performing as it was. There is always an implication of a *causal relationship* when we employ regression. Since the assertion that the passage of time automatically causes anything to happen is patently absurd, we have to rationalize our basis for working by saying that we are using time as a *proxy variable* in place of other determining variables (economic growth, greater affluence of our customers, or some such phenomenon) for which we do not have data. Very often, however, time seems to work pretty well as a proxy for these unknown determinants in explaining some part of the observed change in our data.

If we had better information on the true determining variables we might prefer to use them; but if time performs well for us in a quick and dirty way, then there is a lot we can do with it, and, as we shall see, it may help us to obtain a better understanding of some of the underlying determinants.

In disaggregating a seasonal component, we are again using time as a proxy for underlying behavioural variables which are either imperfectly understood or imperfectly measurable. The seasonal is defined as any component of variation whose periodicity is perfectly regular. This normally applies to sales statistics month by month and many such series reflect a high degree of seasonality. Operationally the seasonal is hardly worth computing in its own right — as Moroney (1956, p. 321) puts it, 'this is the sort of thing that any competent ice-cream manufacturer does in a flash without recourse to statistics'. However, once it is discounted, it helps to clear the ground to get at more interesting aspects of the problem.

Once the seasonal has been disposed of there remains the more intractable, and less regular fluctuation, the cycle. Cyclical fluctuations are distinguished from seasonal by their irregular periodicity, and because, perhaps, their underlying reasons are less easy to distinguish. Businessmen generally know why their sales are seasonal: the weather, Christmas or something which happens regularly and predictably. No one knows the full explanation of the trade cycle and we devote a later chapter of this book to discussing just this level of ignorance.

We are interested in cyclical fluctuations partly for their own sake, and partly because the overall purpose of this exercise is to eliminate from the data all fluctuations which we believe to be caused by some set of systematic influences, whether of a long-term sort, of regular occurrence, or of irregular but periodic recurrence. Theoretically we should be able to get some sense of the underlying determinants of such fluctuations, and the search for them may lead to an explanatory model of what has been happening. Underlying determinants may have to be written off in aggregate form as 'the business cycle' which pretty well defies rational explanation. Alternatively we may see in the data, for example, the effects of price changes, line widening, or promotional campaigns and their withdrawal. Assessment is not easy and the attempt is only worth while if we really care about finding out.

Once we have eliminated to the best of our ability all the regular fluctuations we are left with the 'unexplained variances' which arise from the basic phenomenon that large numbers of order from buyers, of different sizes, spaced at intervals determined by the buyers' needs, will tend to vary in a random manner about some central mean. We saw in the last chapter that randomness is a phenomenon which we can do something to analyse. Some older textbooks label this component the 'irregular component' and leave the analysis at that point with the suggestion that there is little we can do about its existence.

There is more than a semantic problem involved here. If the remaining unexplained variances are merely irregular, there is an implication that they might still be systematic, and we are not entitled to examine them further as if they were random. Irregulars may arise from causal factors which we have so far failed to distinguish and identify, from unforeseeable shocks (e.g. incidence of strikes) or from truly random influences. A fair amount of *ad hoc* manipulation and casting around for testable explanations may be needed to get the data from merely irregular to a point where the analyst may feel happy that the scatter of the residual errors really is unsystematic except in terms of a model which suggests that they have been randomly generated.

Given that the analyst is satisfied that he has isolated the random component and has not been conducting his analysis in a statistical vacuum, so that he has begun to develop explanations for the observed systematic fluctuations, then he is in a position to answer some demanding managerial questions. For example, what are the chances of a liquidity crisis? What are the chances of sales falling below break-even, or profit-generating levels over specified time periods? What are the chances of customers having to wait more than a specified time for deliveries? How much of our output would we be able to deliver from stock under varying demand conditions? And so on. The answers to most of these questions requires a knowledge of the financial and operating structures of the firm as well as the demand structure, but here we can show how component analysis can identify demand structure in helpful ways in relation to such questions as the above.

The information might be used to approach questions concerning the chances of some particular commercial outcome if management pursues a particular course of action. An important component of the outcome is likely to be closely related to sales income over a specified period. For example, liquidity problems may be anticipated if sales over any six-month stretch in the first two years of a project were to exceed a given level.

The specific question, therefore, might be formulated as follows. 'What is the probability that the value of deliveries will exceed £100 000 per month for six consecutive months within the first two years in the life of the project?' Such a question will only be posed in circumstances where the answer is both uncertain and important. In other words, an overall look at likely sales trends has already cast doubt on this aspect of the project, and management needs a more certain answer.

In outline, time series component analysis will help to lead to the answer by discovering the conditions under which the sum of the explained and random components might produce the specified outcome. For example, the trend growth may be based on some complex economic and behavioural model. To this would be added probable cyclical fluctuations over the first two years of the project, when a 'fore and aft' estimate would suffice: on various likely assumptions as to starting and finishing dates of the relevant cycles, an envelope of likely cyclical components, each with some probability of occurrence would be obtained. To these it is simple to add the seasonal timing, but the amplitude of seasonal fluctuations may be variable, so that a band of probable seasonals may be needed. Finally, all the foregoing would be reconstituted on a basis of some form of model, incorporating random and irregular components. Examination of the outcomes would reveal the conditions under which the addition of the components would be likely to throw the total outcomes outwith the warning limits, within the time period.

Before proceeding with the discussion of the integration of the various component projections into the decision-making system, it will be necessary for us to spend some time examining the methodology of analysing each component. This is standard material to be found in a number of business statistics textbooks (e.g. Croxton and Cowden, 1960) and our purpose is simply to summarize an extensive body of statistical analytical techniques.

In summary, what we shall be looking at is the disaggregation of the data into components *describing* the influence of the overall trend, cyclical and seasonal fluctuations, irregular non-random components, and finally the random component. We are still attempting to obtain *descriptions* not *explanatory models*.

4.2 The trend

There are two approaches to trend fitting: the first, by simple linear regression, was fully discussed in chapter 3. The second involves a combination of algebraic and graphical description, and is known as the method of *moving averages*. This gives not a straight line trend, but a fluctuating trend incorporating in a modified form the cyclical, irregular and long-term effects, but reducing (in a perfect world, obviating) the effects of seasonal and random factors.

We shall be meeting moving averages again when we come to consider exponential smoothing as a forecasting technique. Very briefly, this methodology is used to flatten out from a series the effects of *regularly recurring* fluctuations, so that a twelve-month average should in theory eliminate seasonals, while randoms should also average out in the long run. In any case, the effect of even a major random distortion (e.g. through a strike paralysing output) appears on this moving average trend with only one-twelfth of its immediate impact. Unfortunately, a small amount of the underlying cyclical movement will also be smoothed out.

The average for the first year of the series is given by

$$\frac{J_1 + F_1 + M_1 \ldots + D_1}{12} \quad \text{(where } J = \text{January's data, } F = \text{February's, etc.)}$$

However, we wish to place our first average result at the centre of the period to which it refers, and this is simpler with an odd number of observations.

Thus, a *seven*-month moving average, if such were appropriate, could be constructed on

$$\frac{J_1 + F_1 + M_1 + A_1 + My_1 + J_1 + Jl_1}{7}; \text{ Result 1, centred at } A_1$$

$$\frac{F_1 + M_1 + A_1 + My_1 + J_1 + Jl_1 + Au_1}{7}; \text{ Result 2, centred at } My_1.$$

and henceforth by deleting the first observation of the previous set, adding the next in the series and computing a new average a *centred* seven-month moving average would be obtained.

With a twelve-month period (the commonest) what has to be done is compute

$$\frac{J_1 + 2F_1 + 2M_1 + 2A_1 + 2My_1 + 2J_1 + 2Jl_1 + 2Au_1 + 2S_1 + 2O_1 + 2N_1 + 2D_1 + J_2}{24}$$

and then centre the first result opposite the first July.

Thereafter by subtracting $J_1 + F_1$ and adding $J_2 + F_2$ the next entry centred upon August may be obtained. The name given to the numerator (top line) of the above fraction is the thirteen-month weighted sum, and the name given to the result is the twelve-month *centred* moving average. Normally in computation a number of the thirteen-month moving sums are computed centred on each July in the series, and then the intermediate ones are calculated by the subtraction and addition process. This provides a check on the arithmetic accuracy as the July results should coincide with those obtained in spot checks once all the weighted sums are in position, each is divided by 24 (multiply by 0.041666667). (A full account of this technique appears in Croxton and Cowden, pp. 454–7.)

To illustrate the operation of discovering the twelve-month moving average we may refer to Table 4.1 which sets out the deliveries of steel sheets by British producers. The trend from which it is assumed that seasonals and random variations

Table 4.1 *UK cold reduced steel sheet deliveries weekly average deliveries per month (tons)*

1963	January	40 957	1965	January	54 284
	February	46 180		February	54 772
	March	45 861		March	48 437
	April	41 716		April	45 105
	May	43 998		May	53 781
	June	44 603		June	47 565
	July	36 652		July	37 781
	August	43 161		August	48 249
	September	46 956		September	46 059
	October	49 916		October	49 643
	November	50 814		November	50 044
	December	46 078		December	41 294
1964	January	43 578	1966	January	53 764
	February	64 938		February	57 604
	March	59 854		March	55 834
	April	57 498		April	53 412
	May	54 870		May	55 222
	June	53 336		June	50 764
	July	39 110		July	41 154
	August	46 045		August	45 647
	September	49 901		September	50 186
	October	52 517		October	44 772
	November	54 421		November	41 190
	December	42 689		December	36 775
			1967	January	49 006
				February	50 285
				March	44 584
				April	50 849
				May	47 460
				June	47 812
				July	39 688
				August	37 252
				September	49 898

Source: British Iron and Steel Federation, *Iron and Steel Monthly Statistics.*

have been netted out, is shown in Fig. 4.1. The moving average trend may be compared with the regression trend, also shown: both clearly supply different sorts of information.

4.3 The seasonal index

To handle the seasonal component it is first necessary to calculate its value. The steps are illustrated in Table 4.2.

First list the raw data (column 1) and the moving average trend data (column 2). The difference between each of the values in columns 1 and 2 is then listed in

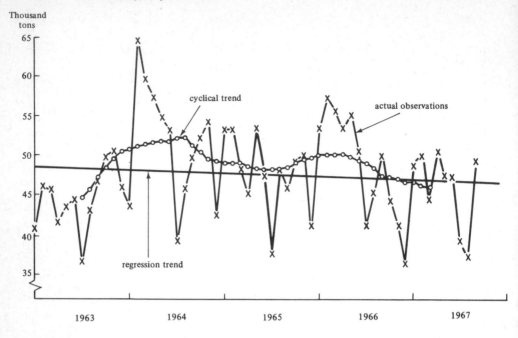

Fig. 4.1 Two types of trend compared

Some five years' data for British deliveries for cold rolled steel illustrate different ways of representing trends. From the data of Table 4.1 we can compute the regression trend using the
methods outlined in the last chapter. It's equation is:

$$D = -\frac{1}{37} t + 48.6$$

   Both the regression trend and the cyclical trend computed using a centred twelve-month
moving average are shown. Had the 1963 results not been included in the regression trend it
would have started from a higher point and its track would have more evenly divided up the
cyclical trend.

   Selection of this set of data illustrates a number of forecasting problems. The February 1963
outturn was the culmination of a long upswing as demand pent up by earlier rationing was
released. There is some question whether mid-1965 is a low point in a small cycle, or merely a
kink in a longer upcycle from mid-1963 to 1967.

   On the information available it is impossible to make an intelligent forecast. However, the
analysis clarifies the course of the data, and interpreted in light of known economic changes
through the period, this type of analysis may serve as one helpful input to the process of
forming a forward view towards 1968.

column 3. Where the trend is rising or falling markedly it may be necessary to
compute the seasonals as percentages of trend values represented by actual data,
rather than absolute differences. This is slightly more complicated arithmetically
but does handle the problem of seasonal swings being proportional to trend values,
hence increasing in amplitude as trends rise (or vice versa).

Table 4.2 *Computation of seasonals: data extracted from Table 4.1*

		Deliveries ('000 tons) (1)	Moving average equivalent (2)	Difference between (1) and (2) (3)*	Average monthly differences (4)*	Seasonally adjusted deliveries (1) ± (4) (5)
	.					
	.					
	.					
1963	Nov.	50.8	49.7	+1.1	−0.1	50.9
	Dec.	46.1	50.5	−4.4	−8.1	54.2
1964	Jan.	43.6	50.9	−7.3	+1.7	41.9
	Feb.	64.9	51.2	+6.3	+8.3	56.6
	Mar.	59.9	51.4	+8.5	+3.8	56.1
	.					
	.					
	.					
1967	Jan.	49.0	47.0	+2.0	+1.7	47.3
	Feb.	50.3	46.7	+3.6	+8.3	42.0
	Mar.	44.6	46.3	+1.7	+3.8	40.8
	.					
	.					
	.					

* In columns (3) and (4), + indicates actual data were *above* the trend − indicates they were *below* the trend.

The following seasonals emerge for the data of Table 4.1, if computed as explained in the text.

Jan.	+1 700		Jul.	−10 400
Feb.	+8 300		Aug.	−3 600
Mar.	+3 800		Sept.	−400
Apr.	+2 800		Oct.	−400
May	+5 400		Nov.	−100
Jun.	+700		Dec.	−8 100

The next step is to take the average for the observed differences for all of the Januaries, Februaries, etc., in the series, which should, with a long enough series, eliminate the random element. (Another sleight of hand which may be used to mitigate any irregular influences is to take these average monthly percentages for all months except the highest and lowest readings for each month. This is an arbitrary business depending on having enough data, over say ten years, to allow the luxury of dropping two, and also on not knowing enough of the true background of events to say which data might really have been subject to irregular influences. One is always suspicious of blind application of sausage machine techniques.)

Before using the average monthly variations as a basis for the seasonal adjustment, two checks can be run on them. First, they can be checked, visually or

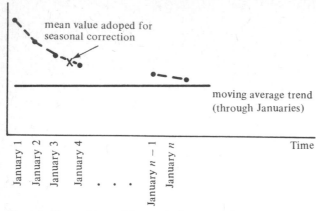

Fig. 4.2 The problem of the wandering seasonal

Computing the appropriate seasonal adjustment for each month involves finding an *average* monthly deviation from the trend. Sometimes the seasonal for a given month or months is found to be changing regularly through time. If it is suspected that this may be happening, a sketch time series of the month's deviation from the trend should reveal it. The appropriate adjustments are those suggested by common sense in the situation.

statistically, to see whether they are tracking in some systematic way; this is illustrated in Fig. 4.2. Clearly any systematic tracking will be built into any forecasts involving the seasonals. This test would also show if the behaviour of the seasonals was such as to indicate that the cyclical trend had not been correctly tracked (Fig. 4.3).

The second possible operation on the seasonals is to compute the scatter band in deciles (or standard errors) about the mean seasonal adjustment. If this is done the seasonals need not be built back into the forecast as a point estimate, but can be incorporated on a probability basis: the analyst can say that although the January

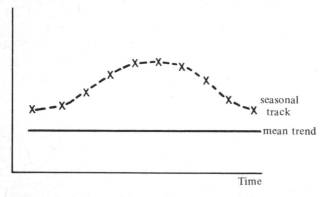

Fig. 4.3 Seasonal—cyclical mix-up

If the track of a given month's seasonal through time betrays this sort of pattern, then we can be sure that some cyclical influence is still present. It needs to be eliminated before proceeding with any further analysis.

seasonal will average x per cent below the cyclical trend, one year in ten it will be y per cent below and so on.

Any decision on this last process will depend on the purpose of the analysis. Thereafter the averages (or in a more complicated but more realistic system, the probability bands) are inserted in the table in column 5. Thereafter it is only necessary to correct column 2 by applying the appropriate factor from column 4 to obtain the seasonally adjusted estimate shown in column 5.

If we arrive at the conclusion that the seasonal adjustment must be changing over time, it is possible to compute a moving seasonal or, if we have grounds to suppose that the appropriate seasonal adjustment has simply shifted bodily at some point in time, we may simply recompute a stable seasonal index for the new situation. The insurmountable problem here is that it requires longish experience of the changed situation before we may be certain of the new seasonal, by which time it may have changed again.

4.4 Cyclical changes

Here we are at the heart of one of the key business forecasting problems, the analysis of business cycles. The fact that we may be able to analyse *past* cycles reliably does not necessarily mean that we will be able to predict the course of future ones. But if, out of the often conflicting cross currents that determine the path through time of any series of economic data we can synthesize the three regular components of trend, seasonal and finally cyclical movements, we have come to the stage of being able to say, the cyclical turning point occurred *then*, and was, say, a more, or less, violent cycle than normal. Further, we may advance hypotheses to explain the timing of the turning points and nature of the rate of change, and to the extent that our hypotheses have any general validity we may look to any recurrence of the same underlying factors to produce a similar effect. Like every individual forecasting technique, this is unlikely to operate with any great reliability; it represents merely one more straw in the wind adding to a cumulative weight of evidence for one conclusion or another.

The problem associated with the prediction of cyclical changes is that, contrary to the inference of their name, they are irregular in the timing of their recurrence and the amplitude of their movement. More than one business forecaster has gone on record as stating that the ability to predict cyclical turning points is what 'separates the men from the boys'. It is here that business has the opportunity to avoid a large number of 'windfall' costs, by controlled stock changes in advance of demand turning, by planned rather than emergency labour recruitment to meet upswings, in the timing of innovation and capacity installation to catch a rising rather than a falling trend, in the timing of new share or debenture issues, in the phasing of raw materials purchases, and many other applications.

But we must be very clear that there is no generalized model of functional value to business of business cycles. If any given cycle — say of stock prices, our firm's market quotation, growth of gross national product, our firm's or industry's sales or any other — has a periodicity of, say, between six and ten quarterly observations on the upswing and a further six and ten on the downswing, then by simply predicting no change in cyclical direction each quarter we can create an illusion of being right on average about 80 per cent of the time. The correct score to keep is the proportion of the time that a turning point occurs which we have predicted correctly, as a ratio of our incorrect turning point predictions. Say we begin in quarter 6 to predict a change; it does not occur; quarter 7, wrong again; quarter 8, right. Not very clever prediction. We are doing worse than by predicting on the basis of the probability distribution generated by the timing of previous turning points in the series. Any system of turning point predictions which we adopt must therefore turn in more consistently reliable results than we would get by applying the above crude approximations of the frequency of turning point occurrence.

The point, therefore, of synthesizing from the total trend that component which may be regarded as cyclical is not, as it is often treated, an exercise in economic history in its own right: rather it is a matter of obtaining a reliable estimate of the course that may be reasonably ascribed to economic-cyclical factors (as distinct from growth trend, seasonal behaviour, and the results of sales promotion or other irregular occurrences) in order, hopefully, to be able to explain what happened in terms of behaviour of economic variables which may give us predictive leads for further assessments.

We have already seen how the twelve-month moving average tracks a cyclical trend (Fig. 4.1), but there is a danger that this process may induce apparent cycles into non-cyclical data. Also the cyclical trend we get still contains in it the effects of the long-term trend of the data. This is of little significance with our steel industry data, but if the long-term trend is strongly upward or downward, we may want to make allowance for the fact that end-of-period observations will be materially different from those at the beginning by virtue of the long-term trend effect. This may on occasion affect our views as to when cycles have changed.

We therefore need to discount data observations for the trend track value, usually expressed as a percentage of the first. In the present case the long-term trend has a negative slope of $\frac{1}{37}$ = 0.027 per cent, a factor which should be added back to the data purporting to represent the cycle. As stated above, with the trend so very nearly horizontal this makes no material difference to the outturn, but the working is shown in Table 4.3 so that anyone interested may follow the method.

Referring to Fig. 4.4, it can be seen that we have now two versions of a cyclical component, one represented by the twelve-month moving average, the other by the deseasonalized data. To our relief, the twelve-month average tracks pretty well through the deseasonalized data, and we can feel that for operating purposes we have a fair view of that particular cycle. The deseasonalized data corrected for trend effect are supposed to measure the influence of the cycle and random components, and are known as the *cyclical relatives* of the series.

Getting at cycles in this way is laborious and one only does it if it is thought that something worth while will be learned in the process. However, the whole business can have one useful payoff.

Table 4.3

Period No.			Thousands of tons				
			Moving average deliveries (1)	Seasonally adjusted deliveries (2)	Trend factor (3)	(1) Adjusted for trend (4)	(2) Adjusted for trend (5)
12	1964	Jan.	50.9	41.9	0.3	51.2	42.1
13		Feb.	51.2	56.6	0.3	51.4	56.9
14		Mar.	51.4	56.1	0.4	51.8	56.5
15		Apr.	51.7	54.7	0.4	52.1	55.1
16		May	51.9	49.5	0.4	52.3	49.9
17		Jun.	51.9	52.6	0.4	52.3	53.0
18		Jul. etc.	52.3	49.5	0.5	52.8	50.0

Trend factor per period = 0.027 x No. of periods.

Thousand tons

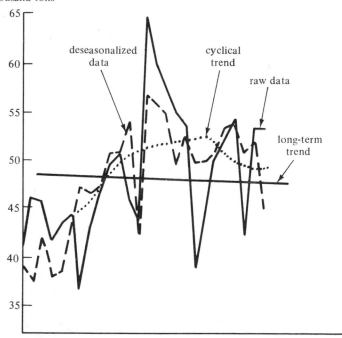

Fig. 4.4 Two representations of the cycle compared

Here we reproduce the first part of Fig. 4.1. After much laborious effort it has been possible to add to our previous information the cycle shape offered by computing deseasonalized data. At least this tends to confirm that the cyclical trend probably is tracking the cycle. The vertical distances between the deseasonalized data and cyclical trend should give us a measure of the random component of the series. If the long-term trend had been rising or falling steeply, we should have wanted to discount this trend effect before being satisfied that we had a reasonable cyclical picture.

If we refer back to Table 4.3, it will be seen that the difference between column 5 and column 4 (seasonally adjusted figures and moving average figures, both corrected for trend effect) gives us a measure of the random component in these data. These differences are as follows:

Period No.	12	13	14	15	16	17	18 . . .
Difference	+9	−5.5	−4.7	−3.0	+2.4	−0.7	+2.8 . . .

In practice we should need the whole series, but there are things we can do with 100 or more random numbers. We shall see more of this in chapter 9, but as indicated in the last chapter we can obtain measures of the probability of dispersion of results about the mean which will find a place in the decision-making system.

If the sole object of the analysis is to isolate cycles, and if great precision is not required, the residual method is somewhat laborious and a direct shortcut may be applied. This will give a quick, if somewhat imprecise, guide to the timing of cycles, though *absolutely no indication whatsoever of their amplitude*. The method is simply to express the data for any one period (e.g. a month) as a percentage of the corresponding month in the previous three, four or five years.

The harmonic method consists of an attempt to fit a mathematical sine-cosine curve to the cyclical or cycle/irregular component of a time series. This technique is only valid where, in the judgment of the analyst, the data exhibit a very high degree of consistency in their periodicity. If the data are indeed so regular, they should probably be investigated as seasonals, not cyclicals. The object of the technique is to obtain a value for the average periodicity and amplitude of the cycle. The method is fully explained in Croxton and Cowden, chapter 19, and has so little general application that the interested reader ought to pursue it there.

4.5 Irregular fluctuations

The final problem remaining is the removal of the I component from the CIR data of Table 4.2. A moving average of the data ought to achieve this end if the I component is strictly randomly distributed with a mean of 0 about the cyclical relative path of the data. The problem is that a sufficiently long moving average to secure smoothness of the data (twelve months) will seriously depress the apparent amplitude of the cycle and may also obscure significant turning points. A very short moving average (say three months) may not induce smooth enough data.

The way round these problems is to adopt a device known as the *weighted moving average*. Simple moving averages over, say, three or five months by inference assign the same weight or importance to each of the three or five readings included. If we introduce *binomial weighting* in the moving average, we give a greater weight to the *middle* readings and lesser to the outer ones. This has the effect of producing a smoother curve, and one closer to the amplitude of the original cycle, than using a simple moving average.

In practice, this means for a three-month moving average assigning the weights 0.25, 0.5 and 0.25 to the first, middle and third members of the average (sum to one). If the smoother results of the five-month moving average are desired, then the weights should be 0.1, 0.2, 0.4, 0.2, 0.1. (Strictly speaking the binomial weights would be 0.0625, 0.2500, 0.3750, 0.2500, 0.0625, but the added complexity of computation is not normally compensated for by additional precision or value in the results.)

For a description of polynomial weighting, a further variant of the same procedure, which is seldom resorted to but which helps to preserve the amplitude of the cycle (rarely a matter of critical importance) the reader is referred to Croxton and Cowden, chapter 31.

In a context of eliminating irregularities probably by the use of the five-month binomial weight, we ought to remind ourselves of some of the important aspects of these irregular fluctuations which, in a context of a test on time series analysis are merely the component which cannot be handled, but on the business forecaster's desk assume greater significance. First, their existence may reflect systematic errors in our seasonal index construction and indicate a need to reassess this index. The second important role of the irregulars is that they offer an opportunity of calculating how precise a forecast estimate may be if the underlying systematic components continue to function in the future as they did in the past. Thus we may say that if the irregular fluctuations are very large relative to the general height of the trend and amplitude of the regular fluctuations, it will be impossible to offer great precision in a forecast estimate. In such circumstances it will generally be necessary to aggregate, say, daily into weekly, weekly into monthly, monthly into quarterly, and quarterly into annual data in order to get out as much as possible of the severe irregular fluctuations. As with the problem discussed above of striking a balance between smoothness and precision in cycle estimates, here again the forecaster must use his judgment and strike a balance between the precision of the forecasts which the data will allow and offering a sufficiently narrow time spread of the forecast estimate for relevant decision-taking.

A further alternative weighting system is that known as *exponential weighting* in which the most recent observation is given greatest weight as the trend determinant, and preceding observations are given less weight. The weights are assigned in an exponential series, for example, 0.2, 0.16, 0.128 . . . in which each weight is four-fifths of the one preceding it. This represents an exponential series (geometric progression) summing to unity. This type of weighting system is commonly applied in automatic forecasting systems (see chapter 5).

4.6 The random component

There are other sources of uncertainty in the foregoing model, which are less susceptible to strict statistical analysis. First, the amplitude and periodicity of the cyclical component may vary, either randomly or systematically (e.g. growing or contracting systematically over time). Now the sort of use to which the present forecasting methodology is most appropriate is to provide a picture of the state of demand one to five years ahead, that is generally within one cycle, and with a cycle periodicity of around four to five years, it becomes difficult to get a good estimate of past data within a relevant time scale as a basis for forecasting the present cycle. Probably the best that can be done is to estimate earliest and latest turning point dates from past data, with perhaps a very crude guess at probable intermediate dates. For example, over five possible time periods, the analyst might be able to do no better than assign a 20 per cent probability to each. Similarly very crude approximations are probably the best that can be made of the amplitude of forthcoming cyclical fluctuations.

Whether or not all this matters depends on the decision for which the information is required. Sometimes such uncertainties make no difference, at other times they may be crucial. The important point to recognize is that since the best the analyst can hope for are rough cuts, it is of great importance to specify *precisely* what the information is to be used for, in order to determine whether available data and analyses can provide the information satisfactorily. A case illustrating these alternatives is discussed in section 4.8.

A second source of uncertainty concerns systematic changes in the data, such as systematic changes in the course of the trend, or in the amplitude of seasonal, cyclical or random fluctuations. We have already discussed in chapter 3 the problem of nonlinear trends, which most are, a problem which may or may not be soluble within limits of cost-efficient analysis.

It commonly happens also that as a trend rises, so the swings about the trend increase in some proportion. Bearing in mind that randomness in an important property which we wish to arrive at, this phenomenon, heteroscedasticity, poses problems.

There are two things which can be done in order to get a forecast impression of error bands. The first is the crude visual method; accepting that swings are getting wider, or narrower, simply interpolate radiating approximations equivalent to standard errors or deciles. If more precision is required, the data can be transformed into the form of percentages of the estimated value.

It is to be hoped that the percentages will turn out to be randomly distributed about the true value; if not, the analyst may require to seek out a subtler model designed to explain the systematic swings.

The first step in doing so is to find the regression of the residuals on the estimate: for every value estimated from the trend line there will be a residual representing the difference between the true value and the one estimated from the trend. The method of conducting this analysis and inherent problems are the same as that explained in chapter 3. If the changes in the swing are truly systematic the points should cluster closely round the regression estimator, and the new set of residuals (*second order* residuals so called because they are the residuals discovered by plotting residuals against trend estimates) should be random.

Forecasting problems in which this level of analysis are required in real situations are infrequent — I have only encountered them two or three times — and the only advice which can be given on further processing is that the remainder of the analysis tends to involve fiddling around to find an optimal way of applying the new information to the decision problem in hand. If the analyst is reduced to tracking down heterostedasticity in seasonal, cyclical and random components altogether, the exercise becomes much too involved to have much operational significance — we are dealing with fine distinctions of statistical uncertainty in a context in which the larger uncertainties of data quality and futurity are more important by several orders of magnitude.

4.7 Theoretical objections

A fullblooded classical analysis of a time series is a complex, lengthy and somewhat cumbersome process. One of the first questions to be asked of this technique is, how much may it be expected to achieve? General trend-fitting precedes the main body of the analysis and may be conducted independently. If a general trend is to be extrapolated it requires a fairly adventurous type of forecaster to be prepared to add back a projected cyclical on the trend. The seasonal index has in its own right only limited applications, and seasonal corrections of projections are rarely needed.

Among reasons for being unwilling to base too much prediction upon the cycle-upon-trend projections are a number of theoretical objections to the forecasting techniques of time series analysis. The first of these was mentioned on p. 76 when attention was drawn to the problem of building a seasonal index in such a way that the cyclical component was not distorted. The second objection is that moving averages are capable of inducing apparent cycles in non-cyclical data, and two stages of classical time series analysis depend upon taking moving averages; the third is that an entirely random series may exhibit behaviour indicative of a systematic trend effect, and this result is almost impossible to detect.

In short, an attempt to use classical time series analysis suffers from a number of drawbacks, in addition to those inherent in all forecasts, such as the problem of confidence that the parameters of the underlying model are not going to change as soon as a valid set of explanations of the history had been devised. These particular drawbacks include cumbersomeness, especially if large numbers of projections are needed; lack of precision in distribution of cyclical component; no intrinsic explanation of causation of the cyclical component; lack of confidence that the cyclical component produced is real and neither distorted nor entirely illusory. It is hardly surprising that most analysts regard this type of model as no more than a tentative first approximation to cyclical descriptions.

A final objection to any method using an unweighted moving average is that the longer the period of the moving average, the further back in time we have to go to obtain the termination of the moving average. Thus a twelve-month moving average has its terminal entry six months behind the latest actual observation. For this reason it is very slow to pick up changes in the trend; the picture it offers of cycle history may not only be distorted, it can rarely come near enough to the present to allow much confidence in its behaviour into the future.

Despite these theoretical objections, the elements of time series analysis may be justified in particular medium-term applications of the type outlined at the beginning of the chapter, where they may with all their imperfections represent the only available method of arriving at probability based estimates of demand relevant to specific decision problems. The provisos involved are that the analyst should know why he is trying to disaggregate the components and be trying to understand the reality behind the time series components so as to use them if possible as a basis for a model of interactions rather than a description of events. The trouble is that the methods are so simple, especially with the innumerable standard computer programs available, that they offer a great temptation to unthinking projection-casting, rather than conceptual forecasting.

4.8 Example of an application

Enough has been said by now to indicate the essential conceptual crudity of time series analysis; it must, like all forecasting techniques, be applied with caution, and never in isolation. That said, its principal application lies in situations in which good benchmarks are required from one to five years ahead, and where the analyst needs leads to possible models on a basis of very little information except past time trends. Especially where the decisions are important.

For example, the Steel Fabrication Company, located in Scotland, completed a capital investment programme in the late 1960s just in time to catch the particularly severe recession of the early 1970s, which included the collapse of one of its largest customers, Upper Clyde Shipbuilders Ltd, with considerable consequent losses to SFC. By mid-1972 the company was in severe cash straits, with its short-term borrowing capacity fully used up, and long-term capital very expensive if available at all. The company was generating only a minimal positive net cash flow.

The problem was that, while much of its still new capital equipment had a range of applications, many details, especially in finishing equipment, was directed to markets now in decline, and were inappropriate to the immense new opportunities opening up to the company as a possible subcontractor on North Sea Oil extraction plant building. Reorganizing equipment to take advantage of this opportunity called for an investment of around £1m, borrowable at not less than 12 per cent, and in the event that capacity was filled, the company would need to find a further £1m to £1.5m for working capital, at an average interest rate assessed at 8 to 9 per cent from all sources.

The company had a twofold problem: what was the maximum level of sales it could afford to generate without running out of cash, and what was the minimum level which would enable it to service the new capital it required? More relevantly: what were the probabilities that demand would be so high that the company could not meet it without running out of cash, or so low that it would be unable to service its capital?

Only a very simplified version of the approach to this exceedingly complex fore-casting problem can be outlined here. Both financial and market analysts were

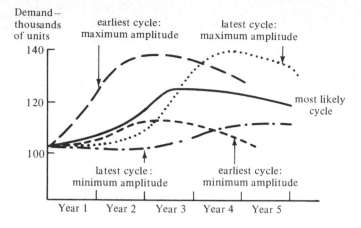

Fig. 4.5 Envelopes of cycle projections

We know there will be cycles, but there is likely to be much uncertainty about their timing and amplitude. In this example these were rather important so a set of possible cycles was charted, and based on past cycles and management's and the analysts' views of business and the economy probabilities were assigned to their likelihood. One possibility proved to be of critical financial importance, and at a later stage of the project was investigated in great detail, down to the seasonals and bands of random error.

involved: for purposes of this exposition, the financial inputs are taken as givens, although in practice they evolved in the process of intra-team dialogue.

The sales projection had two components: existing business and oil business. Existing business was easily charted historically according to the methods outlined in this chapter. Projected for the next five years, it appeared in the form shown in Fig. 4.5.

A cyclical trend projection of earliest and latest expected cycles, maximum and minimum expected amplitude, giving, it was thought, eight cases of potential interest for analysis.

	Earliest cycle	*Latest cycle*
Maximum value	Max. amplitude Min. amplitude	Max. amplitude Min. amplitude
Minimum value	Max. amplitude Min. amplitude	Max. amplitude Min. amplitude

These are eight extreme trend values, and much effort was expended in expressing their probabilities of occurrence. In the end, an intermediate period trend was also examined, at maximum and minimum amplitude, since it was thought to have a high probability of occurrence. The final matrix of probabilities was as follows

Amplitude	Cycle period			
	Earliest	*Latest*	*Intermediate*	
Maximum	0.03	0.03	0.15	0.21
Intermediate	0.09	0.09	0.4	0.58
Minimum	0.03	0.03	0.15	0.21
	0.15	0.15	0.7	1.0
	Probability of various cycle occurrences			

The most serious possible outcome for the company would have been the earliest cycle/maximum amplitude combination, following the investment which at the seasonal peak, and given more than modest growth on the North Sea Oil side, would have led to a cash runout. However, the probability (0.03) was small, and when combined with a probability (0.6) of the growth of North Sea being at the critical level, a joint probability of 0.6 x 0.03 = 0.018, = 18 chances in 1 000. Also the consequences were easy to guard against once the possibility had been noticed. Here the forecast provided a small possibility danger signal.

Another serious outcome, latest cycle, irrespective of amplitude, had a probability of 0.15 of occurring. In fact danger lay not only in the latest, but also 'less latest' combinations, so for this phase of the analysis 0.15 of the probability attributed to the intermediate outcome was borrowed. In other words, the analyst said there was a three in ten chance that the cycle would firm up late enough to cause serious trouble. This was a more dangerous case than the previous one, and involved looking closely at the joint behaviour of the existing market and North Sea.

First a control chart was evolved as follows

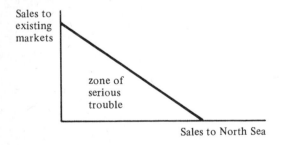

Second, a set of probabilities was evolved for the scatter band around the 'latest cycle' trend. Third, elementary multiple regression and input-output models were devised (on bases discussed earlier and later in this book) to try to get a feeling for the likely growth rate of North Sea business. These expectations were expressed in the form of cumulative probability tables and charts. An example of the latter is

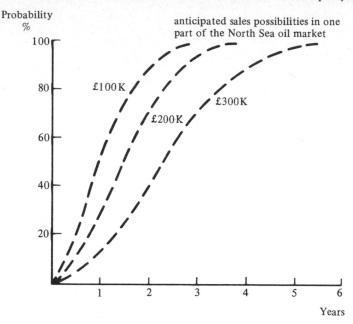

Fig. 4.6 Management's estimate of likely sales under uncertainty

This cumulative probability distribution of sales in a new market represents management's estimates of what might be sold. The same sort of chart can be produced from the scatter bands about a trend projection or series of projections. In the exercise from which these bands were derived, it was necessary to combine these estimates with those drawn from another market in which the company had a long trading history, so that the cumulative probability charts were derived from projections of fully analysed time series.

This example illustrates the importance of producing forecasting output in the form required for decision input.

(All data in this example have been disguised at the company's request.)

shown in Fig. 4.6. The joint probability of any point on the control chart in a given year can then be found by multiplying the probabilities from each of the cumulative probability charts for existing and North Sea.

For example, 'serious trouble' occurs if in year one the latest cycle ($p = 0.3$) is combined with North Sea sales of £200 000 ($p = 0.3$). The joint probability ($p = 0.09$) was regarded as large enough to give management serious food for thought — nearly one chance in ten that the proposed investment would lead to bankruptcy in the first year.

Management's dilemma was that: not to invest led to a near certainty of steady atrophy for the company, leading to a high probability of eventual collapse; to invest led to a probability of 0.15 (the highest found in any of the demand outcomes obtained from visual inspection) of bankruptcy. The probability of recovery to levels which the company could regard as fully healthy was 0.3. Management decided to accept the risk and invest. The outcome is not known at the time of writing.

4.9 Summary

Classical time series analysis involves attempting to dissociate various components which are thought to have governed the path of the data in the past so that due allowance can be made for them in the future. These components are the trend (which may be either a regression trend or a moving average trend); the effects of the trade cycle; the effects of seasonal movements; the effects of irregular movements imposed by non-recurrent shocks; the randomly distributed error component.

Doing all this is complex and cumbersome, although computer programs are available which will cope with all but irregular (non-recurrent) shocks. It is worth doing nowadays probably only for the difficult area of medium-term forecasting where we are particularly interested in evaluating the effects of economic cyclical phenomena. In this context it must be related to more deepseated economic analysis of the type discussed in chapter 7.

An important and previously neglected use of these techniques is to enable the analyst to obtain a measure of the random component which can be handled stochastically so as to produce relevant inputs to the decision-making system of a type more fully dealt with in chapter 9.

REFERENCES

Croxton, F. E. and Cowden, D. J. *Practical Business Statistics*, Prentice-Hall, 1960.
Moroney, M. J. *Facts from Figures*, 2nd edn, Penguin (Pelican), 1956.

5 Automatic forecasting systems

5.1 The forecasting problem

We have seen that while the traditional methods of analysing time series are of some value in isolating the random component and giving the analyst a sense of the consequences of likely cyclical fluctuations, the whole methodology is subject to some theoretical objections and is very cumbersome, although computer programs are widely available which will give readings of the trend, cyclical, seasonal and random components and forecast these into the future.

Except for particular applications in medium-term forecasting, however, it must be questioned whether the classical method is worth doing. Multiple regression, we shall see, is normally a more powerful tool for general medium- to long-term forecasts, and there are neater ways of doing short-term forecasts. It is in the short term in particular that automatic forecasts come into their own.

Like any forecasts, these are not an end in themselves; in this case they usually form a component in a stock control system. The criteria by which they are to be judged is not, as with most forecasts, their value as an input to a decision-making process, but their value as a component of a system whose purposes are to improve customer service and reduce costs.

The essential inputs to a stock control system are decision rules regarding the extent to which management is *willing* to be out of stock in any line (in general, the cost of ensuring against *never* being out of stock is prohibitive), actually receiving the merchandise (which may be variable) and forecasts of turnover through to the next time when goods might be received. Complicating this last factor is the existence of more than one source of supply (e.g. factory *v* wholesaler) offering different delivery speeds and costs.

To do justice to the area compressed into the above paragraph would require a complete book on logistics; and the principles are generally well recorded (see e.g. Heskett *et al.*, 1964). The present purpose is to sketch only the context of applications for the forecasting subsystem, for the justification for the whole business lies not in its being 'good' forecasting in its own right, but in the context of overall system efficiency.

Automatic forecasting systems are finding widespread application where a large number of stock lines has to be managed. Its most successful applications occur where demand offtake is relatively steady compared with the basic demand trend, e.g. in commodity items. Systems have been devised (e.g. IBM's Impact System) which can cope with situations in which offtake is very lumpy relative to the baseload demand, but these are inevitably less satisfactory.

The justification for the use of such systems is their ability to control stock more efficiently, rather than to forecast better; and integrated automatic stock control/forecasting systems may be able to cope more efficiently even with lumpy demand patterns such as might be found, for example, in fashion merchandise or Christmas lines. This ability arises through editing and grouping procedures operated on the various stock lines on the advice of the system suppliers.

A particular problem arises with the definition of a stock item. Many applications involve definitions which may be divided into many fine variants of size, style, colour and so on, as well as price and use. Careful judgment has to be exercised in order to achieve definition on the one hand useful to management and on the other which confines the number of lines to proportions which can be analysed economically, and which ensures that the sales of individual lines are sufficiently large, so that trend and seasonal factors are not obscured by random variations. In other words, some aggregation is almost always necessary. The lines are therefore grouped into stock control units, *on a basis of similarity of demand behaviour.*

Various sets of decision rules may be appropriate in different situations, with a trade-off between lower stockholding costs and an increased probability of being out of stock. It is possible to perform simulations which will show management the expected consequences of different rules involving the stock levels at which replacement lines should be ordered and the size of the orders to be placed, in terms of the cost of holding stock and the frequency of out of stock positions.

Management's role in the operation of such a system is to authorize the decision rules on a basis of their expectations as to consequences and periodically to monitor the operation of the system. They are also involved in aspects of the physical creation of the system. This requires the creation of devices physically to record inward and outward goods flows. The former is generally no problem, being handled by a stock-keeper, as is the verification of proper system operation through periodic stock counts. Recording outward movement of goods, often from widely dispersed points through the hands of an indifferently motivated group of sales or despatch personnel, can be more tricky.

One method is to have each item tagged with a small card containing a punched code which must be detached at the point of issue. A recently developed method involves scanning the tags with a light pen in order to input the relevant despatch data to the control system, another is to have a code for each item entered on a till or other register at the time of sale, and these entries electronically recorded.

Where goods are despatched against order with invoices, rather than against cash, an electronic record of the invoice or despatch note numbers can be retained. Elaboration of these systems is required to deal neatly and inexpensively with the problems of returns or errors in recording. The procedure thereafter is to collate these sales records, normally weekly, in order to find the current stock position in the store. Where the system becomes complex is when the company operates a multilevel distribution system involving, say, central and branch warehouses or stores, when the most economic reorder point for any one store is likely to be different from that of the system as a whole. Management has two alternatives: to keep every unit independent and not normally permit interstore transfers to make good stock deficiencies (thereby sacrificing some system efficiency in favour of greater administrative convenience and a clearer cut control system), or to permit such transfers in the interest of system efficiency, but incurring the additional costs of operating a transfer system and a more complex management control system. Here simulation procedures could help show which alternative, if any, makes a material difference to costs and customer service.

The detailed work of integrating forecasts with the stock control system involves two main areas: the type of system hardware and software available from specialist suppliers on the one hand, and management's objectives and criteria for efficient system operation on the other. Information on system design is available in comprehensive detail from the manufacturers and suppliers: the critical problem is that of communication between the systems experts and the managers based upon clear definition of managerial objectives for the system, and unambiguous statement of the limitations of the system by the supplier, each in terms which are clearly meaningful to the other side. Among those limitations we must include limitations on the capacity of the forecasting component of the system.

5.2 The forecasting system

The principle underlying automatic forecasts, more properly known as *adaptive* forecasts, is that of trend extrapolation using weighted moving averages, as discussed in chapter 4. In the present case we are concerned with short-run extrapolation, and our concern is not to produce forecasts which are excellent in their own right, but which operate effectively as a component of a system (for stock control) which is, overall, more efficient than alternative methods. The distinguishing features of adaptive forecasts are this integration with computer-based systems, the extreme cheapness of producing an individual forecast, and the fact that the system can operate for considerable periods with neither managerial nor analytical intervention.

It will be recalled that the purpose of taking moving averages of trends was to cancel out random and regular seasonal effects from the data in order to get a clearer picture of the trend behaviour, as an alternative to the development of a straightline regression trend. We discussed the alternatives of assigning equal weights to each observation, binomial weights to highlight cycles, and exponential weights in order to give greatest importance to the most recent observations. The only criterion to be observed was that the sum of the weights must equal 1. It is possible to approach the creation of adaptive forecasts in the same way, bearing in mind the availability of a computer to do the calculations and transfer the results to the rest of the stock control system.

Before proceeding to the explanation, mention may be made of a fairly crude system which can be operated manually to produce similar results. This is the *seasonal differences* method. This method essentially postulates that sales in a given month this year will be the same as those of the same month last year (thereby coping with seasonal effects) plus a trend factor, thus S (March 1974) = S (March 1973) + trend. The only problem is to decide how long to track the trend — normally a year. Adaptive forecasts are more sophisticated but before deciding to install an adaptive forecasting system, managers should remember that in essence they do not necessarily provide a more accurate prediction than the seasonal differences method. If an electronic stock control system is not required then forecasting by seasonal differences will work practically as well as adaptive methods. The latter, however, possess the facility of being self-correcting when trends change sharply, whereas the seasonal differences method requires personal intervention. The principal advantages of the adaptive method are that it does readily pick up short-run trend changes, and will automatically incorporate corrections into future forecasts.

Bearing in mind that adaptive forecasts are intended to operate for long periods without intervention (except in the case of serious malfunction), it is important to establish at the outset that the data to be used as the basis of the forecast are what they purport to be — that is, actual *demand* (unmodified by restraints on supply) for the product in question, with consequent problems of defining where one product ends and another begins, and the extent to which restriction on supply on one product is creating artificially inflated demand for a closely related variety or product.

5.3 The statistical method

One very crude short-term forecasting method would be to take a simple moving average of some convenient data base, say seven or nine months, and in the absence of any long-term trend projection simply extend the most recent trend direction somewhat into the future more or less visually.

This type of moving average suffers from two objections: in using it for forecasting the earliest data in the data base are given precisely the same weighting as the latest, and the midpoint occurs some months in arrears. We can devise a method of giving greater weight to the later observations so as to improve the reliability of our short-term extrapolations. In order to preserve the essential characteristics of a moving average, that it should indeed be an average, the weights attached to each of the data in the series should be fractions which in aggregate sum to unity. For example 0.5, 0.25, 0.125, 0.0625 . . . is a series of fractions which extended to the limit of infinity would theoretically add up to unity. One special characteristic of such a series is that it forms a geometrical progression, that is, each member is a constant fraction (in the above case one-half) of the preceding member. Stated another way round, each is a constant multiple (twice) the succeeding member. Such a serious declines or increases *exponentially*.

There are many ways in which we might weight a set of seven, say, monthly observations for June back through the preceding December which let us label Ju, M, A, Ma, F, Ja, D. We could give Ju weight 1, and assign weight 0 to all the others. This would not be an exponential series and would imply that the only member we were interested in for forecasting purposes was the current Ju reading. At the other extreme of reasonableness, we might assign a weight of one-seventh to each member, meaning that each was equally important. This is what we do when we take a simple moving average. If we used the weights 0.5Ju, 0.25M, 0.125A, 0.0625Ma, 0.03125F, 0.015625Ja, 0.0078125D we would clearly be assigning considerable weight to June and almost negligible weight to December. (One might question the taking of a seven-month average when data for seven months ago is regarded as so unimportant.)

However, the series 0.5 + 0.25 + 0.125 + 0.0625 + 0.03125 + 0.015625 + 0.0071825 . . . is a true geometric progression summing to unity, so is a properly exponentially weighted moving average. It can be rewritten $(0.5 + 0.5^2 + 0.5^3 + 0.5^4 + 0.5^5 + 0.5^6 + 0.5^7)$.

The square, cube, fourth power, etc., are called *exponents*, hence the description *exponentially weighted* for the moving average associated with such a series. The moving average (m) would then be given as

$$m\text{Ju} = 0.5(\text{Ju} + 0.5\text{M} + 0.5^2\text{A} + 0.5^3\text{Ma} + 0.5^4\text{F} + 0.5^5\text{Ja} + 0.5^6\text{D}).$$

Now the moving average for May will have been created in the same way, so that
$$m\text{M} = 0.5(\text{M} + 0.5\text{A} + 0.5^2\text{Ma} . . .)$$

mJu is therefore equal to $0.5\text{Ju} + 0.5m\text{M}$.

That is to say, the moving average for June may be expressed as half of the recorded demand for June and half of the moving average for May.

Thus taking one-half as our constant fraction we assign very considerable weight to the most recent observation in determining how far the moving average will follow individual fluctuations. The average will in fact tend to fluctuate about half as wildly as the irregular components. This would perhaps be unhelpful.

Say we chose four-fifths as our constant fraction, so that the coefficient of each term (the 0.5, 0.5^2, etc., in the previous example) would form the progression 0.2, 0.16, 0.128 (each being four-fifths of the preceding). The moving average in this case would be

$$m\text{Ju} = 0.2(\text{Ju} + 0.8\text{M} + (0.8)^2\text{A} + \cdots + (0.8)^6\text{D} + \cdots)$$

which may be simplified to 0.2Ju + 0.8 *m*M, i.e. one-fifth of the demand for June plus four-fifths of the moving average for May.

This means that as the June sales become known a new moving average m_t (*t* for present time period) will be calculated, composed 80 per cent of m_{t-1} (the moving average for the previous time period) and 20 per cent of d_t (demand in the present time period).

A more general form of expression for the moving average under these circumstances would be

$$m_t = 0.2d_t + 0.8m_{t-1} \qquad (1)$$

Using a little mathematical sleight of hand we can write

$$m_t = m_{t-1} - 0.2m_{t-1} + 0.2d_t \qquad (2)$$
$$= m_{t-1} + 0.2(d_t - m_{t-1}) \qquad (3)$$

which means that the current moving average can be found by adding to the previous moving average one-fifth of the difference between current demand and the previous moving average. Say the previous moving average was 1 000. Current period sales 1 500. Difference 500. Of this, one-fifth equals 100. New moving average 1 000 + 100 = 1 100.

Alternatively, substituting these numbers in equation (3)

$$m_t = 1\ 000 + 0.2(1\ 500 - 1\ 000)$$
$$= 1\ 000 + 0.2 \times 500$$
$$= 1\ 000 + 100 = 1\ 100$$

The general form of equation (3) is

$$m_t = m_{t-1} + a(d_t - m_{t-1}) \qquad (4)$$

where *a* is a constant fraction. The meaning of the value of 0.2 assigned to *a* in the above example then is that we are saying that of any observed fluctuation, 20 per cent is regarded as being part of a trend shift, the other 80 per cent is irregular. In practice, values between 0.1 and 0.3 are generally found to give reliable results. In general we can say that the larger the value of irregular fluctuations relative to changes in the average, the smaller should be the value of *a*, and vice versa.

In the absence of any trend, m_t is the best available estimate of the trend level of demand for the present as well as the future. If demand is thought to be increasing or decreasing an allowance must be made for the underlying upward or downward trend. If the trend is thought to be steadily upwards at, say, 0.5 per cent per month, the forecast for six months ahead would be m_t + 3 per cent. Generalizing, if we say the trend rate of change is *T*, the forecast for *k* months ahead would be $m_t + kT$.

Formula 4 may be modified to take account of the trend by replacing m_{t-1} with $m_{t-1} + t - 1$ so that it becomes

$$m_t = ad_t + (1 - a)(m_{t-1} + r_{t-1}) \qquad (5)$$

where *r* is a variable denoting the trend factor.

$m_{t-1} + r_{t-1}$ is the latest forecast for month t and m_t is a weighted average of the actual and expected demands for the month. The difference between the *actual* and the *expected* can be denoted by a new symbol e_t, then

$$e_t = d_t - (m_{t-1} + r_{t-1}) \tag{6}$$

and we can say

$$m_t = (m_{t-1} + r_{t-1}) + ae_t \tag{7}$$

Any change in the value of the trend coefficient can be picked up by a formula

$$r_t = r_{t-1} + be_t$$

where b is a small positive fraction.

The effect of the foregoing, which is a simplified presentation of a more comprehensive material contained in an ICI statistical monograph (Coutie *et al.*), is that using these types of formulae a computer can print out a moving average trend which takes into account forecasts it has itself produced for the current month, and the difference between its own forecast and the actual observation. Some of this will be accounted for by random variations, but the programme will allocate some of the error to a change in the trend. In many situations seasonal factors are also required. Typically these are handled by computing them in accordance with the methodology described in chapter 4.

The details of the foregoing description are unimportant, reflecting as they do one system which was extremely thoroughly reported some years ago (Coutie *et al.*). The important aspect is to understand the underlying principles, that what such a system is attempting to do is systematically to track changes in the cyclical trend of demand net of random influences and seasonal variations.

Adaptive systems have been much developed since the account on which the above was based was written, although the principles remain the same. The suppliers' analysts can be expected to give generally reliable advice on problems of grouping of stock lines, estimating values for m, t, a and b in the formulae, and setting up control limits at which managerial action is required.

5.4 Summary and conclusions

There are a number of variants of this general class of adaptive forecasting techniques such as Brown's method, the Box Jenkins method, and Holt's method, basically the one described here. It has been shown that they all amount to much the same thing, and recent development work has tended to concentrate on different classes of application for such methods, for example situations in which the seasonal factor is becoming more or less pronounced, situations in which there are exceptionally wide random swings (e.g. with infrequently ordered large unit value lines) and so on. There is little point in describing such developments in detail in a work such as this, since most such developments have been undertaken by computer software companies, and come as part of standard computing packages either direct from the manufacturers or through bureaux. The best source of information on such operations is the software supplier.

Managerially, the problems in this area lie in the selection of the most appropriate systems for the firm's operation. Generally speaking, such systems will be selected on a basis of their value to the firm as information systems in general, and perhaps stock control systems in particular. The precise configuration of the forecasting subsystem is therefore unlikely to be of critical importance and managements should find any subsystem offered by a reputable supplier totally satisfactory provided a few simple conditions are observed.

These conditions relate to the clarity of management's own thinking, and the manner in which they specify their objectives. For example, it will be necessary to specify the most appropriate forecast time periods (week, month, quarter, year) for each stock line, to delineate precisely what is to be taken as a stock line, to define the objectives of the stock control system, to define acceptable error levels in the forecasting system and so on.

It is not necessary for management to understand the precise mathematics of the process: the computer is there to master that: the necessary skill is to be able to communicate meaningfully with the software representative.

The important point to recognize is that in this type of system the forecast is merely a mechanical tracking device which adopts a number of compromise positions which have been programmed into it in advance. The further ahead the time period goes which the analyst is attempting to forecast, the grosser will become the errors in forecasting.

The justification for these systems lies entirely in their proven record of being able almost invariably to improve stockholding costs or customer service levels (or both together) by comparison of any alternative available method of operating a stock control system.

The availability of hardware, software and specialist advice is now at such a routine and inexpensive level through bureaux that the place for the type of description contained in this chapter has moved in less than a decade through from journals dealing with development of statistical method to elementary textbooks on general management.

REFERENCES

Coutie, G. A. *et al.*, *Short Term Forecasting*, ICI Monograph, No. 2, Oliver & Boyd, 1964.
Heskett, J. L., Ivie, R. M. and Glaskowski, N. A. *Business Logistics*, Ronald Press, 1964.
Institute of Business Management *Retail IMPACT, Inventory Management and Control Techniques*, IBM Ltd.

6 Relationships among economic variables

6.1 Role of relationships in forecasting

The theme of chapters 3, 4 and 5 was the interpretation of time series with a view to extrapolating them in a manner meaningful to decision-makers. It was stressed there that all the variants of time series analysis are subject to theoretical and practical shortcomings, and when regression analysis was discussed it was pointed out that the underlying rationale for computing the regression of an economic series on time was to say that we were using the passage of time as a *proxy variable* for actual economic forces for which we lacked data, or which we could not use for technical reasons. In other words, we said that for practical purposes we would regard the passage of time as determining the trend changes shown in the regression estimate.

In many sets of circumstances, however, the analyst may have access to data which he feels actually represent the path of the true determining phenomenon. For example, he may believe that sales are determined by the activity of buying customers, profits are determined by sales or cost changes, or that demand for a shop's merchandise is determined by size of frontage and the number of passing shoppers. These situations suggest that the analyst has in mind a *model* relating the variable to be forecast (the *dependent* variable) to the behaviour of other (the *independent* variable).

There are various sets of circumstances under which such a model may be a valuable basis for forecasting. First, when the analyst can obtain, or thinks he can create, a more reliable forecast for the independent variable than the dependent one in which he is interested. Second, when changes in the independent variable are found to *precede* by some fixed period, changes in the dependent variable. Third, when (as in the store location case) a number of variables are involved which can be measured simultaneously over a number of cases (as in the case of a store chain).

There are particular problems involved in the first two categories, namely situations involving finding regression estimates of one time series from the behaviour of others. These are so demanding that a separate subject, econometrics, has grown up which deals with them. This is the field of the econometricians, trained in both economics and statistics, and although the basic methodology is common to that used in the more direct case, the scope of this book will allow us to do no more than indicate the special problem areas associated with econometrics. It should be observed that econometrics in practice is a more powerful tool for analysing the behaviour of major economic segments, e.g. coal, power, steel, foodstuffs generally, etc., than for the majority of individual firms dealing with markets of more limited scope.

We can return to the special problems of econometrics shortly, after examining the general methodology underlying this type of model building, namely *multiple regression analysis.* Before proceeding even this far, however, mention should be made of one crude but very useful simple application of comparison of time series called *lead-lag* analysis.

We spent considerable time in chapter 4 on the problems of predicting economic cycles. These come in many forms – the 'trade cycle', a measure of fluctuation in the rate of growth of gross national product, being perhaps the best known. There are also fluctuations in such economic cycles as the level of bank clearings, the balance of payments, unemployment, credit and money supply, the retail prices and ordinary share indexes, physical stock levels, building industry starts, manufacturing industry orders, investment in plant and machinery, savings and expenditure, and many others, recorded regularly in *Economic Trends* (HMSO).

Individual firms are also subject to cycles – sales, costs, profits, stocks, employment and so on, which are often thought to be related to underlying economic cycles or cycles affecting their customers. For purposes such as stock planning, manpower planning and materials purchasing it would often be very desirable to be able to get a good estimate of when a particular cycle (e.g. orders) was likely to turn. Management may not need details of the extent of the change nearly so much as a reliable signal on its timing.

The method adopted is crude but frequently highly effective. It consists of finding some economic time series whose turning points regularly lead the one in which management is interested by a usable time interval. Such time series are called *leading indicators* and the technique is labelled *lead-lag analysis.*

Finding such series is a matter of trial and error. The basic economic series for Britain are in *Economic Trends.* Industry and customer series are found in trade association returns and trade journals, as well as directly from customers. But not all series are usable. Many do not work with a consistent lead time. Many do not lead by a margin greater than the time in which they become available. Some which appear to work do not fill the analyst with any confidence because he can see no rational reason why they *should* work. It is a fortunate analyst who has one or two that work reliably. Although the search is time-consuming, the payoff for success is very high in an industry where prosperity is subject to underlying cycles.

The problem of unreliability can be mitigated to some extent by the creation of a tool known as a *diffusion index*. This is an index composed of a number of indicators, each of limited reliability. The theory is that although no one will perform reliably, the consensus of the leading indicators can be used with greater reliability. Ideally a diffusion index should be created of series whose data are reported monthly, and the analyst exercises a judgment such as 'when one-third of the leading series have turned, we take this to offer e.g. a five to six month indication of the turning point in our sales'. Such judgments are based on experience.

The reason for suggesting one-month reporting is that monthly data are generally published four to six weeks in arrear, whereas quarterly data are frequently not available until as much as a quarter in arrear, so that there may be a delay of some five months between the occurrence of a turning point and its reporting. Since a leading signal of about six to nine months is the most that can normally be expected, quarterly data tend to come in too late to be of much use.

Monthly data should be deseasonalized, and if six to ten indicators are contained in the index, the random component is normally expected tolerably to cancel out.

As well as leading indicators, many analysts like to keep track of current or even lagging indicators, to help confirm that the observed turning point was not merely a false start, but that a new cyclical trend has really become established.

6.2 Building simple models

The kind of model of the economy implicit in the analyst's mind when he is using leading indicators must be described as crude. It may work in a generalized sort of way, but it lacks any kind of detailed specification. It is analogous to the notion that a rough cylinder ought to run downhill: this is a long way from designing even a simple effective wheel, far less the sophisticated undercarriage of Concorde.

To obtain an easy approach to one of the most powerful model-building techniques available for business analysis, not only in forecasting but in many fields of investigation, let us consider the very simple, but true, example of the operator of a small shop chain who felt that the sales in his shops were determined principally by the number of shoppers per hour passing in the street and the floor area of the store. This was his crude model. He wanted to know whether the data he had could be used to predict sales in two alternative stores he was considering purchasing. The data for the existing stores were as follows:

Shop no.	No. of passers by per hour	Floor area (ft²)	Sales per week (£)
1	564	1 300	490
2	1 072	1 400	580
3	326	900	400
4	1 127	1 000	565
5	798	1 100	520
6	584	1 300	500
7	280	1 350	370
8	970	1 500	625
9	802	1 250	540
10	650	1 000	438

Using a simple linear additive multiple regression program, the computer prints out information in the following form (Z is sales, X is traffic and Y is the floor area).

Simple correlation coefficient of Z with X = 0.902 4

Simple correlation coefficient of Z with Y = 0.429 8

Simple correlation coefficient of X with Y = 0.165 6

The parameters of the regression equation

$$Z = A + B1^*X + B2^*Y$$

Are given below

A = 192.839 5

Bl^* = 0.232 1

$B2^*$ = 0.117 7

Partial correlation coefficient of X with $Z(r)$ = 0.933 5

Partial correlation coefficient of Y with $Z(r)$ = 0.659 7

Multiple correlation coefficient (R) = 0.946 1

Residual standard deviation = 29.737 2†.

From this printout we can define the model of sales determination for shops in this group as

$$S = 192.8 + 0.23 \times \text{Shoppers} + 0.118 \times \text{Floor Area}$$

However, we are a little concerned that there is a low correlation between the sales and the area of the store, with the result that addition of floor area to traffic adds very little to our ability to explain variations in the dependent variable. Nevertheless, the partial correlation coefficients of traffic and area with sales appear fairly impressive, and the multiple correlation coefficient (R) shows that we have explained a very impressive 95 per cent of the variation in the dependent variable.

The question which arises at this point is what is the precise meaning of the correlation coefficients? A multiple correlation coefficient of sales with traffic of 0

---

† These terms all have precise meanings in statistics. For the non-statistical reader, the correlation coefficient measures how well the estimating equation fits the original data. If the correlation coefficient is up towards 1 then we have a good fit, down towards 0 then we have a poor fit. Here store size and traffic are slightly correlated, and traffic is almost overwhelmingly powerful as the sales predictor. The partial correlation coefficient does the same job, but in this case the influence of the other variables is discounted and held fixed. The partial correlation coefficient is the one normally used: for practical purposes the simple correlation coefficient is meaningless in multiple regression models. The multiple correlation coefficient (R) tells us how much of the variation of the dependent variable has been explained by the independent variables. One word of warning to the uninitiated. This example occupies this place in the book because it comes out so beautifully and simply. It is easily the best result this author has ever obtained so simply. Usually, especially in econometric work, we are content with Rs of around 0.3.

would mean that there was no relationship between the two. A coefficient of 1 would imply a perfect one — for one relationship. Some figures between 0 and 1 reflects an imperfect but nevertheless measurable relationship. We are all familiar with chance relationships: coincidences. The question then is, could the correlation coefficients have arisen by chance? They could: they always could, but statisticians have developed tests to determine how likely it is that a given correlation coefficient arose by chance. The tests are applied using tables one of which is reproduced as Table 6.1.

The column headed n refers to the number of sets of observations available in the regression model. Reading along the row n 10, we see that $r_{0.1} = 0.4973$. That is to say, if the value of r is equal to or greater than 0.4973, then there is a probability of 0.1 ($\frac{1}{10}$) that the observed correlation arose by chance. There are more stringent tests. Further along the same row we see that if $r \geqslant 0.8233$ then there is only 1 chance in 1 000 that the observed correlation arose by chance. Our correlation of sales with passing traffic (0.9335) is therefore highly unlikely to have arisen by chance, and a reasonable jury should be prepared to find the case proved beyond reasonable doubt. The correlation between store area and sales looks fairly impressive at about 0.66. However with ten sets of data this can be taken as statistically significant at only the 0.02 level; that is to say, in one case in fifty such a result could have arisen by chance rather than as a reflection of real phenomena.

As is evident from the table, some correlation coefficients may be 'significant' at one level, but not at others. It is up to the analyst, or the manager, to decide how to interpret such information. In this case, the store owner told the analyst that he reckoned area was important, and if the statistics could not prove this, that merely demonstrated the deficiency of the statistics. He was no doubt perfectly correct, and the store area coefficient was retained in the model.

Forecasting using such a model is of course very simple. You can do it manually or the computer will do it for you. Insert the appropriate numbers for shoppers and area in the formula and solve it to obtain expected sales. The last line on the computer printout tells us that the standard deviation of the residuals of this model is about 29.7 (say 30). Since we know that roughly two-thirds of all observations should lie within one standard deviation either side of the mean estimated by this formula, 95 per cent within 2, and 99 per cent within 3, we have a useful measure of uncertainty of the forecast. Programs also exist which will give the dispersion of the residuals in terms of deciles, which may be more useful for certain decision-making purposes.

6.3 Regression of time series

Few problems in practice yield as neat solutions as the example in the previous section. In solving that problem the analyst had a rare combination of circumstances: a model which the analysis confirmed, clean, relevant and readily accessible data, linear relationships, independent variables which truly were independent and variables whose behaviour is not being tracked through time.

The correlation coefficient

Table 6.1 *Values of the correlation coefficient for different levels of significance*

n	0.1	0.05	0.02	0.01	0.001
1	0.98769	0.99692	0.999507	0.999877	0.9999988
2	0.90000	0.95000	0.98000	0.990000	0.99900
3	0.8054	0.8783	0.93433	0.95873	0.99116
4	0.7293	0.8114	0.8822	0.91720	0.97406
5	0.6694	0.7545	0.8329	0.8745	0.95074
6	0.6215	0.7067	0.7887	0.8343	0.92493
7	0.5822	0.6664	0.7498	0.7977	0.8982
8	0.5494	0.6319	0.7155	0.7646	0.8721
9	0.5214	0.6021	0.6851	0.7348	0.8471
10	0.4973	0.5760	0.6581	0.7079	0.8233
11	0.4762	0.5529	0.6339	0.6835	0.8010
12	0.4575	0.5324	0.6120	0.6614	0.7800
13	0.4409	0.5139	0.5923	0.6411	0.7603
14	0.4259	0.4973	0.5742	0.6226	0.7420
15	0.4124	0.4821	0.5577	0.6055	0.7246
16	0.4000	0.4683	0.5425	0.5897	0.7084
17	0.3887	0.4555	0.5285	0.5751	0.6932
18	0.3783	0.4438	0.5155	0.5614	0.6787
19	0.3687	0.4329	0.5034	0.5487	0.6652
20	0.3598	0.4227	0.4921	0.5368	0.6524
25	0.3233	0.3809	0.4451	0.4869	0.5974
30	0.2960	0.3494	0.4093	0.4487	0.5541
35	0.2746	0.3246	0.3810	0.4182	0.5189
40	0.2573	0.3044	0.3578	0.3932	0.4896
45	0.2428	0.2875	0.3384	0.3721	0.4648
50	0.2306	0.2732	0.3218	0.3541	0.4433
60	0.2108	0.2500	0.2948	0.3248	0.4078
70	0.1954	0.2319	0.2737	0.3017	0.3799
80	0.1829	0.2172	0.2565	0.2830	0.3568
90	0.1726	0.2050	0.2422	0.2673	0.3375
100	0.1638	0.1946	0.2301	0.2540	0.3211

Table 6.1 is taken from Table VII of Fisher and Yates: *Statistical Tables for Biological, Agricultural and Medical Research*, published by Longman Group Ltd., London (previously published by Oliver & Boyd, Edinburgh), and by permission of the authors and publishers.

These conditions cannot be encountered when attempts are made to apply the same methodology to time series, for example, with a view to operating lead-lag analysis with greater precision. One condition which is probably never met in practice with time series is the condition that there should be no systematic relationship between the independent variables themselves.

Consider three time series

Dependent variable	Independent variables which it is postulated determine the dependent variable	
	A	B
15	30	45
20	40	60
25	50	75
30	60	90
35	70	105

A glance at the table shows that either *A* may determine the dependent variable, or *B*, or both. Equally, however, *A* may determine *B* or *B* determine *A*. There is no power on earth which can tell which (or if both, the relevant role of each) determines the dependent variable. This is an extreme case of a phenomenon known as *multiple collinearity* of the independent variables.

A glance at *Economic Trends* will show that economic time series tend to behave in the same way, at the same time or at regularly spaced intervals. In general, over the past fifty years, economic and business series have tended to go up together. Additionally, as we saw in chapter 3, business and economic series rarely remain linear for long. This means in effect that while it may be safe to try to get a regression estimate of the influence of one leading series on, say, our sales, to do so for more than one may be futile, although our 'model' suggests that more than one may be relevant.

One device which analysts adopt in attempting to overcome this problem is to suggest that while the trends may be multiply collinear, the difference between one period's observation and the next on any one trend, used as an indicator of the appropriate differences in the observations for the independent variable, may be found to be subject to less multiple collinearity than the crude trend observations. The regression model then attempts to state that the crude difference between each pair of observations of the dependent variable will be determined by the crude difference between each pair for the respective independent variables. This means that instead of predicting the series of observations of the independent variable, the analyst tries to predict each of the differences in the series. This is known as the *first differences* method. What this technique boils down to is an attempt to put precision into the diffusion index as a cyclical predictor. Perhaps this can be made to work where the independent variables tend to be volatile and disconnected, and where they offer a long lead.

One elaboration of this idea has been put to work with some success in large sector industries, and may be applicable to some firms which feel confident that changes in their sales, costs, profits, etc., are accounted for by one or two identifiable, mutually independent determining variables, such as growth of consumers' disposable income, changes in hire-purchase availability, or the size of the sales force. The model then states that sales in any period, t, will be most heavily determined by sales in the previous period $(t - 1)$ and the changes in other independent variables. In other words, the dependent variable is thought to be *serially correlated*.

Computation is extremely cumbersome and demands a computer, but the principle is easily expressed, and a forecast can be extended indefinitely, so long as the analyst is willing to predict the future of the independent variables. If these are very deep-lying which exhibit great stability (such as changes in gross national product) the analyst may be happy to try a linear regression extrapolation for a long period ahead based on a long historic series. Similarly, if they are under the control of the firm, he may well be willing to try out the consequences of a number of alternatives, and project them a long way ahead. Since the method is susceptible to very long period extrapolation, it tends to be basic to long-term planning projects. Its operation is simple in principle. Knowing existing sales (say) and projecting changes in the independent variables to next year, it is possible to derive an estimate for next year's sales.

How should the analyst decide whether to adopt actual data or first differences? Actual data give a measure of the difference in the dependent variable *from its average* (the first stage in computation by the graphical method) produced by varying the independent variables: on the other hand, use of first differences shows the relative importance of the independent variables in causing a change in the dependent variable *from one time period to the next*. Generally first differences are preferable where strong trend influences are present, where intercorrelation of the independent variables is greater using actual data, and where the residuals from the final analysis exhibit serial correlation. A combination of first difference and time trend can produce a very powerful long-term forecasting model of the firm.

Sales in any time period will be determined by sales in the previous period and the change in (say) GNP or advertising or buyers' orders and a constant and residual error, or

$$S_t = S_{(t-1)} + a\,\Delta X_1 + b\,\Delta X_2 + C + \phi$$

Δ is the sign for difference.

The problems involved in creating such a model are less mathematical than operational. The mathematical theory is well understood by statisticians but this only makes a beginning to the story.

This model says really that there are only two major influences on sales ΔX_1 and ΔX_2, let us say changes in advertising and changes in consumers' income. Now this conclusion did not emerge out of blue sky. It began with an unspecified model of a shape such as, 'we think sales are determined by prices, sales promotion, retail discounts, income of consumers, competitors' prices and sales promotion, and the state of the weather'. To get from there to a model has involved someone in weeks of fiddling around (*a*) to specify the *shape* of the model and (*b*) to specify the relevant independent variables.

On shape, decisions have to be made whether the dependent or independent variables shall be in the form of actual data or first differences (or one other little-used form, *link relatives* which involves expressing data in time *t* as a *proportion* of data in $t - 1$). A second major decision is whether the model should be *additive* or *multiplicative* in other words, should the effects of varying independent variables be *added to* or *multiplied by* each other? A third is whether to incorporate a time trend component (e.g. S_{t-1}).

A fourth major decision is whether any of the independent variables should be lagged; for example it might be argued that the effects of a price change would only show up after a lapse of one or two months. Finally, there will arise the question of distributed lags in the effects of independent variables; for example, how much of the effect of advertising will occur in the period in which the advertising takes place, and how much will be carried over to later periods?

Figuring out the answers to these questions is time consuming, and involves continuous attempts to improve the specification of the model in light of management's evaluation of what is in fact in repeated interaction with the results of the computing, and this raises all sorts of questions about the common sense of what someone, somewhere, is doing. As well as specifying the shape of the model by trial and error the analyst is also trying to specify the relevance of the independent variables chosen for investigation. Suppose he gets measurements for the various variables, and cranks out a regression estimate, so what?

First of all, he will not be sure that he is using the best available measure of the independent variables implied in the unspecified model. Second, he will not be sure that each of these individually fits best with the dependent variable in a *linear* form. The best fit might involve logarithmic relationships; in other words, the model is multiplicative in that term, and he will have to examine the trend of the residuals to see whether this is the case. Third, he will not know how much multiple collinearity there is among the independent variables, and even if he produces a device known as a correlation matrix to check for this, he will probably still not be sure whether the degree of intercorrelation is too great until he has tried out various combinations.

In all this the analyst has two yardsticks: the first is to produce a model that in a few terms explains in an intuitively satisfying way a large proportion of the behaviour of the dependent variable. To do this he is operating partly on intuition, but is materially aided by a measurement known as the *coefficient of multiple determination* which has the handy property that it tells the analyst how much of the variation in the dependent variable he has explained by his current group of independent variables modelled as they are.

The coefficient of multiple determination is known for short as R^2 and can be calculated as follows

$$R^2 = 1 - \frac{\Sigma(d)^2}{\Sigma(Y^2) - (\bar{Y})^2 N}$$

where d = the unexplained residual deviations in the analysis

$\bar{Y}$ is the mean of the Y values (values of the dependent variable)

N = the number of observations in the analysis.

R^2 always has a value between 0 and 1 inclusive, and if the analyst obtains an equation which gives an R^2 of 0.5, this means his model explains 50 per cent of the behaviour of the dependent variable.

Now the game is not to maximize the value of R^2, although this is a short cut to producing a forecast by means of standard computer programs known as step-up regression programs which will search out the individual R^2 for each of the independent variables, and select first that variable with the highest individual R^2. It then searches through the remaining variables to find the one which, in combination with the one offering the highest, gives the highest joint R^2 for the two variables, and so on until all the variables are down in the list and the program has spewed out the R^2 for the lot. This is a horrible method of analysis. For one thing it is entirely mechanical and completely ignores the first, and most important, analytic criterion set out above, that the model should be an intuitively satisfying description of events in a real business context.

It is also technically unsound, and may well mask important relationships; say, for example, out of a dozen possible independent variables thrown into such an analysis, one is tremendously important (e.g. growth of consumers' credit) whereas two others (e.g. growth of bank advances and growth of hire-purchase debt) are only slightly less important individually. Let us say the respective individual R^2s are 0.4, 0.3 and 0.3. Clearly these three measures to a considerable extent overlap, and will themselves be intercorrelated. As a result, once consumers' credit is in the equation, neither of the other two will be in a position to raise R^2 very much, adding perhaps only 0.025 each, hence they will appear very much among the also rans in the step-up regression output, contributing jointly only 0.45 to R^2. Quite conceivably the bank advances and hire-purchase debt used *independently* of consumers' credit but taken together could contribute 0.55 to R^2, an explanation of a full 10 per cent additional variation in the dependent variable. Hence the importance of modelling in terms of what the variables *mean* rather than their numerical properties. (Without going into the mathematical properties of correlation it is a little difficult to explain why R^2 should go down by adding a third variable, but what this depends on is that R^2 is partly an inverse function of the number of explanatory variables put into the system.) The best approach is to obtain two or three intuitively good explanatory variables, put some work into getting good data to measure them, and then put a lot of work into specifying a commonsense model shape in which they work well. If they explain 70 to 80 per cent of the observed variation in the dependent variable then the analyst should be pretty happy. Unless he is an academic he ought to have better things to do with his time than fooling around trying to add another 2 per cent to R^2.

Working this way it is unlikely that the analyst should get into much trouble over *significance tests*, but their existence is worth registering just in case. Their purpose is to suggest whether or not the existence of a regression equation can be regarded as representing a real phenomenon, or just a quirk of the statistical sausage machine. It is possible (though unusual and unlikely to arise where the modelling has been intelligently done) to obtain large R^2s which quite probably mean nothing at all.

This can arise because the standard error of estimate (the width of the error bands either side of the regression estimate) is very large, so that although the estimating equation does explain a substantial proportion of the dependent variable, the observations are so widely dispersed that the apparently strong correlation might have arisen through misfortune. Two such tests are commonly used in econometric analysis, the Chi-squared (χ^2) and Student's T tests (the latter generally used where the number of observations is small, say around ten). The use of such tests involves comparison of the results of formula calculations with tables or charts containing control limits for accepting or rejecting the view that the association observed between the dependent and independent variables might have arisen through chance. The statistics is standard, obtainable in any textbook and should be pursued there.

6.4 Multiplicative or additive models?

Models of the situation under investigation may be of a form which suggests that a given increment for the independent variable(s) will produce a constant increment in the dependent variable, irrespective of the value of the independent variable. For example, a fifty-unit increase in consumers' disposable incomes will produce a one-unit increase in sales, or a ten-unit increase in advertising expenditure will produce a one-unit increase in sales, irrespective of the value of the independent variables. This relationship therefore holds across the whole range of variables under investigation. We can say that a given increment in Y (income) or A (advertising) will always have the effect of adding a constant increment to S (sales). The estimating equation for this sort of situation then has the form we have already investigated

$S = K + 0.02Y + 0.1A$

(S = sales, K = a constant, Y = income, A = advertising).

If we reason, however, that a 100-unit increase in advertising expenditure will have a different effect when the base level is 1 000 units rather than 10 000 units — arguing for example (*a*) that a 10 per cent increase will have proportionately smaller effect than a 1 per cent increase; or (*b*) that a 1 per cent increase would hardly be noticed while a 10 per cent increase would have a greater than proportionate increase; or (*c*) that at 10 000 the effects of advertising would be exhibiting diminishing returns — then we could hardly be confident of the linearity of our model. If we go on to reason further (*d*) that the effects of increasing advertising will be greater with affluent consumers than with poor ones, then clearly we will be mis-specifying the model if we suggest that the effects of adding a constant A to Y when $Y = 1\ 000$ will be the same as when $Y = 2\ 000$.

In such circumstances (and most intuitively satisfactory econometric models suggest that the simple linear additive relationships are inadequate) we might want to respecify the model in the form

$$S = K \times Y^a \times A^b$$

i.e. a *multiplicative* form.

An equation of this form involves two changes by comparison with the linear and additive model. First, we have added an exponent (*a*) to the income variable and (*b*) to the advertising variable, suggesting that the scatter diagram may follow a curve

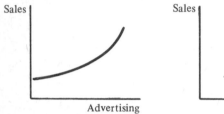
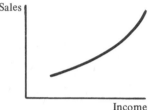

a change which will not matter even if the relationship turns out to be linear, since then the exponent will take the value 1; second, we have multiplied the independent variables suggesting that we think that the effects of the variables are in multiplicative form, that is to say, the model will give better predictions when the effects of Y are multiplied by the effects of A than when they are added.

It is fortunately very easy to turn this type of estimating equation into the form which we are used to handling; all that is necessary is to take the logarithms of both sides of the equation, when it can be rewritten

$$\log S = \log K + a \log Y + b \log A.$$

Tables of logarithms are used to obtain the *transformed* values of Y and A, and the *logs* of the original data are used for the estimating equation.

Here again, the practice involved is tedious to do manually, although conceptually perfectly simple, and computer programs are widely available which will do all this laborious calculation instantly, and also instantly give back forecast values for S with standard errors or probability bands of error for any value of Y or A which the analyst cares to insert.

One practical warning may be in order in using variables such as advertising budget as predictors of sales; very often advertising budget is determined by management as a fixed percentage of historical or budgeted sales. Obviously using historic data generated in response to this condition will produce perfect correlation, but the direction of causation is the wrong way round and the analysis is valueless. To use advertising as a predictor it is normally necessary to set up long-term experiments in which advertising is systematically (or randomly) varied through time or between different markets.

Let us now reconsider what we have been doing: we started with a number of possible models of the situation we were trying to analyse, suggesting that the variable we were trying to forecast was related to a number of other variables. We may have been highly unsure of the precise nature of the model, whether it was linear and additive in all its terms or not, whether there was multiple collinearity amongst some of the independent variables, what was the importance of serial correlation, whether all the suggested independent variables really had a significant effect or not, whether the data were homoscedastic, whether the directions of causation were all as we supposed them to be, and what were the best timelags (or distributed lags) for the various variables.

Answering these questions involves a good deal of trial and error, creating first attempts at the equation and judging them in light of the contribution to R^2 of each of the terms and the contribution of the model to our understanding of what actually has been going on in light of real time. We have perhaps used significance tests to determine whether a variable should be retained or rejected as an element of the explanation. Eventually the quality of the equation as a predictor would be tested by backcasting to see how well it would have worked in predicting the past history of the independent variable.

The route to the estimating equation finally adopted will have been littered with rejected alternatives — rejected both on technical statistical grounds, and grounds of commercial common sense and significance.

Until very recently, manual computation was so laborious, and batch processing by computer so time-consuming in terms of real time elapsed between each of the iterations required to obtain a good model, that the use of this technique was confined to crucial applications where it was worth while to give a team of statisticians a year to come up with a model. In the end the sheer laboriousness of the process, and problems of communication between managers and the analysts so awe-inspiring, that probably the company had to be content with a second-best model.

Recent developments in computer technology have vastly altered this picture, with the advent of time-sharing systems operated by commercial bureaux. Here the analyst, who may well be a manager with no more knowledge of statistics than that expounded in this chapter, can produce in two or three hours models which less than a decade ago would have taken several men years to work out.

By calling up a multiple regression program and punching in the values of the independent variables he can obtain immediate feedback of the values of the estimating coefficients (including the constant) together with their standard errors and the value of the R^2 for the whole equation. He can attempt all sensible combinations of the independent variable in a few minutes. By calling for the residuals he can have these listed to inspect them for lack of linearity. By calling for logarithmic transformations he can repeat the whole process for multiplicative and non-linear forms of the model. By returning the residuals to the system as an independent variable (at the press of a button) he can operate *step regression* techniques. In this technique the dependent variable is regressed against the residual errors of the first model: if there is a correlation, then clearly the term contains some important explanatory variable which ought to be in the model. He can test the residuals for randomness and for heteroscedasticity. He can instruct the computer to operate on a time trend basis, using the value of the independent variable with various lags ($t - 1$, $t - 2$, etc.) as an independent variable. Press another button, and he can pick up distributed lags for any of the variables, yet another button and he can instruct the computer to attempt a one, two, etc., period lag for an independent variable. After a couple of hours he can have an equation which represents an astronomical quantity of highly sophisticated statistical manipulation, all performed in seconds and directly under his own immediate control as he evolves a route to a model which is not only technically optimum but which is also in line with what the manager with all his insights into the actual situation can regard as acceptable.

On this route, incidentally, the manager bringing to bear his insights on the real world to the results of the computations, will inevitably find himself obtaining fascinating insights into the value of his own beliefs and the nature of his own uncertainties about how his commercial milieu operates. Suddenly he will find himself saying: 'Of course! I suspected *that*, but never realized it was so strong', or 'goodness, I would have thought *that* mattered more'.

Perhaps, of course, his intuition is still right at that point, and the model is still deficient. This is why the technical statistics and manager's judgment must interact closely in getting a model which the manager can believe in thoroughly, albeit at the expense of some previously cherished notion.

What all this boils down to is that the new computing tools move multiple regression from the area of experimental methodology into that of tools for regular use. Models involving highly sophisticated statistics in interaction with managerial judgment can now be produced by managers themselves and used as a basis for forecasts in which large numbers of variations in the values of the independent variables can be assumed. It thus becomes possible to uncover the profitability boundary conditions of the determining variables in so far as profitability is determined by sales, or some alternative determining variable.

The reader who wishes to pursue regression analysis further in a context of a specific forecasting problem is advised not to go into the literature of econometrics but to seek out a computer bureau in the Yellow Pages telephone directory. Armed only with the information in this chapter, and given about an hour's instruction in using an interactive computing system, the whole business of econometrics is open to him.

6.5 Summary

Many forecasts are built on leading indicators of various sorts. The two main types are data series whose movements correlate with the variable we wish to forecast, with a regular timelag between the leading indicator and the forecast series, and data series for which we can obtain long-term economic forecasts of high reliability (e.g. GNP).

To use such leading series it is necessary first to postulate a relationship between them and the variable being forecast. The form of such a relationship will be functional.

Testing the precise nature of the relationship is a complex task involving inter-action between management's judgment on the realities of the situation and statistical judgment in the complex area of regression analysis.

Regression analysis is not ideally suited to the creation of models of the relation-ship between time series. Although the principles are simple, the conditions under which it may be applied are stringent and are generally violated by time series of economic or business data.

The complexity of the statistical task required to get around these restrictive conditions has hitherto seriously limited the value of multiple regression as a practical forecasting tool, not only for lack of econometricians to do the job, but also because of the sheer expense involved in getting the analysis technically (far less commercially) acceptable.

The conditions require, among other things, that the data should be linear, additive and homoscedastic, and that the independent variables should be neither intercorrelated nor serially correlated. Finally, it is necessary to guard against the possibility that the direction of causation is the opposite way round from that which the analyst supposes.

While the techniques for overcoming these problems (as far as the data will allow) are well known, they are highly laborious to apply either by calculating machine or even by batch process computing.

The advent of on-line computing enables an astronomical amount of statistical manipulation to be done almost instantaneously, so that the essential trial and error nature of regression modelling ceases to be a hindrance to the production of reliable models inexpensively.

Once the model is created it can be tested by backcasting — trying the model on past data —and the forecasting programs associated with the regression programs enable the analyst readily to determine a large number of possible outcomes for the dependent variable, given different possible values for the independent variable.

7 Economic forecasts

7.1 The business cycle

There are two broad classes of approach to the problem of creating models of economic activity which will be of value for forecasting applications. We have already spent much time on the first of these — the production of conceptually naive if statistically complex descriptions of economic behaviour in the past. The second class of approaches is that of trying to formulate some sort of model of the economic system (or subsystem) we are trying to understand. Within this class there are a number of subapproaches. One of the commonest is to try to construct a verbally presented model of the economy and how it interacts. All the material in this category comes into the well developed subject area of macro-economics, of which the forecaster should possess a working knowledge, but which is far beyond the scope of this book.

An alternative approach lies in the production of quantitative statistical models of some aspect of economic behaviour, a field known as econometrics, which requires a mastery of both macro-economics and of statistics, hence in a field very much reserved to the specialist. Despite the technical complexities involved in the production of econometric models, the principles underlying them are easy to grasp, and the two main types have already been discussed, namely input-output models and models based on multiple regression analysis.

When these classes of economic models were being discussed we observed that problems of data availability and the applicability of the models to specific situations limited their usefulness to the individual manager, and perhaps their principal validity lay in their ability to help block out a rough picture of what the relevant aspects of the economy might look like a decade or two hence.

We can say, therefore, that in this book we have dealt with two broad and conceptually simple areas of forecasting: the relatively long-term and broad sweeping type handled by econometric types of model, and the very short-term specific type handled by adaptive forecasts. We discovered in dealing with classical time series analysis that it was technically somewhat unsatisfactory but we had to retain it in order to get some sort of line on medium-term (say six months to five years) and medium-complexity problems, such as planning plant or product line expansion, planning cash flows in the medium term and so on.

It was suggested then that the key technical problem in making acceptable predictions of economic behaviour relevant to such problems was the issue of forecasting the path of the relevant trade cycle. *Economic Trends* regularly plots time series of cyclically significant economic variables; many institutions such as the Bank of England, the National Institute of Economic and Social Research, the London Business School and the *Sunday Telegraph* have complex econometric models, reporting generally quarterly; many well equipped students of the economy spend much of their time attempting to forecast some of its finer variations. The plain fact is that despite all this activity there is no one who can predict with a precise probability measure the likelihood of a change in the pace of the growth of gross national product to within commercially significant and tolerable limits for even a few months ahead. No one.

Such changes in the rate of growth of national output and income, savings and investment, exports and imports, and so on are what we refer to as the *trade cycle* or the *business cycle*. Our purpose in the first part of this chapter is to explain why the business cycle is so difficult to predict, and later to see whether, despite the obscurity of the whole business, there is anything in it that is of value for the practical manager.

Business cycles are a type of fluctuation found in the aggregate economic activity of nations that organize their work mainly in business enterprises : a cycle consists of expansions occurring about the same time in many economic activities, followed by similarly general recessions, contractions and revivals which merge into the expansion phase of the next cycle. This sequence is recurrent but not periodic; in duration business cycles vary from more than one year to ten or twelve years; they are not divisible into shorter cycles of similar character with amplitudes approximating to their own (see Burns and Mitchell, 1946, p. 3).

Business cycle principles, whether implicit or explicit, are basic to the formulation of any business forecast. The fact that there has been a vast amount of research into the business cycle which has not been able to provide a final explanation as to its causes, does not mean that the business forecaster working for an individual firm can afford to ignore these vitally important and disturbing fluctuations. It is necessary for the forecaster to use the behaviour of cycles to predict the future whether or not he fully understands their causes.

The interest of the forecaster for the individual firm is unlikely to be so much in understanding the causes of cycles as in the use of these cycles as an underlying factor in the prediction he is making about the activity of his own firm. To predict the likely future course of a cycle, however, it is manifestly necessary for the fore-caster to have a reasonable understanding of some of the more important aspects contributing to the behaviour of cycles. There are probably about as many theories of cycle behaviour as there are analysts working in the field.

A cycle view is of paramount importance in constructing medium-term forecasts in, for example, the heavy capital goods industries. This is well illustrated by the dilemma posed in 1973 by the managing director of a major shipbuilding group. Should he take orders for 1976? Given that there was a strong probability of a very severe rate of inflation (though *which* rate was difficult to forecast), that only fixed price contracts were available, and that there was currently a lot of such business on offer for 1976, should he fill his yard capacity? The potential penalties, as he expressed them, of wrong decisions were that if he booked the business in 1975 rather than 1973 he could be much surer of his prices (and they would almost certainly be higher), but if he did not book in 1973 he could conceivably find it impossible to obtain profitable business at a later date. The outcome would depend, of course, on the business of demand and supply of shipowner's business by 1975—6, in turn a function of the trade cycle. If trade would be booming by 1975, he should hold off: if trade would be in recession, he should book now. The differ-ence between a right and a wrong decision could be measured in terms of millions of pounds. In the face of this dilemma he employed an interesting strategy. He pur-chased the most thorough (and expensive) set of relevant economic forecasts he could find and took his decisions on the basis *that they would be diametrically wrong.*

This example is interesting from a number of viewpoints, for in essence it contains all the elements of a forecasting problem which is insoluble in the present state of the art, but nevertheless one in which the forecasters should still be able to give some useful guidance to management, using techniques we shall discuss in chapter 9. At this stage, it might be instructive to highlight some of the uncertainties which have to be dealt with.

First of all, the statement of the problem itself includes uncertainties concerning the rate of cost inflation. Since inflation is a phenomenon affecting every advanced economy more severely than the economic managers regard as desirable, it is clear that the economists' knowledge of the causative factors and potential control mechanisms is at any given time deficient.

The second uncertainty concerns the role of market expectations. If the customers *expect* to need more shipping in 1977, they will order for 1976 not later than 1975. So in predicting whether there will be a net demand pressure in 1975 we are predicting whether there will be a favourable balance of expectations by the customers at that time. Whether such a balance of expectations is favourable or not depends at least in part on the character of the trade cycle up to that point. But if it had, say, been rising strongly, then some customers are likely to be predicting a continued rise while others are predicting the end of the boom. Given that business expectations tend to be self-reinforcing, what we are trying to predict is a point in time when a balance of views occurs, as votes are transferred from optimism to pessimism.

The next class of uncertainties in this problem is physical uncertainties, such as oil strikes or wars, and their effects, such as the closure (or reopening) of the Suez Canal. The timing is unpredictable: the effect on the delicate supply and demand balance for shipping services can be cataclysmic.

Finally, there is the class of uncertainties concerned with our very deficient knowledge of the causes of the trade cycle, deficiencies which conceivably will never be remedied. The difference between a boom and a slump in today's conditions represents a tiny difference between two vast aggregates. Perhaps the clearest model for illustrative purposes is to view the economy as a pair of scales, around which are lots of people, each carrying two handfuls of sand. From one hand they are steadily pouring sand into the pan marked 'Demand', From the other, into the pan marked 'Supply'.

There is a dimly understood system which keeps them fed with a continuous supply of sand. The objective of the game is to pile on sand as quickly as possible while keeping the scales exactly in balance, but the only way the controller can do this is speeding or slowing the supply of sand destined for one tray or another. So naturally he makes mistakes. Besides, the needle on the scales is a bit inaccurate at the best of times, and usually takes time to catch up with real swings.

Forecasters are not told, except in broad terms, what the controllers are doing. They have virtually no up to date knowledge of what the participants are doing. Even if they had, they would have to second-guess what the participants would do next. So they watch the late and inaccurate gauges, and hope to make some kind of sense out of what is going on. Since they are not merely observers but players too, it is hardly surprising if most of the time they are predicting that present trends will continue (all gloom together or all glee together) and that collectively they are all wrong in their predictions more often than they are right.

The purposes of this exposé of professional ignorance are to demystify the whole business of economic analysis, to discourage managements from taking too sanguine a view of the predictive abilities of the profession of economists, and to encourage them to believe that it is vitally important that they, as managers, must be in a position to have a view which is intelligent and well founded of business cycle futures in so far as these are relevant to the prosperity of the company. In this area the well informed manager can do at least as well as the professional economist when it comes down to the steely business of predicting what the economic cycle will be doing.

7.2 Cycle theories

Two major types of cycles have been detected. Schumpeter distinguished between the one- to ten-year cycle and a very much longer underlying fluctuation with the periodicity of perhaps some thirty years. His theory probably provides a more plausible explanation of the longer-term cycle. It is that the cycle is basically influenced by the phasing of innovation. According to this theory innovation in business constitutes the chief dynamic factor in economic life.

Inventions and discoveries which add to technical knowledge are the basis of innovation. Inventions and so on, however, arise at random through time; innovation amounts to finding new methods of combining factors of production in order to provide new ways of satisfying an economic want. It is suggested that innovations tended to be bunched in time, when a relatively small number of entrepreneurs make the initial ventures into new fields, and once the profitability of the successful ventures has been established many others are quick to follow the lead of the innovators.

Such innovation results in an increasing demand for capital and an expansion of investments. This continues until the new equipment and technological processes have been completed and are turning out consumer goods. At this point it is suggested the condition of over-optimistic over-capacity which will have developed will have reduced profits and discouraged further expansion. As the pace of innovation lags and finally stops the boom ends and forces of contraction become operative. The abnormal production levels are followed by liquidation of weaker business enterprises, fall in prices and profits and a general readjustment of the economy to a new equilibrium level.

One of the principal problems with this innovative theory of the business cycle, though it has a great degree of plausibility to commend it, is that it is impossible to measure statistically the phenomenon which the model implies, and hence it is difficult to see how the forecaster can use this theory as a basis for business cycle predictions.

We may be helped a little by an attempt to explain why the 'bunching' phenomenon of innovation should occur. The most general explanation is based on business expectations. It seems a plausible idea that executives should be more willing to innovate and to undertake the investments implied by innovation at a time when they expect high and expanding profits to materialize from the decision. In other words, to attempt to time the coming on stream of their new capacity to coincide with a buoyant period in the business cycle.

Unfortunately, there is a fairly large number of practical reasons why this theory is very difficult to validate. First, different groups of managers are likely to interpret the future of the business cycle differently. Secondly, the difficulty facing management of controlling the lead time between the decision to make an investment and actually getting it operational is very great. However carefully planning may be done, avoidable and unavoidable delays are likely to mean that the actual commissioning date is something of a guess. Thirdly, empirical research which has been done (among others, by the author) suggests that businessmen regard other factors influencing the investment decision as being much more important than any attempt to guess at any likely future course of the trade cycle.

The most important of these alternative determinants of the investment decision which is generally cited is that of availability of investible funds, irrespective of the cost of these funds. It is reasonable to expect a favourable response to attempts to raise funds following a period of cyclical boom when profits have been easy to earn, company saving is likely to be high, and there has probably been an upswing of stock market. Similarly, levels of bank deposits will have been high and banks will be more willing to extend credit than they might otherwise be. The record seems to show that it has been at such times that managers have made decisions to increase capital investment, being willing to take the rough with the smooth of the business cycle. This raises the question whether it is important to forecast cyclical changes in the context of fixed capital investment decisions. Until recently the answer would have been that it was not of vital importance. Apart from anything else the inability of the tools of investment appraisal in the past to distinguish between the inflow of funds from the early part of an investment's life and that of the later part meant that timing was not seriously regarded.

This has changed a great deal since the general adoption of discounted cash flow as a basic method of investment appraisal. As is probably well known the criterion for acceptance of an investment under the DCF principle is that the cash flows in the earliest parts of an investment's life are counted as being of greater importance than the later cash flows, hence if cash flow over the first two or three years of an investment is below expectations this could have a very serious effect indeed on the standing of that investment in DCF terms. This would be all the more true in the event that the firm in question had been allocating funds on a 'marginal' basis, that is allocating right up to the point where the DCF rate of return was equal at the margin to the cost of capital. In the case of the first few years fund inflows showing a shortfall on expectations this would make such investments entirely submarginal.

It has long been recognized nevertheless that business anticipations may have a profound effect on the course of the business cycle. For example, if the majority of businessmen hold the view that the economy is entering a recession, there will undoubtedly be a strong tendency for them at least to intend to postpone investment decisions for a time and to hold their funds in more liquid form, say in the form of government securities, until such time as they feel more confident about the business outlook. Similarly, at a time when they anticipate that the economy will be moving into a boom period, they will probably be more active than normal in seeking for credit facilities from all possible sources in order to pursue expansion plans.

Although this is a fairly naive theory of the business cycle it is probably an explanatory one, though the extent to which the explanations are of value has never been tested statistically. Data on business anticipations is collected in Britain quarterly by the Confederation of British Industries published as their *Industrial Trends Inquiry*. Comparison of business anticipations as revealed by this *Inquiry* and the actual outcome of the variables on which the businessmen were asked to give their view of the future of business investment, output, export prospects and so on, indicate very little relationship between what they expected they would be doing in the next quarter and what the later record actually showed them to have done. The more so then it could be taken that the record of businessmen's anticipations would fail to coincide with the general movement of the economy. At best, therefore, anticipations data may be used as no more than a fairly rough check on other forms of projection.

So far our explanations have treated the business cycle in terms of business investment, including investment intentions by managers. Two theoretical devices link business investment with economic cyclical development generally. The first of these originally described by J. M. Clark is the *accelerator* mechanism. This principle indicates the relationship between the volume of investment and the *rate of change* in current output. It is a common observation that production of invest-ment goods fluctuates more violently than production of immediate consumer goods. If we take it that the demand for consumer goods is the determining variable then we can say that changes in demand for consumer goods result in *accelerated* changes in the demand for capital goods, investment goods, or producer's goods. The relationship is also observed to hold between the more and less durable con-sumer goods. A simple example will make this principle clear (Table 7.1).

Table 7.1 *Illustration of the accelerator principle*

	(1) Demand for and output of consumer goods	(2) Value of machinery required to produce 1 unit	(3) Deprecia- tion cost (say)	(4) Value of new machinery installed (incl. deps.)	(5) Increase in (4) ——— Increase in (1)
Year 1	100	1 000	100	100	–
Year 2	110	1 100	110	210	11 times

It is evident that a 10 per cent increase in demand for, and production of, finished consumer goods gives us an increase of 110 per cent (given the assumptions of Table 7.1) in the annual production of capital goods. It also follows that the derived demand for plant and equipment will fall absolutely as a consequence of a mere decrease in the rate of increase of demand for the finished consumer goods.

The second of these fundamental economic devices is that of the *multiplier*. This device was developed by J. M. Keynes in *The General Theory of Employment, Interest and Money* to explain the connection between income and employment on one hand and investment on the other. The idea is that when money is spent on creating fixed capital, that is to say when money is invested in for example produc-tive plant, then a very large proportion of that money is used to pay wages of the men involved in producing the investment, salaries of managers and income for shareholders and subscribers of capital to the enterprises in which the investment is being manufactured. Thus an increase in investment creates personal incomes which lead to an increase in demand for consumption goods.

Of this new income, those who receive it will consume a portion and will save a portion. Keynes argued that there was at any period a fairly stable ratio of the proportion of income which people would consume and a proportion which they would save. He called this ratio 'the propensity to consume'. It does not follow that the propensity to consume out of incremental income will be the same as the propensity to consume out of previous income. It is suggested in the theory that the propensity to consume out of incremental income will in fact be lower than out of existing income for a number of reasons. One is that the receivers of the incremental income will be that much closer to having satisfied their immediate consumption demands and will therefore be more willing to save. Another is that since the income is new, consumption patterns and tastes will take time to adapt upwards to the new level of income, again for a number of psychological reasons including security with the result that the *marginal propensity to consume* of such new income will, at least for a time, be lower than the propensity to consume as measured in terms of the old income.

Now the multiplier depends entirely on the marginal propensity to consume and varies directly with it. If marginal propensity to consume is, say, two-thirds (that is two-thirds of a given increase in income goes into consumption and one-third into savings), the multiplier is expressed numerically as 3 or the reciprocal of the fraction saved. Again if the marginal propensity to consume is four-fifths, then the multiplier is 5.

Assuming a multiplier of 5, £1 of new investment will lead to a £5 increase in income. The £1 investment expenditure will produce an increase in income of £1 of which 80 per cent will be spent for consumption. The 80 per cent will, however, again add to income since 80 per cent of that will be spent for further consumption and by a succession of such rounds of expenditure, the addition to income will reach a limit where the aggregate increase of income will be five times the original investment. In this process accumulated fractions of newly created income which are saved will be equivalent to the amount of the original investment.

The multiplier explanation of the business cycle works as follows. In the boom period the *marginal efficiency of capital* (in practical general terms, the expected profitability of new investment in capital equipment) is high because each new increment of investments stimulates consumption and increases income by way of the multiplier principle. As the cost of new capital rises and the increased output made possible by capital already in use lowers some yields below original expectations, optimism ultimately gives way to pessimism and a sudden fall in the marginal efficiency of capital results. The multiplier works in reverse as decline in investments produce a reduction in employment. Entrepreneurs will then for the time being prefer to become more liquid and interest rates rise causing a still greater decline in investment.

Recovery is thought to take place in this model when some development occurs which increases the attractiveness of investment. In time capital wears out and becomes obsolete. Excess stocks of goods are worked off, a decrease in the amount of money required for transactions brings about a reduction in interest rates. When these factors of recovery heightened by a return of business optimism provide a basis for an increase in the marginal efficiency of capital a greater volume of investment is expected to take place and the expansion theories of the cycle will again get under way. The key factor determining the cyclical fluctuations under this theory is variation in investment.

As we saw when discussing the accelerator, an increase in consumer demand tends to produce an accelerated demand for investment so it is evident that the accelerator and multiplier principles tend to reinforce each other.

So far the discussion has been couched in terms of the business cycle being induced by changes in business behaviour affected only by changes in the rate of increase of finished goods consumption. This has been the only 'exogenous' variable built into our model. Apart from consumption all the other explanatory variables of the business cycle are themselves indigenous to the business sector of the economy.

A somewhat more comprehensive approach, taking account of broader economic issues, is suggested by the following somewhat crude attempt to describe the model a modern analyst is likely to use. He regards the economy as being divisible into four major components, final consumption, investment (generally taken to be equal to saving), government expenditure (equal to taxation plus the government's net borrowing requirement and can be used for purposes equivalent to consumption or equivalent to investment) and, finally the balance of payments. Together the value of each of these adds to the level of gross national income. The model can be simply expressed as

$Y = C + I + G + P$ where Y = gross national income

$\qquad\qquad\qquad\qquad\quad C$ = consumption

$\qquad\qquad\qquad\qquad\quad I$ = Investment

$\qquad\qquad\qquad\qquad\quad G$ = government expenditure

$\qquad\qquad\qquad\qquad\quad P$ = net balance of payments

It is taken that there are basic forces operating to force up the level of C and G inexorably. For C this might include the power of organized labour, an inability on the part of society to adjust consumption expenditure downwards from any level it has attained, and general expectation on the part of consumers of economic growth, and hence of growth in their own affluence.

In the case of G the basic influences driving this upwards include the power of bureaucratic machinery and the same kind of influences as affect C. It is then postulated that the rise in C and G is likely to outstrip the rate of expansion of resources available to allow growth of C and G to occur. Some of the increase in C and G may be attributed to an increase in resources arising through the multiplier and accelerator principles. To the extent that aspirations have outrun resources, the fulfilment of these aspirations might be at the expense of saving and investment, implying that there has been, at least for the time being, an increase in the marginal propensity to consume and hence a change in the level of the multiplier, resulting in a very rapid increase in demand and the expectation of a powerful accelerator phenomenon setting in.

Alternatively, the increase in C and G may be at the expense of resources which are being devoted to the balance of payments. This can be visualized as occurring because there are insufficient resources at home to meet the increased expenditure, or because the increased demand on home resources is such as to divert production from export-orientated ends. The next round of this postulated cycle is that as a result of the increase in consumption the accelerator principle applies and produces an increase in investment. The demand for investment funds, however, comes up against a by now relatively inadequate level of savings which have been at least partly raided in order to provide the consumption. At the same time the demand for investment in equipment will increase demand for imports of such equipment which will arise at a period when the balance of payments is already under strain to the extent that resources have been diverted from exporting to home consumption. Then interest rates will rise in response to the increasing demand for investment in the face of inadequate savings. However, the rise in interest rates is likely generally to be much too little and much too late to make any material difference in the supply and demand balance for investible funds.

The deteriorating balance of payments is expected to be of much more immediate moment for short-run economic policy. The government will recognize the need to redirect resources towards improving the balance of payments and hence will attempt to achieve a cutback in consumer demand at home and in its own consumption, the consumption orientated expenditures in particular. Of course they will also attack those expenditures which take place overseas and directly contribute to the adverse balance of payments. The cutback in domestic consumption which may take place either through taxation policy or through an effect in the level of money available to make purchases (especially credit) provides a clear signal, perhaps up to a year in advance of the impending end in the consumption boom. As a result prudent businessmen are likely to curtail any grandiose investment policies they may have had, as confidence begins to become eroded.

Bear in mind that if the cutback in consumption intended by the government achieves its end very rapidly then businessmen will almost inevitably find themselves with an increase in undesired investment on their hands in the form of an involuntary run-up in stocks. This is often taken by businessmen as the first signal to curtail investment projects. This explanation is essentially an over-simplification because it leaves out of the argument entirely the problem of monetary changes in their own right. The whole argument has been couched in terms of real economic variables; it becomes very much more complex when the fact that money tends to assume a kind of life of its own is included in it.

For example it has recently been argued that the 'power of organized labour' assertion used at the outset of this discussion to explain the strength of the aspiration to increase consumption takes on added force when one of the expectations of organized labour is that there will be a continuing inflation. Then demands may be couched so as to compensate for the erosion of value of money being earned through the inflationary process. Severe inflation is likely to provide a disincentive to save, with a resulting increase in the marginal propensity to consume and an increase in the level of the multiplier.

If the home economy is inflating faster than those of export customers when prices of home produced goods are likely to get out of line with international competition and the resultant difficulty in selling exports will increase the problem of the balance of payments and the necessity for cutting back on home consumption so as to contain the inflation. There is evidence that the rate of inflation in Britain has in recent years been running at about the same level as those of our overseas customers but that both the balance of payments and business profits are much more sensitive to inflation in Britain than abroad. One reason for this undoubtedly is the generally low level of profitability of business in Britain (arising no doubt from what Denison of the Brookings Institution described as 'the quality of management and the manageability of labour' in Britain, together with the apparent psychological attitude in Britain that things there are always worse than anywhere else in the world). For this sort of reason the rate of increase of export prices is in Britain as fast as the rate of increase in the domestic price level, whereas for most of Britain's international competitors the rate of increase in the domestic price level far outstrips the rate of increase of the international price level. This can be accounted for by the ability of the overseas company to adopt a marginal cost pricing policy on international business for the sake of filling its lines, knowing that it can absorb all its overheads on domestic production. Where the domestic market is growing more slowly, and where the amount of profit is reduced by restrictive practices and managerial lack of imagination in terms of product differentiation, domestic industry is much more susceptible to inflation than is the foreign competitor.

The role of saving and investment are crucial to this crude model, the former being determined by a general set of attitudes towards thrift or spending, the latter being determined in part by the innate instability of the marginal efficiency of capital. If saving is reasonably stable over time we are forced to return in our business cycle theory to a further inspection of the role of investment. This has now to be disaggregated into two parts, fixed capital investment and investment in stocks. The latter competes for available funds with the former, and in the face of an economic performance which does not meet expectations can be increased involuntarily.

Investment in fixed capital is probably determined by four variables: availability of funds, investment opportunities recognized, short- and long-run confidence in the future of the economy, and attitudes to innovation. In much of this kind of economic theorizing as a basis for forecasting it is probably necessary to incorporate some set of economic theories like the foregoing into an economic model.

The purpose of this section has been to give the reader previously unfamiliar with economics some idea of what is going on behind the production of the arcane symbolism inherent in forecasts produced by the kind of agencies referred to earlier. There are three or four areas in which this type of background is important. First of all, it is necessary for the individual manager disposing of resources to have his own view of the future of the economy, he has to be a bush economist of sorts in his own right, because in the present state of the art *no one can predict the path of the trade cycle.* If a manager's decisions depend on what the cycle is doing, then he is on his own.

In a field in which no one can guarantee the right answer there is a babel of 'experts' promoting their pet formulae, often very expensively. Management needs enough knowledge to be able to distinguish between the 'experts' and the experts.

Nevertheless, there is a lot of genuine work in the area, published regularly by reputable agencies, in which the conclusions are less important than the careful and detailed reasoning presented with the conclusions. Managers making decisions in cyclically sensitive areas need as many 'reasoning' inputs as possible. The importance of forming the 'right' view may be only slightly greater than confidence in the basis on which the view was founded, and recognition of the sensitive variables which, were they to change suddenly, would lead to an alternative conclusion. Being right may be little better than recognizing sooner than anybody else that you were wrong.

7.3 Predicting changes in cyclical activity

We shall be concerned in this section with forecasting which can be done without going the full length of complex econometric models and systems of equations to formulate a view of the likely future of the business cycle.

One conclusion which emerged from section 7.1 was that the use of the term 'business cycle' may be misleading, in that for many purposes we can regard the economic cyclical behaviour as being not one but a number of different cycles each affecting business in aggregate. Among the cyclical fluctuations which we can isolate we might include consumers' expenditure, investment, balance of payments, finished goods stock, company liquidity, company profits, stockmarket prices, gross national product, government expenditure, domestic capital expenditure, construction expenditure and consumer expenditure on durable and non-durable goods. In addition to these fairly broad economic sectors it is possible to separate out less highly aggregated economic data such as motor-car sales (registrations), steel industry output, fuel and power output, and others which no doubt the manager will recognize as being relevant to his own firm. There are two possible uses which can be made of any of them. One is to attempt to relate their behaviour to the behaviour of the economy generally in terms of the sort of exercise which we attempted in section 7.1; the other is to attempt to relate the sales of the product which we are in the process of forecasting to the behaviour of some of these sectoral cycles. In this way, while it may not be possible to relate our product directly to the economy as a whole, it may still nevertheless be possible to relate it indirectly through some of the disaggregated cyclical series.

Each of these is a special case of a general set of techniques known in business forecasting as *sectoral analysis* which probably serves as the basic forecasting platform for any of the major utilities and basic industries (e.g. steel, fuel and power, aluminium, transportation, construction). In this procedure, the various components of demand are separately evaluated and then combined to form a total. Forecasting the future course of any of these sectoral series can be done on a basis of any of the techniques outlined in this book, including regression against time, correlation with what are regarded as being determining variables, for example, those which lead the variable under forecast, exponential smoothing and other adaptive techniques, input-output analysis, or economic or econometric model building. Some components will, in fact, be non-cyclical. For example, consumer spending on services and to a less extent on non-durable goods tend to be very stable. National and local government expenditure on goods and services are also unlikely to be cyclical in their nature. Much more cyclical will be such components as business fixed investment in plant and equipment and in stocks, consumer spending on relatively expensive durable goods, and so on.

Once approximations have been made for all components and for the total of gross national product, the most important task is to refine these first estimates into final form. This phase involves careful appraisal that there is internal consistency between the parts and the total. In this sort of context input-output analysis is of great assistance.

Generally speaking there is probably a great deal more virtue in using economic forecasts as an aggregate, rather than individual firm's forecasts, as a basis for industry. This would, of course, not be true for large national or international companies. In addition, however, forecasts of the general economic cycle may be required for reasons other than direct sales forecasting. For example, a firm contemplating an investment decision at a specific date in the future may wish to have a clear view on what is going to be the likely state of availability of funds from outside the firm at the proposed date. Timing in relation to the business cycle might also be relevant to such decisions as launching a new product, entering a new market, floating a share issue or seeking a bank loan. But what has to be stressed is that this particular aspect of forecasting can do no more than offer the manager a reasonably informed view of the likely course of the trade cycle. It is, indeed, one of the least reliable guideposts, a will-o'-the-wisp which has led far more business economists astray than it has guided successfully. As Butler and Kavesh (1966) put it:

> Most importantly [the business forecaster] will (or should) have a deep understanding of how the economy and its sectors operate and interact in practice. This latter quality is the most elusive to capture and generally serves to set apart the superior forecaster from his inferiors. Experience and study may help in part to acquire this understanding but in many cases they do not. And, perhaps it is because the ultimate tool — the one that combines and synthesizes all the others — is that indefinable 'judgment'. Without it the forecaster may become amired in a swamp of statistics; with it he may be able to create order and form.

I suggest that the following ingredients are necessary before anyone sets himself up as being capable of predicting turning points in the business cycle from an analysis of economic data.
1. He must possess a clear concept of the basic working of the economic structure — as it were a model of the business cycle either of the sort outlined earlier in this chapter or in some other which seems to him to contain basic theoretical plausibility.

2. This should be supplemented by the up-to-date data referring to each of the variables which interact in his model, being operated upon in a logical manner, or alternatively at the very least he should have knowledge of the working of an operational econometric model of the economy. He should be a relentless student of periodicals such as the *Financial Times* and the *Economist* the National Institute of Economic and Social Research's *Economic Review* and the Bank of England's *Economic Review*; he should be regular in his study of *Economic Trends* and he should be in complete touch with opinion within his own industry.

3. He will be at some pains as far as possible to verify his cyclical projections using a well worn, naive method than the one of basic economic analysis, for example, lead lag analysis, diffusion indices or by licking his finger and holding it in the air to see which way the wind is blowing.

> Like any craftsman assembling a product, he will try to make sure that each piece fits together into a unified, consistent whole. And if the total seems un-realistic or somehow wrong he will adjust and adapt until the artist in him is satisfied. Thus, the forecaster is like an artist or a craftsman: he will ponder, appraise, improvize — until he feels satisfied with his final product (Butler and Kavesh, p. 144).

7.4 Taking the long view

It was suggested in the previous section that the use of economic analysis can enable the forecaster to take a view of the likely immediate future of the business cycle in its effects on the variables he is forecasting. In a longer-term sense, it is important also for the manager to be able to take a view in order to set a context for his forecasts. One suggestion made in section 7.1 was that business cycles fall into a context of a much longer set of cycles, perhaps based on the rate and bunch-ing of innovatory activity. For this purpose, the usual practice is to take an arbi-trary date a long way in the future, say twenty or thirty years, and attempt to list and describe the sort of factors we think may influence the shape of things to come. The reason for using such generally crude factor listings is that we are unable to cope with probable occurrence of inventions and consequent innovations, as well as fundamental shifts in, for example, cultural attitudes.

Before beginning his factor-listing exercise, the crystal ball gazer, for this is what he is at this kind of remove, generally begins by citing some of the political and other assumptions under which he is operating. For example, he may assume that there will not be a major war but that minor military outbreaks will continue to occur (there has been no day in the world's history since 1930 when there has not been some armed conflict somewhere). Others might be that, for example, there will be no major basic shift in the form of government or the form of enterprise in the economy being forecast: that Britain will continue to operate as a parlia-mentary democracy with a mixed enterprise economy; and that the changes in social patterns will not produce impossible strains on social organization: there will be no revolution in the domestic economy. Then there will continue to be innovations which cannot be forecast and which will materially reduce the cost of satisfying consumer wants in the period. Finally it might be assumed that the relative importance of manufacturing conversion in satisfying consumer wants will decline and the relative importance of selling, distribution and all the service industries will increase steadily over the period. In Britain, given these assumptions, it is relatively easy to predict the kind of life style which will be enjoyed by the population in thirty years' time. It will be roughly equivalent to that enjoyed in southern California now in economic terms. In social terms most commentators would suppose that the British with their much higher level of social sophistication than the Americans will be able to avoid many of the mistakes into which the Californians are plunging. (No criticism is implied here of the Californians — Britain was itself making the same sort of pioneering social mistakes 200 years ago.) In taking a long look forward, the first thing to notice is that most of the important aspects of life in thirty years' time are already in existence now. Most of the means of satisfying consumer wants are already there. For example, the houses most people will be living in thirty years from now are already in existence.

We can guess that world population will be double its present level by the end of the century: the problem of hunger among the poorest members of the world's population will be diminished but by no means solved (unless the 'have' nations as a matter of policy devote a greater part of their resources to the solution of the hunger problem). The effects of the contraceptive pill will be such that Britain's population will be substantially lower than 70 million presently forecast by the Registrar General; probably 60 million is a more realistic estimate. The Commonwealth, the sterling area and Britain will continue to decline in importance individually and collective institutions will gradually break up as the purposes which they serve come to be seen as being archaic. There will be vast strides, for example, towards the provision of an international money which will help to render the sterling area provisions obsolete. Tariff barriers will generally have become pretty well obsolete, but progress towards greater political unity in the various large areas of the world will be proceeding at a very slow pace so that it is doubtful whether any substantial achievements will have been made by the end of the century.

The proportion of income taken in taxation will continue to grow and we shall continue to live with a rate of inflation which, by the end of the century will probably be under control at perhaps 1.5 to 2 per cent per annum throughout the world in the developed countries. Perhaps economically the more significant developments of the next few decades will be vast improvements in urban transport and national and international communications. It is in these areas particularly that the greatest social investments will take place.

Finally, it has to be acknowledged that some of the basic assumptions on which the forecast is based may themselves be open to question and we may be at risk from, for example, war, revolution, famine or pestilence. There is, however, no future in brooding on this prospect.

In Britain the most important influence on the rate of economic development will lie in the business sector, despite the fact that government will probably escalate experiments within planning and centralized control of the economy. Innovation, investment and a willingness to work so as to extract from these the full economic fruit will determine whether the rate of growth of GNP accelerates from its present low level. Since the 1930s Britain's productivity has been increasing at an accelerating speed, and this contrasts with the North American economies where the rate of growth of productivity has been increasing at a declining rate. British productivity and national income per head are now so very far down the league table of developed countries, there seems little reason why the rate of acceleration should not continue. The question is whether it can be hoped that it will increase at a higher rate than historically.

A key figure on this question is the proportion of national product devoted to investment. In 1958 about 12 per cent of total British national product was devoted to investment in fixed assets and stocks, a ratio which has risen to over 20 per cent. It is, however (early 1970s) increasing at a decreasing rate and present indications are that it will level off by about 1980 at some 25 per cent. This change reflects a very different attitude towards fixed capital investment between the 1930s and the 1970–80s and 1990s. The international level of the proportion of GNP devoted to investment is of the order of 30 per cent. When the rate of investment is translated into a rate of investment per person employed the rate of increase is much greater than that implied by the previous figures.

The rate of increase of British GNP over the past ten to twenty years has been of the order of 2.7 per cent per annum compound. The question is whether it can rise to the higher reaches of 3 per cent and perhaps even break through the 4 per cent barrier. Most of the developed countries, it should be borne in mind, can easily achieve substantially more than 4 per cent, and in some cases over 5 per cent. Even at the lower rates we are still faced with the prospect of average family income being by the year 2000 in the region of £5 000 to £6 000 per annum as measured in presentday prices. It is a very interesting speculation how the British will choose to spend this amount of purchasing power.

Unlike the countries of the world which have achieved personal and family incomes approaching these levels, the United States, Canada and Sweden, Britain does not have vast empty spaces of land available for the ownership of second homes, country cottages, massive road systems to accommodate the two, three and four cars per family which are common, massive areas available for the shopping centres to make one-stop shopping possible and so on.

A curiously mixed political system in which a socialist orientated government alternates with a capitalist orientated one (in contrast with any of the three countries mentioned before) means that the British way of life by the end of the century will almost certainly not be any kind of imitation of that of other countries. We could speculate for a long time on possible outcomes; a few of the obvious ones are suggested here.

Anyone contemplating using this kind of perspective as a basis for company strategy today should bear in mind that they are investing in a long-term future and there may be a lot of money to be lost in the short term developing of their hoped-for markets. It might, for example, be pointed out that the 'leisure' industry has been the cause of many shattered company illusions. The question is not so much *whether* things will come about, as when, and in what form, and who will be competing for the business.

By 2000 much more money will be spent on disposable items than at present. Much more will be spent on electronic equipment and other forms of hardware for communication and entertainment as well as for control of processes about the home, factory and office. Automatic garage doors will be commonplace, infrared ovens will be the accepted order of things, lunch will be by automatic vending cooked on the spot, much urban transport will be encapsulated and automated and, hopefully, Britain will be pioneering the world in resisting the devastation of its cities by the motor car, replacing them with more logical forms of transportation within towns such as travelators, automatic monorail services and so on. The demand for greater living space will have led to a vast encroachment on agricultural land and a massive increase in factory farming. Much more will be spent on remedies for ill health and all forms of health and leisure pursuits. No home will be complete without its own fully equipped workshop. None of the foregoing would be regarded by most people as being in any way exciting or controversial.

One of the most interesting challenges to technology will be posed by the steady depletion of the world's oil reserves, set against increasing demand for transportation and oil-based manufacturing. As the price of crude oil escalates in response to these forces an era of prosperity based on cheap, storable, mobile energy will come to an end. Personal and materials transportation will become vastly more expensive, for the alternatives can never be as cheap as the oil we have enjoyed. The basic energy source will be electricity from natural or nuclear sources. But while this will be adequate to power commuting vehicles, with a nightly top up, there is no immediate prospect of a technology which could power aircraft from this source. Whether rocket-type propulsion will be available for aircraft is debatable. Certainly air travel will become relatively much more expensive. The oil alternatives one sees most clearly are first, a revival in trains and trolley vehicles drawing their power from a grid, development of nuclear propulsion for merchant ships, and a massive improvement in electronic communications to reduce the need for business travel. What we are going to use to replace plastics is far from obvious.

It has been estimated that about half the economic activity of the highly developed world is based on cheap oil — motor vehicle manufacture, servicing, etc., aircraft manufacture and transportation, plastics and so on. Manifestly the next three decades are going to witness shifts of economic resources on a staggering scale.*

The ten- to thirty-year period is the important timespan over which it is difficult to predict the profitability of today's investments. This is a period so long that it is impossible to be in any way precise about what is going to happen but, neverthe-

* The foregoing was written before the October 1973 Arab—Israeli War and its later consequences.

less, which will encompass the lifespan of many investments which are in their initial planning stages now.

It is necessary for practical purposes to be much more precise than we have been able to be in the foregoing about specific economic and industry trends over that sort of planning period. The important point is that this kind of time horizon should be investigated in the context of a specific kind or set of decisions, either long-term strategic planning decisions or fixed investment decisions. For these purposes over this sort of time period it is important to get the general orders of magnitude correct. It is not necessary to be precise. What the forecaster wants to be able to do is to specify that the demand required to keep a production line or group of factories fully employed over the period in question is likely to be at such levels over the whole period of the investment's life, and that the decision takers today can feel reasonably confident. It is easier to pose the problem the opposite way round and to ask whether there is any serious doubt about a level of demand being maintained. Can we list any factors which might enter the situation, leading us to suppose that the demand will be cut away from our investments in due course? When we have such a list, how probable do we suppose that each event will be? There is probably only one forecasting technique which can allow us to give any kind of reliability to those sorts of estimates and that is technological forecasting.

7.5 Technological forecasting

The role of technological forecasting is to provide information about the kinds of future development which are possible. It should provide a probabilistic assessment of the likelihood of each development, giving the urgency with which it is desired. It is a way of charting the range of possible or alternative futures (see Jantsch, 1967).

Today about 600 large and medium-sized American firms carry out technological forecasting on a regular basis and spend together about 1 per cent of their research and development budget on it. Some cotton companies deeply involved in innovative markets have been able to double their new product sales by employing this technique.

The object is not to make precise forecasts. In the materials field, for instance, it would not be possible to establish the precise chemical or physical form of the properties of materials over the next thirty years, but it is possible to outline something of their general properties. The first approach to such a problem might be the study of the basic physics of materials, from which it is possible to discover the absolute theoretical limitations of the specific properties such as hardness and flexibility. A curve can be drawn up of the increase in these properties over the past century. A variety of the available curve-fitting techniques could then be used to attempt to extrapolate those curves over the coming years between the current values and the theoretical limits. In fact, a number of curves can be constructed to show how the time scale might be expected to vary with demand and with the amount of effort and funds devoted to a particular field of material science. For instance, one of the greatest requirements in the field is for a stiff high temperature synthetic material which is also light. Progress towards such a material is likely to advance faster than it is towards, say, a heavy and flexible high temperature material.

An important point is that each step in the argument is quantified to give a framework within which future advances must fall. Where they are likely to fall has to be determined from the knowledge for the need for a material which may also demand a forecast and such other factors as the current state of technology, the future possibilities of fundamental breakthrough and the relative importance of advances in related technologies. The survey carried out in 1967 for the Organization for European Co-operation and Development listed twenty different basic approaches to technological forecasting with approximately 100 different versions or elements of techniques being adopted in the United States in that year. The most important of the methodologies are the Delphic technique, trend extrapolation, input-output analysis and morphological research.

The Delphic technique is a development of the idea of taking the opinions of people who might be expected to be specially knowledgeable about probable future technological and economic trends. The aim is to sharpen expert group consensus in a succession of iterative rounds. In seeking the views of many experts, procedures are used to make these experts sharpen their own thinking and to prevent them from exchanging opinions with one another. They never meet, but their first estimates are used to produce modified second estimates. For instance, an initial survey might be made asking experts what breakthroughs they expected to see in the next forty years. The first results will be analysed and the first twenty breakthroughs listed. The same experts would then be asked what probability they attached to these breakthroughs occurring within forty years. This would provide a further list of breakthroughs in order of probability and the experts would then be quizzed as to which decade and with what probability the breakthroughs might be expected. At each stage the replies are successively refined without introducing extraneous psychological features, as would be done, for example, in face to face discussion.

As well as trying to use polite cross-examination techniques to obtain a view of the future development of technology, it is also necessary to integrate such a view with one of the development of the economy. To this end probable technological events are interrelated with probable economic events, it being recognized that the probability of an innovation is greater under the pressure of an exigent economic situation. In this context it might be recognized that the relevant variable for technological forecasting is *not* the existence of an invention, but the need for innovation. There might be a dozen conceivable inventions to fill some given economic/technological need; which one will come first, or eventually prove best, is highly speculative.

Just as we saw the possibility of producing long, if somewhat speculative, extrapolations of economic trends, it is also possible to construct extrapolations of technological trends, which frequently make fascinating viewing. The longevity of man, his mean speed of long distance travel, his capacity to communicate, the size and capacity of devices he uses to do so, and so on, can be measured over fairly long spells. The outstanding feature of all these graphs (if a long enough time scale is chosen) is the breathtaking acceleration of the capacity of technology in the past half-century or so.

There is then a dangerously seductive temptation to believe that the rate of change of the trend will continue. But trends never go on upwards at an accelerating rate (except possibly the intergalactic system's relative movement). We can take it as a first principle that social trends are S-shaped. Rather than be dazzled by his own ingenuity, man would be better employed explaining why the technico-economic trends of the world's twenty leading nations have so little reflection in the other fifty or so. For if the dazzling predictions are not to materialize, how are the poor to be prevented from becoming poorer? Certainly not by continuing our social systems in their present form.

On the technical side, however, we have seen earlier how difficult it is to fit an S-shaped curve to a set of data. There is a large family of curves which will tolerably fit most systems of data observed over time. Trends of this sort must be regarded as one of the inputs towards the formation of a long-term view of the business environment. They cannot and never will be able to provide firm guidelines for company decisions.

One of the principal strengths of input-output analysis, described earlier, is its ability to take a comprehensive view of economic means and ends, and if the output from such analyses is compared with the availability of resources, it becomes possible to detect in time to take action the areas in which innovation will be required. The development of aluminium as a substitute for copper in overhead transmission drives is perhaps the best known example of successful use of input-output analysis in technological forecasting.

Morphological research is an attempt, still very much in the development stage, to do a sort of technological input-output analysis by attempting to break technological development problems into their basic parameters. For example, a jet engine characterized by eleven basic parameters can be constructed in (so it is said) 25 344 combinations of these parameters. Some of these represent highly novel devices which might not have been thought of without morphological research. The great benefits claimed for morphological research are comprehensiveness and rigour.

7.6 Summary

It is necessary for the business analyst to have a view of the economic background to his company's activities, in order to take a reasonable view of the relevant future. The problem is that economic theory is diffuse, and econometric models tend to offer conflicting advice. This is especially true in areas (involving for example the investment decision) where it is necessary to take a view of the medium-term future, and where some of the relevant economic variables are highly unstable.

Although a crude set of economic theories can be formulated, and these can be refined into sophisticated econometric models, in the end they tend to be of little general use in a practical decision-making context. However, much use can often be made of the specific reasoning in published forecasts of the economy as a basis on which a manager may make a decision based upon his own reasonable view of the economic future.

A similar sort of role is ascribed to long-term economic and technological speculation which, despite substantial efforts to introduce rigour and quantification. remain largely areas for specialist speculation out of which decision-makers may select the little bits which may from time to time be helpful.

REFERENCES

Burns, A. F. and Mitchell, W. C. *Measuring Business Cycles*, National Bureau of Economic Research, 1946.

Butler, W. F. and Kavesh, R. A. *How Business Economists Forecast*, Prentice-Hall, 1966.

Jantsch, Garrick, 'Forecasting the future', *Science Journal*, October 1967.

8 Surveys as a basis for forecasting

8.1 The role of survey investigation

So far we have concentrated on two aspects of the forecasting process: the formulation of some type of model to explain the behaviour of economic variables, and the interpretation of such a model by the analyst or manager responsible for making the decisions to which the model purports to be relevant.

It is by now apparent that the whole business is speculative in nature, and the purpose of all the economic and statistical exercises is to help sharpen the awareness of the analyst of the relevant determinants of the economic scene, and to help him get a better specified feel for possible outcomes under different situations. The process should add clarity to intuition and precision to the specification of uncertainty. What we are trying to do is not to define what will happen, but to reduce our uncertainties concerning the future, to assign measures to them and to use our defined uncertainties as a basis for building a speculative model of the future.

Such is the nature of the human animal that when faced with uncertainty its commonest first reaction is to ask for help. This is essentially what surveys are about. In attempting to resolve his doubts, the business forecaster usually seeks additional facts and other opinions. Frequently in the course of a complex forecasting process analysts will resort to some form of survey, as a formalized and structured vehicle for gathering and using additional facts and opinions.

In the category of facts may be included basic market research, designed to establish existing usage of some product or service group. Market research is a field in its own right, already well documented, whose role in forecasting is to provide benchmarks about areas unfamiliar to the firm, from which extrapolations can be extended (for example, Moser and Kalton, 1971; Ferber and Verdoorn, 1962).

When deciding whether to conduct market research for this sort of purpose, the analyst must bear in mind the long lead times normally involved and the fact that the information will turn out to be imperfect. The costs and uncertainties are normally such that this type of work is usually confined to investment decisions incorporated in important diversification strategies. It has, however, recently become possible to measure the worth of conducting such research, by applying Bayes' Theorem to the relevant decision system. Although the literature has as yet no record of a successful application of this analytical technique in an actual decision situation, the principles are easily understood. The outlines of this type of decision analysis are contained in chapter 9.

Another type of 'fact' which can be collected is intentions data. Here the idea is, say, to ask customers what they intend to buy, or use in their processes, or what their processes might be, sometime in the future. Perhaps the best known intentions survey in Britain is the *Industrial Trends Inquiry* conducted by the Confederation of British Industries, in which key businessmen are asked to comment on whether they expect such things as sales, exports, production, employment and investment to go up, down, or remain the same over the ensuing four months. Unfortunately, studies of the value of this *Inquiry* as a predictive device seem to show that there is very little relationship between businessmen's expectations and intentions and the performance which emerges. Many economic and market research surveys include 'intentions' questions of either a direct or hypothetical type. 'Do you intend to increase output of widgets next year?' is an example of the former, while the hypothetical type runs: 'If the XYZ company were to introduce a line of chromium plated plastic doorhandles, would you incorporate them into your products?'

There is a great deal of evidence, both from the direct experience of practitioners and in economic literature, to suggest that this type of survey, and these types of question, are frankly not worth the ink used to print them (National Bureau of Economic Research, 1960). In short, people cannot give reliable answers to such questions.

One minor but important exception to this generalization is the obvious case in which such a survey turns up a firm indication of interest with an important potential customer; but this is the sort of thing that any aware manager should be doing without recourse to forecasting research.

If fact gathering surveys have only limited application in forecasting, and intentions surveys turn out in practice to have zero value, is it worth while going on to consider opinion surveys at all? It must be said straight away that there are a good many analysts who mistrust opinion research in all its forms. Nevertheless there is a case for using opinion research, at least depending upon whose opinion is being sought and how the information is being used.

There are a great many areas of speculation relevant to the future on which the views of salesmen, wholesalers or retailers, development engineers, technical consultants or other managers may be of great value in assessing whether an idea is likely to be operational or not.

The task is to uncover these opinions in a meaningful way, and weight and collate them into a composite picture of informed opinion, as yet another input into the decision-making structure. To the extent that the investigation reveals *reasons* why opinions are held, then information can be got which is relevant to the task of building a model of the future. In particular, the reasoning underlying opinions may draw attention to an important set of possible influences moulding the future which cannot normally be incorporated into a statistical model, namely institutional, organizational or behavioural determinants of the way society organizes itself, and its trade and consumption patterns. In addition, opinion research may draw attention to overriding technical constraints on ability of management to carry through some intended programme, for example, that a particular raw material is not available, a necessary process is exclusively patented by a competitor, and so on.

There is a staggering amount of 'random' knowledge of this sort in people's minds, and an important objective of opinion research is to release it into the relevant decision-making system.

8.2 Surveying customer behaviour

An obvious place to seek data regarding future sales is among likely future buyers: customers who might, depending on circumstances, be final consumers, wholesalers, retailers or other distributors, or manufacturers purchasing components or materials from the forecasting firm. The reasonable manager might suppose that these sources would know better than he could the current state of retail or intermediate demand (to be reflected ultimately in his own demand), the shifting emphasis of competition, and plans they might have for developing their end of the business.

Already agencies sell as an ongoing service to manufacturers (particularly in the food and pharmaceutical industries) up to date brand share data derived at retail or consumer level. Such services provide invaluable benchmark facts which may have a lead time long enough for them to be incorporated into production, marketing and other short-term decisions.

Getting at intentions or opinions is trickier. First of all, the investigations are time-consuming and costly, except in markets with strictly limited customer numbers. In such markets the seller customer liaison is generally so close that there is (or should be) a pretty free flow of information. Secondly, interpretation of qualified estimates or qualitative information takes a lot of time, and intentions data are likely to be worthless after a few weeks. Thirdly, the behaviour of buyers in conditions of demand changes can lead to changes in orders placed on suppliers which are widely out of line with underlying demand changes. This phenomenon has been described as 'escalation' whose principles are illustrated in the following trivial example.

Assume that there has been a steady state of demand for some time equivalent to 100 units. For some reason consumers in a period choose to buy 110 units. This is interpreted by the retailer as a 10 per cent increase in demand, hence he wants to increase his order to his wholesaler by ten units, but in addition he is lower on stock than he likes, hence he needs another ten units to replace his depleted stock, hence his wholesale order is 120. This is multiplied by all retailers, leaving wholesalers with an impression of 20 per cent increase in demand associated with 20 per cent stock depletion. The wholesalers' orders to manufacturers will then be increased by 40 per cent. A simple levelling off of consumer demand in the next period will result in only 110 units being absorbed, leaving thirty units in stock. The subsequent period's orders on the manufacturer would then swing far below the 110 of actual demand.

In the face of the many commercially realistic situations illustrated by this example, industries in which changes in demand are likely to be frequent and which need to react quickly and sensitively to such changes prefer to attempt to assess their market position from surveys taken much closer to the consumer than at the level of their ex-factory sales compared with trade association ex-factory sales. There are basically two techniques for so doing which are operated by specialist independent market research companies. The A. C. Neilsen Company has developed a technique of taking a physical stock count of a sample of retailers. By adding to or subtracting the level of stock change from the level of the retailer's purchase invoices in a month in question it is possible to arrive at a fairly accurate figure of any change in sales which the retailer has made in the period. Providing the sample is representative, this technique should give for each of the brands which have been separately investigated a very clear idea of the change in their sales over the period. The alternative method is the one operated by Attwoods Ltd. This costs a little more to operate but gains in accuracy. A sample of households is asked to record purchases in a given period. These purchases are then analysed in order to find precisely the quantities of the various brands bought in the period in question. Thus it is possible, for example, to tie changes in actual consumption very closely with, say, television advertising campaigns.

None of these exercises is designed to do more than tell the producer what his market share is at a given point in time. By comparing this with its history, it is possible for the producer to discern any trends, and if need be to take action in light of this information. Further, at his own risk the producer is at liberty to extrapolate other trends and to make of such extrapolations anything he wishes. However, sales analysis is not inherently a forward-looking or projective technique.

By comparison market research is much more likely to involve futurity. Market research may be distinguished from sales analysis in that it involves the survey worker in determining from someone, say the distributor, the shopkeeper or the consumer, not only precisely what his purchases are and have been but also a set of opinions with regard to some factors regarded by the producer as significant for determining the course of the market. The taking and evaluation of opinions which may or may not be useful as a basis for projection distinguishes market research from sales analysis. As defined here, therefore, market research is specifically a forecasting tool.

It is unfortunate that in many of the conventional approaches to forecasting the business of opinion polling is regarded as being one of the naive techniques available. In fact the reverse is true. Every technique available for business forecasting depends ultimately for its validity on someone giving an opinion to the effect that such is N per cent probable and such another is M per cent probable in occurrence. Ultimately all the 'objective' methods of forecasting come back to someone's opinion somewhere. Insufficient attention has, until recently, been paid to the business of ensuring that such opinions are as well based as it is possible to make them before large sums of money are involved. It cannot be overstressed that it is vitally necessary to recognize that forecasting is essentially an exercise in opinion formation, and it is necessary to ensure that management accedes to, accepts and contributes to the opinion bases of all the forecasting techniques in operation.

Although it was suggested above that market research is essentially a predictive technique, there are a large number of specific uses of surveys which, although basically predictive in their content, nevertheless are more directly designed to produce information of specific relevance to a single given decision. Thus, for example, a piece of motivation research may have been designed to uncover why a level of market penetration is not as high as it was supposed it would be at a specific time; its purpose would be perhaps to enable management to modify a product specification. Although essentially a predictive tool, such a study would not generally be available to help measure the future potential of a large number of different market trends. This kind of market research has therefore, been excluded from the present account.

In summary, we may distinguish between sales analysis and market research by saying that sales analysis tells us specifically and precisely where we are, while market research should be able to help analyse the reasons why we arrived where we are and therefore help to provide signposts indicating the direction in which we are next most likely to go. As is well known, any given market research investigation often contains large elements of both sales analysis and market research. Thus a poll of an industrial market is very likely to involve asking buyers both precisely how much they buy of a number of given components in a given period as well as setting them a number of skilfully designed questions which, when analysed and computed by the researchers, will give a clear idea of why in fact the pattern of purchases has evolved as it has done.

8.3 Respondent groups

For forecasting purposes it is possible to distinguish different types of respondent groups who may well have to be interviewed separately and for different purposes. These are managers, the sales force, distributors, retailers, customers, consumers and 'oracles'. Each of these groups of individuals who have an interest in the products being moved through the market has a different perspective to offer on the reason why a product is performing as it is and on likely future trends. Surveying different groups can help to put some texture into the forecast. To do the exercise comprehensively would be a cumbersome undertaking involving a large number of interviewers over a long period of time. This sort of exercise is only justified for applications such as long-range planning and investment decisions. As we saw in the last chapter, this type of method is central to technological forecasting. The more relevant parts of it, however, can still be utilized for some shorter-range applications including, indeed, very short-run sales forecasting. Curiously, although most of the present interest in survey and polling methods is in long-term applications, this type of technique originated in very short-term sales forecasting. This is still heavily biased towards the technique of asking salesmen for their projections of what their sales are going to be in the next time period (say three months ahead). Let us now examine the use of each of these respondent groups.

Managers: the first stage
We have already argued that managers' opinions should be woven into the total texture of a forecast. The assumptions on which it is based, the opinions sought in determining its validity, the techniques of projection to be used, and the validity of the data fed into it. Their role in this context arises, of course, from the fact that if a forecast is to be accepted by management it needs to have been endorsed by them at every stage. If a forecast is not accepted by management then the total exercise involved in producing it is a waste of time. Once it has been accepted, therefore, there is an implication of management's commitment to it, and it is then possible to define the manager's job, as has been done in the past, as 'making forecasts come out'. It is, however, in the alternative context of being one of the contributors to the forecasting process in terms of their opinions as to potential customers being of value that we now wish to consider the role of the manager *vis-à-vis* the forecast. For this purpose it is necessary to distinguish between different types of manager. The perspectives of the marketing manager, the research and development manager, the purchasing manager, the production manager and the finance manager are all likely to be different, if only in shades, and all are likely to be equally relevant to the problems of determining what is likely to be the shape of markets in the future. The view of the managing director or chief executive is, of course, of greatest significance in this exercise. Ultimately the whole forecasting exercise is a delegation of one of the kernel responsibilities of the managing director. His primary responsibility is to shape today an organization which will meet the needs of the future.

Much of the apparatus of forecasting is a means for supplementing the vision of the entrepreneur. What may often misguidedly be taken as hunch or insight as a basis for top executive prognostication of the future of sales, costs or profits, may frequently reflect the fact that the managing director of all the people in the firm has the most comprehensive knowledge of the global state of the market and the firm, and the most detailed appreciation of the influences which are shaping it.

Frequently the chief executive will be the most widely read and best informed member of the managerial team. Not infrequently the fact that formal forecasting has taken place is a matter of the managing director having responded to the wishes of the Board to obtain some kind of formal confirmation of what he has decided is going to happen. One of the most authoritative starting places, therefore, in the pursuit of some knowledge about the future is to interview the managing director. The process of interviewing to obtain the guide to the insights which the managing director possesses is subtle and complex. Probably it is best done away from the office and its pressures: perhaps in a completely informal environment, over dinner or on the golf course. What the interviewer in this situation requires more than anything to bear in mind is that as the managing director reveals his innermost thinking he is giving up a significant part of those secrets which distinguish him as the entrepreneur from his colleagues.

Often the great man will reply by devious hints rather than give a direct answer. For example, he may suggest that the interviewer looks back on some back numbers of a particular columnist in one of the management magazines or the *Financial Times*. Apart from making it clear that the level of confidentiality involved in such an interview will be respected to the hilt, and that the revealing of confidential information in no way poses a threat to the position of the managing director from the interviewer, the other necessary condition for success in an interview of this sort is that the interviewer has done his homework thoroughly. His homework in this case involves briefing himself as thoroughly as can reasonably be expected from all published sources and from colleagues within the firm in question as to the total state of knowledge about the project he has been asked to investigate. It should be clear to the respondent in the course of this sort of interview that the interviewer already knows more about the subject than any other single individual in the firm.

There are two reasons for this degree of preparation. First, it will mean that the managing director is more likely to respect the man and to give frank and full answers; second, and perhaps more important, it enables the interviewer to know what is the state of play, to know on what issues he ought to probe more deeply into the answers he is getting and on what issues he has already been given all the information the managing director is likely to possess, and to determine the sort of angle or direction he might take in asking questions in order to elucidate the frankest and fullest replies. In other words, the interviewer must make sure that he is fully briefed before the interview begins and the only person who can brief him is himself.

It follows, therefore, that the interview at managing director level will take place fairly late in the forecasting process and will only be justified in those cases where major decisions hang on the outcome of the forecast. This process is totally qualitative, but nevertheless highly significant in commercial terms. The interviews with other managers in the firm will precede the key interview with the senior decision-maker. Frequently, however, the forecaster will have met the senior decision-maker, probably briefly, when initially instructed on the project. It is important at that point to make it clear that he will probably wish to conduct a much fuller interview with this man at a later stage of forecasting, and to refuse to allow himself to be drawn into asking half-baked questions at the initial briefing meeting. Many managing directors are notoriously impatient people who will want to overhurry the process.

By interviewing individually a number of members of the top management team, the interviewer is able to obtain cross-bearings on the target. One question which frequently arises in this context is whether the interviews should be conducted with the top management decision-making group all together, or whether each individual member should be interviewed separately. It is probably preferable to interview the individuals separately, but the nature of the political game in many companies makes it inexpedient to do so. In many cases the individual directors or senior managers will be unwilling to have an outsider interview one of their colleagues on a matter of major significance which might well involve a political cut and thrust of development of one department or division unless all are party to all the proceedings of such discussion. The greater the number of same-level colleagues (e.g. several Board members) confronting him in an interview the more the interviewer's political antennae should alert him to the potential dangers in the situation. Any forecast he makes, however soundly based, may prove unacceptable to the management team because it conflicts with some basically held political position.

The two managers who generally have most to contribute to the forecaster's understanding of the project under investigation are the marketing manager and the research and development manager. Very often the interview will be conducted with these two together and it will well repay the forecaster to work out very early on whether the atmosphere between them is mutual cooperation or mutual hostility. Both are found in practice. If the atmosphere is one of mutual hostility it will probably be advisable to curtail the interview with the two together and arrange separate interviews at a later stage.

Where the opposite atmosphere prevails the interviewer is likely to find himself in one of the more fruitful situations of his career. These two managers can separately contribute to the forecaster's understanding of the situation: (a) the market basis for having a project, e.g. the way in which some kind of gap or empty market segment has come to be identified; (b) the sort of historical sales trends available for the product being forecast or the products from which the new development is being derived; and (c) the history of alternative offerings in the market with which a proposed one is to compete. The sales analysis section (which should be under the marketing manager's control) should be on top of these kinds of figures. The marketing manager should also be able to indicate the extent to which, as a first approximation, sales of the product under review will be a function of total general growth of market size, the general development of the economy, or a response of some form of sales promotional input such as advertising or direct selling. Cross-bearings on this position can be provided by the research and development manager who can indicate whether the segmentation of the market involved in the differentiation of the product is real in technical terms or whether it is somewhat illusory and based on marketing techniques. This kind of information has a very important bearing on whether consumer loyalty for a product will build up or whether it will be subject to frequent brand switching. A second vitally important area in which the research and development manager will be concerned, is in defining who the buyers for such a product might be and the range of uses from a technological viewpoint.

Especially if the product is a new one, sales forecasting has to be derived from the use of the technology offered by the product being offered for sale rather than by extension of past trends of sales of a similar type of product.

The executives in charge of production and finance can perform a somewhat different type of service for the forecaster. They can warn him about the feasible limits of attainment outside which his forecast should not fall. It is not uncommon for a forecaster to produce an outcome which cannot be achieved within the resources of the firm.

The fundamental idea behind the technique of *long-range planning* is contained in this area of unexploited potential and limitations on enterprise. It might, for instance, be market potential available to the firm which existing resources are insufficient to enable it to exploit.

From the foregoing it will be clear that there is an order in which it is desirable for the interviews to be conducted. After the briefing interview would come the marketing and research and development staff who might have relevant information to offer. Following this would come senior marketing and research and development managers who can help to identify the opportunities which the firm sees as underlying the need for a forecasting project.

The third group of interviews should be with production and finance management; if properly conducted this should leave the interviewer with a clear perception as to the limits within which a forecast will be regarded by the firm as acceptable. The final interview will be with the managing director. All these points, together with the results of the desk research the interviewer will have done, can then be brought to bear on the one man whose role in the exercise has probably been that of the motive force in establishing that there was a potential project there in the first place, and to whom ultimately the results of the forecasting process will have to be sold and established.

Customers

There are two situations in which the customer can help the forecaster. The first is in the area in consumer markets of motivation research, in which numbers of people selected as representative of typical customers are subjected to a battery of tests involving them in making decisions from a number of choices of potential product qualities or forms of presentation, supported by different kinds of sales promotion methods and so on. Despite the high level of sophistication of the tests operated, the results required from them are conceptually extremely crude.

Essentially the researcher in this situation is attempting to establish which among a number of alternative possible offerings to the public will be easiest to sell, often with no clear perception of the quality in absolute terms which will be sold. In other words, the task is to rank the various alternative possible offerings ordinally, rather than place cardinal numbers on any of them. Although in its restricted context this kind of technique has its uses, the fact that the consumer is for very good reasons incapable of giving a sensible answer to any question involving how many of such and such is likely to be bought next week, means that this kind of technique cannot be used as a basis for making quantitative estimates, except by reference to some baseline measure equivalent to a real value or volume increase.

This point may be illustrated with reference to a manufacturer in a fashion goods industry, in which any specific design might remain in production for one to upward of ten years. With five or six new designs being introduced each year (and four or five being withdrawn) the problem is to determine which of the available designs under development ought to be introduced.

The use of attitude research, together with a scoring system to measure consumer perceptions along specific relevant dimensions enables the researcher to rank the new designs in order of customer preference, at least along the measured dimensions. The important stage, however, is also to measure designs from the existing product range along the same dimensions. If the study has been well conceived it ought to be possible to correlate attitude scores with sales value for the existing lines and, subject to regression errors, this can be used as a basis for forecasting sales of individual designs, assuming of course that tastes either are not changing, or that changes are being monitored and have been discounted by an appropriate term in the regression equation (if one is used), or by an appropriate allowance in a less formally formulated model.

The situation is different in industrial markets. Here, because purchases are normally tied to much more clearly defined uses, it is often possible for a customer or potential customer for a product to give a clear idea of the likely potential purchase of it in answer to a direct question. In this sort of context what matters to the forecaster is not so much the sophistication of mathematical or economic content in his analysis, as his relationship with the significant purchasers of the commodity under investigation, so that he can ring them up, invite them to dinner, or, on a small inquiry, simply ask them outright if they will assist him in his exercise, and tell them the figures he requires.

This sort of relationship with customers is an important part of the stock-in-trade of the industrial market forecaster. As in interviewing his own management, however, the important aspect of this type of interviewing is not to ask the naive question but to make it clear that he already possesses sufficient knowledge of the situation to be able to formulate intelligent questions about it which are capable of being answered on a basis of, and only on a basis of, the specific knowledge of trade which the respondent can be expected to possess.

This type of general approach, which may involve as much as anything simply getting at the requirements of the process and the products of the customer in general terms rather than in terms of any specific kind of supply which is for the moment designed to meet such a use, is of particular value in the forecasting for new products. Only a customer's production or research and development manager can give a meaningful answer to the questions involving, for example, a potential and new component on the market, whether such a component would fit with their processes, and to what extent it would have applications in their plant and products. At this stage we are beginning to talk about a rudimentary form of technological forecasting.

The sales force

Probably the most popular of the interview approaches are those based on the sales-men's estimates of future sales in their territories. These are often required from the sales force as a matter of routine weekly or monthly reports. Such projections are added together to arrive at the total company sales projection for the short run. In almost all cases the salesman is required to fill up his set *pro forma* with a record of past sales before him. The past records, which may range from a few quarters to as much as five years, are necessary to give the salesman a perspective and provide him with a base figure from which to work.

It is possible also in this context for management to give the salesman certain broad guidelines on economic outlook or company policy and thus help to improve the viability of the estimates he is making. Normally such projections are broken down by type of product, type of customer, geographical area and so on; frequently, they are projections revised and/or ratified by the individual salesman's immediate manager. In another case, the sales manager of an individual product or division may make the basic forecast the basis for spot checks of the individual salesman's views.

Probably a more desirable approach is for the individual salesman and the sales managers to make up entirely separate forecasts without having had sight initially of each others' estimates, and for the composite of the sales force and the manager's estimates to be forwarded separately with a reconciliation arising out of the meeting explaining any discrepancies between them.

There has been no recorded instance so far of such a *sales force composite* fore-cast or a *jury of sales executive opinion* forecast having probabilities of outcome at different levels of attainment assigned to it. This is a pity because, despite the very much greater complexity of the form which the salesman and the manager would be required to complete probability-based estimates when combined with the computing power of modern data processing equipment would probably give rise to forecasts of much greater usefulness than have commonly been obtained from such anticipation surveys of sales personnel. The sort of form which would be required to enable such a process to take place is shown in Fig. 8.1.

Salesmen and sales executives anticipations data are normally regarded essentially as a tool of very short-run sales forecasting of the three-month to six-month type. This is probably fair inasmuch as this is a period over which, in consultation with the buyers to whom they are selling, the salesmen can develop a reasonable feel for the movements of their markets. In any event any company which is not utilizing this type of data is failing to tap an important potential resource in the company.

On the other hand, there is no record of this type of data being used at any time as a basis for long term sales projection or for the projection of potential demand for, say, new products. An objection which is commonly lodged to the use of sales force anticipations as a basis for forecasting is that salesmen are frequently too optimistic (or occasionally consistently too pessimistic) in their expectations as to the outcome of their sales effort. While it is very easy to see where the theoretical basis for such an objection comes from, in practice there is rarely found to be any

XYZ Company

Sales Territory Predictions

Name. _ _ _ _ _ _ _ _ _ _ _ _ _ _ _ _ _ _Territory. _ _ _ _ _ _ _ _ _ _ Period _ _ _ _ _

Past sales									Product line	Expected sales assuming				
Years					Quarters					Worst cond. $p = 0.1$	Poor cond. 0.2	Most likely 0.4	Good cond. 0.2	Best cond. 0.1
−5	−4	−3	−2	−1	1	2	3	4						

Fig. 8.1 A suggested *pro forma* for recording sales anticipations by salesmen or management

The conventional *pro formas* used for this job normally request a point forecast, or at most a best, average, worst prediction. The differences in the *pro forma* outlined here are that five bands are identified, and each of these is associated with some expressed numerical likelihood of their occurring. Personnel are instructed on the meaning of the bands, namely that what they are saying is that they expect 'worst' conditions, leading to the lowest prediction, to occur once in every ten occasions ($p = 0.1$) and so on. As well as being able to integrate information in this form into decision-making systems, it is possible, once a track record is established, to check and discount each individual's tendency towards error.

justification for it, provided the salesman is faced with a record of his past sales achievement as a guideline on which to base his projection of the future. Secondly, and of critical importance, the salesman must be confident that the projection he is offering is what he believes can reasonably be attained, and will not later be turned round and used as a target element in a bonus or commission system on which his remuneration might be based. It is vitally important in this exercise that salesmen should clearly and confidently in their minds dissociate the projection being made from anything which has to do with remuneration.

In view of the extent to which bonus schemes are related to targets, this requirement poses a considerable problem for sales management, but there are a number of alternatives. First, of course, the short-term projection business can be confined to target-setting and it is therefore necessary to accept that as a basis for forecasting it is of little value. Second, bonus and commission target sales levels may be set independently, for example, by managerial assessment of territory potential; alternatively, managerial forecasts may be used for forecasting, and salesmen's estimates for remuneration planning. A third option is to drop the sales target working through remuneration as a motivating device. Finally, more devious mixtures are also possible, bearing in mind that as well as this particular area of endeavour as an input to both the forecasting and the sales motivation process there are also parallel inputs to both processes.

In the case of forecasting, these are principally forecasts derived from earlier statistical and economic analysis. In the case of management they are non-financial motivating devices, and targets based not on sales, the output of the sales effort, but on the degree of effort *input* in terms of number of sales calls, minimization of journey and other non-productive time, ratio of successful calls to all calls and so on.

Some ingenuity is required to dissociate the forecasting from the motivation process, and the extent to which it is worth while putting effort into the attempt depends on the value to the individual company of improved forecasts, compared with the costs of alternative motivation systems. The main point is to recognize that there is a managerial problem here, which deserves attention in a way that, as far as the record seems to indicate, it does not normally receive.

There are a number of managerial advantages in using a sales force composite type of forecast for short-term projections. First, this approach makes use of the knowledge of the men closest to the market and places responsibility for the forecast in the hands of those who must produce the results. Second, knowledge that they are contributing in one of the key planning exercises for the company often shows beneficial results in salesmen's morale and obviates the feeling that they are being manipulated by academic boffins sitting in back rooms. Third, being involved with the forecasting process inevitably involves the salesman with the management process. Fourth, though there are frequently good reasons for not using the sales force as a basis for market research, nevertheless there are pieces of information relative to forecasting which the salesman is often better placed to pick up than any other member of the company. If he is involved in the forecasting process generally, he will be willing to pursue specific lines of inquiry when requested to, and, because he will recognize the necessity, will obtain pertinent and accurate information.

Robert Reichhard (1966) quotes a particularly devious case of sales forecasting techniques which were made possible with a good workforce. Apart from anything else this example highlights the basic message that, while techniques are all very well, managerial flair in the design of a forecasting methodology can count for more than all the mathematics and economics in the world. The story is that when the owner/manager of a small company developing plans to market an item used by the steel industry was attempting to create a forecast of likely usage of this product, in order to determine his working capital needs, he was able to utilize knowledge that the use of the product in question in a steel plant was likely to be proportional to the amount of water used by the plant for cooling purposes. Each salesman was then asked to ask the question 'how much water do you use?' on his rounds. The owner/manager then compared these water use figures with each plant's known capacity for producing steel, pig iron and coke. Thus he worked out a ratio between production capacity and water use. He then used statistics from the American Iron and Steel Institute to calculate the total amount of cooling water used by the steel industry. In this way he arrived at an estimate of his potential market. The estimate was accurate enough to use for forecasting purposes.

Managers: a more sophisticated approach

The interviewing of managers discussed so far has been in the context of fairly long-term forecasting for purposes such as decision-making or strategic planning. An alternative approach to forecasting via managers, called the *jury of executive opinion* method, is often practised regularly on a monthly, quarterly, six monthly or annual basis, and involves bringing together sales or marketing managers, or, occasionally, senior executives of the company, and asking them to bring to a meeting their estimate of sales for the period under review. These estimates are then pooled, averaged or otherwise reconciled through the give and take of executive discussion until at last a final forecast evolves.

In most cases where this method of forecasting is employed the various departments, including the professional forecasters, supply the executives with data on sales, industry trends and so on. Such an approach is valuable for producing or modifying a sales strategy for a fairly short period ahead. The professional forecasters should always attend such meetings for, in the course of them, many salient facts about the likely future course of markets which would otherwise go unrecognized by the professional forecasters are likely to be brought to light. Such asides may point the way to declining and dying products and to unexploited market opportunities facing the firm which may in return provide a basis for dynamic planning opportunities for the future.

One manifest disadvantage of the jury of executive opinion approach is the danger that it will degenerate into a blind guessing game exercise in which the company power politics structure rather than rationality will dictate the eventual outcome of the 'agreed' vote. In order to have meaningful discussions it is essential that those participating in the meeting should be fully briefed by the professional forecasters in the company with all the salient background market trends, sales position and market penetration estimates as well as the current state of the technological variables and likely future economic, business and market projections. For this reason it might be suggested that this approach to forecasting is not suitable for a company which does not possess the resources to make available a comprehensive set of the necessary statistical and other factual data and information to form such a necessary basis for the jury of executive opinion approach. Just as we have stressed through the statistics-based forecasting techniques the importance of executive judgment, here we must stress that in the techniques utilizing executive judgments as the primary input it is of greatest importance that this should be guided by factual estimates.

Another common objection to this form of forecasting is that unless the meetings are to be protracted and very wasteful of valuable executive time they may be liable to become no more than a rubber stamp vehicle for the views and wishes of the chief executive. This view is probably valid, and whether or not the exercise is worth doing depends on the importance to the firm of reliable and

valuable forecasts. If the amount of additional reliability, precision and acceptability built into a forecast by running a meaningful executive opinion jury session
and repeating it at a later date for completion if necessary is not as valuable to the
company as the amount of executive time which is devoted to it, then of course the
procedure should be dropped. To curtail it to a level where it becomes a mere
endorsing body is probably the worst of both worlds. A lot of executive time would
still be wasted and the exercise would be of no value for forecasting. Indeed, the
executives involved may well become sufficiently disgruntled at the process that
they are all the more resistant to the idea of forecasting and the whole exercise
could be counter-productive.

One objection, of less validity, is that the process spreads responsibility which
rightfully is the prerogative of the managing director over a wide range of executives. It must be made clear that the setting and implementation of targets based on
forecasts is essentially the responsibility of the managing director and no amount of
commitment by subordinate executives to his set of targets can take away any of
his responsibility. To the extent that in a given firm the forecasting process is an
integral part of the objective setting process, the managing director requires to be
the chairman of the executive jury which endorses the forecasts. If this role should
be specifically delegated it has to be made clear that the responsibility for the
objectives and their fulfilment which derives from the forecasts has not been
delegated.

Distributors and retailers

Merchants, agents, wholesalers, retailers and other distributors earn their living by
being at the crossroads of the marketplace. The structure of many markets is such
that a very small number of the middlemen in the market are in a position to 'make
a market' for the goods or services which are transacted there. In recent years there
has been a growing tendency for purchasing power to become increasingly concentrated in fewer and fewer hands in each of the economy's markets. The opinions of
the men in control of these organizations can be of critical importance to the forecaster from two points of view. First, by refusing to handle a product when it
comes on the market they may be in a position to sound its death knell. The forecaster who is able to ascertain that in key areas of the market the product will not
gain acceptance in distribution for any set of reasons will have established a
critically important piece of information.

Of a good deal more importance however, in their forecasting role, is the fact
that these critical members of markets frequently have a great deal more market
knowledge than any other participant. Their finger is very close to the patient's
pulse and they can detect often with much greater accuracy than can the employees
of the firms which are supplying into the market, the likely scope of developments
in the marketplace. The principal problem with attempts to poll such individuals
lies in devising a vehicle to obtain the required information from them. A more
sensitive grasp of the trends in the market than that possessed by their competitors
is the fundamental stock in trade, of which such people often make their living.

This sort of information is not a commodity lightly to be dispensed to any casual inquirer.

Here again the critical factor is the integrity of the relationship which can be built up between the forecaster and his respondent. It is the same as the problem with polling managing directors only multiplied to a more acute degree. The managing director of our own firm at least has a vested interest in getting a reliable forecast. The managing director of a firm of brokers in the market has no interest whatsoever in securing a more reliable forecast for us in particular and, indeed, he may frequently feel that he is in danger of breaking the confidentiality of information from one of our competitors if he answers our questions directly and honestly.

Panels

Perhaps the most sophisticated and systematic technique so far evolved for taking the soundings of the opinions of people whose opinions are likely to be worth having is the construction of a *panel*. In forecasting this is an extension of the technique which has long been in use in motivation research. In the latter panels are selected as being typical of the potential consumers of a product, and their likely purchasing pattern is investigated in great psychological and sociological detail in order to help ascertain the likely acceptability of a product.

A point about panels in motivation research is that it is by no means easy to enrol representatives in a sample of a market each of whom is likely to be a reliable and consistent respondent to market research approaches over a period of time. The drawback with panels on consumer research is that having been selected as being a typical cross-section of the consuming public, the moment they know themselves to be members of panels the respondents *ipso facto* become untypical. The degree of untypicality tends to grow through time as they become increasingly skilled at answering questionnaires and at detecting the kind of responses the firm ideally would like them to make. Since they become identified with the firm for whom they are operating, they of course desire to please and therefore become unreliable, so that panels in this context have to be turned over fairly rapidly. A panel kept for forecasting purposes, however, is likely to suffer from none of the disadvantages of the consumer motivation research panel. Furthermore, the advantages which it can offer are probably greater than those which can be offered by a consumer panel.

A forecasting panel is selected not for its typicality of membership of the market but for the degree of knowledge it is supposed to have about what future trends in the market are likely to be. Thus the sort of people to be selected for the forecasting panel for an individual firm would be that firm's managing director, marketing director, research and development director and sales director; possibly also purchasing managers from some of the key customers in the market. In addition or as an alternative to these the panel could include key distributors, brokers, agents, merchants who are sufficiently heavily committed to the products of the firm in question to be willing to put the input into that firm's forecasting process which members of a panel would demand.

Where personnel from outside the firm are being employed on this type of panel valuable professional services are being employed and should be remunerated at the appropriate rate. A panel is exposed, either through a questionnaire or in the form of an extended interview, to questions designed to form the basis for a forecasting operation. Thus it is being used in many respects in the same way as the jury of executive opinion drawn from the firm's own executives.

It may not be necessary in the case of a panel to arm the respondents with statistical background to the market but as a matter of general principle this should normally be done.

From this process the forecaster should obtain a set of opinions of the people most likely to have a valid and reliable view on the likely future trends of the market under investigation. Whether the forecaster uses a large or a small panel is immaterial; he will probably want to use as many people as he thinks can offer reliable opinions. Whether they are asked to give their answers together in the form of a committee or working group or individually in their own offices is also a matter for decision by the forecaster. There is probably no special reason why one method rather than the other should be adopted, apart from the obvious and practical one that it is normally very much easier to conduct individual interviews with busy executives than to attempt to find a time mutually convenient for all of them to meet.

Since a panel, if it is to be worth while, is going to employ some very high-powered brains, it will be necessary to impress members with the importance the firm attaches to the exercise. Probably the best way of doing this is to arrange to consult members on a regular basis, say once a month or once a quarter, and to have a regular *pro forma* of interview so that they can prepare the basic answers required. There will probably always be a large number of 'one off' opinions about which the firm wishes to sound members of the panel. These can normally be attached to the end of the *pro forma* questionnaire.

Also arising from the fact that the people selected for membership of such a panel will by definition be high-powered minds, it is not necessary for the fore-caster to confine his questions to the fairly simpleminded structure required in consumer market investigations. It is quite in order for a forecaster in this context to ask the panel respondents to assign probabilities to the outcomes which they expect. This can be done in terms of conventional probability distribution, for example by asking the respondents to estimate the probability of their being within, say, 5 per cent either side of their target, 5 or 10 per cent above or below and more than 10 per cent out on either side of their target estimates. There is no reason why the questions asked should not be associated with a complete tabular or graphical picture of the market situation up to the present with some possible projections sketched in. The questions, then, may be complex, certainly much more complicated than would normally be tolerated in the consumer market investigation.

There is no objection to putting leading questions and asking for comments on them. Once again the sort of people who are on a panel are there because of the force of their opinions; they are just as likely to object to, as to accede to, a sugges-tion which is put to them. It is more important to explain the logical pieces of the suggestion being made and to ask for comment than to put the question in a simple and contextless way; in the latter form they may be reluctant to give it the time and attention it requires because they can see no reason for its having been asked. The context, therefore, may be very important in securing the required level of attention.

A further great advantage of this type of panel structure arises when we turn to the question of the processing of the results of the questionnaires. Once experience has been gained over a number of years in working with an established panel it becomes possible not only to take account of the probabilities assigned by panel members to various possible outcomes for our market behaviour, but the forecaster can privately assign probabilities to the likelihood that the responses of any one member of a panel will be correct.

Over a period a pattern of consistent error on the part of each member of the panel may emerge, one being generally over-optimistic, another pessimistic, another offering much too wide a range of probability of error and so on. With a panel of, say, ten respondents a level of consistency of 60 or 70 per cent and above (that is to say in 30 or 40 per cent of cases the response which is given is wrong in a way that is out of line with the normal way in which this particular respondent's answers are wrong) would be tolerable and when merged with the total set of ten responses will hardly be noticed. This type of approach has been used to give very reliable results for forecasts in the six-months to two-years range used for short-run planning budgeting, market planning, production planning and financial planning purposes.

The high degree of value placed on this type of panel operation by firms using it may be accounted for from two points of view. First, the calculations of the statisticians and the opinions of the executives are being subjected to a third and independent scrutiny which results in the projection probably attaining additional reliability. (Once again the question has to be posed and answered whether the cost involved in obtaining this additional reliability is going to be fully compensated for by additional value to the firm.)

The other reason why this method of forecasting is regarded by its users as being successful is much less tangible and more psychological in its nature. It is that having subjected their forecast efforts to an independent arbitrator, as it were, the managers who are responsible for the forecasts feel even more confident in it than they might otherwise have been, and feel more confidence in having a high degree of commitment to the forecast and in making it come true. The imponderables may not be lightened but they are shared by this process, and management can feel that all have been subjected to as expert a scrutiny as is possible to give them.

8.4 Uses of survey techniques

It will by now be clear that surveys are designed to contribute two types of input to the forecasting process. First, to indicate buyer or consumer intentions, and second, to find out and assess the opinions of the people consulted. The elaborate structure which is required to make opinion surveying a worthwhile exercise means that this is a relatively expensive technique and therefore best reserved for strategic decisions. It is probably best regarded as being not a provider of a primary quantitative input into the forecast so much as a check on hypotheses developed by the forecasters.

The poll of a panel or of executive opinion will provide a cross-bearing on other forms of forecasting. This type of forecasting, however, comes into its own particularly when the task in hand involves forecasting the likely demand for a new product or of the likely size of an application for an existing product which has previously not been tried. It is not uncommon for cases of this sort to arise under conditions in which there is no quantitative record or any history of experience relevant to forecasting the product in question. In such cases the survey approach may be the only one open to the sales forecaster, at least as a starting point in the analysis.

In dealing with surveys of buyers' intentions the implicit context of the discussion up till this point has been that such surveys are being conducted for purposes of *ad hoc* forecasting. In other words the methodology and use were very much the same as for opinion surveys. A forecaster wanting to get some kind of benchmark on the likely sales of a particular line over a particular period might telephone a few of his contacts in the buying departments of some of the major purchasing firms to get from them an indication of their likely requirements over the next few periods and, indeed, to enlarge on this information with reasons for any changes from present buying patterns.

There are formidable obstacles in the way of attempting to use surveys of buyer intentions for any more elaborate forecasting purpose. For example, it is hard to conceive how a wide ranging survey of buyer intentions could be set up which would provide a basis for periodic forecasting. It is hardly conceivable that industrial buyers would be willing to participate on a regular basis in such an exercise.

The best approximation to this would be to have salesmen fill out 'likely purchase' statements in the report which they complete on visits to customers. Whether such a 'likely purchase' statement could ever be a comprehensive document except in the cases of firms offering only one or two products is very doubtful. Hence, in the majority of multiproduct firms, it is probably undesirable to add this complexity to a sales call. It is a general rule that salesmen should not be used to collect market information unless a very strong positive case can be made out for this procedure. Their job is a different one. But the decision on whether this kind of role should be assigned to the salesman is purely a matter for a decision on a basis of the realities of the individual sales session.

We have in Britain one fairly crude and somewhat unspecific approach to the collection of anticipations data in industry in the form of the Confederation of British Industry *Industrial Trends Inquiry*. This, however, is designed to gauge overall expectations with regard to such parameters as output, exports, profits, labour turnover and so on; any implications drawn from it with regard to purchasing decisions are likely to be extremely hazardous.

As the CBI *Industrial Trends Inquiry* shows clearly, businessmen have no very clear idea of what the next three months hold in store. It is even less likely that a representative panel of consumers would have a clear idea of what the purchasing pattern of durable goods will be over and during a three-month to six-month period. The expectations on which anticipations data are based are likely in themselves to be founded on no more than arbitrary hunch. In the United States both the Department of Commerce and the University of Michigan Survey Research Center produce quarterly reports on consumers' intentions to buy. Both ask families about their future plans for the purchase of such items as new cars, household durables, used cars, houses, etc. These figures for the past have had a small degree of predictive accuracy on changes in consumer buying patterns. (This type of information has some value to the appliance maker in the United States in providing a cross-reference for him on the direction of cyclical change of consumer purchases.)

In view of the fact that the cycle of purchases for consumer durables is probably the most difficult of all the forecasting jobs attempted, any additional indicator, particularly of where a cyclical turning point is likely to occur, is more than desirable. An expensively constructed panel and an expensive research method, mainly using direct interviews, are the necessary bases for such a consumer purchasing intention survey. It is probably, therefore, best conducted by a specialist market research agency selling the service to its subscribers, and, despite difficulties, it is somewhat surprising that such as exercise is not undertaken on a regular basis in the United Kingdom.

8.5 Summary

Surveys cannot be left out of the forecasting operation, despite attempts by some early writers in the field to suggest that survey techniques were naive and 'unscientific'.

Surveys can do a number of jobs for the forecaster. First, they are a source of benchmark information relating to the present state of the business or the market. Second, they are a vehicle for involving managers in the forecasting process. Third, they may be necessary to enable the forecaster to define the full ramifications of his brief. Fourth, they provide a source of informed opinion as to present trends and their likely future evolution. Finally, they are a source of estimates of the probability of outcomes in various unique situations in which there is no history to serve as a guide.

Operation of surveys involves a good deal of management to ensure that data collection conforms with decision-making needs, and collection of anticipations data in particular has been shown to be an extremely insecure foundation for decisions as experience tends to show that there is little correlation between anticipations and outturns. For this reason various complex panel methods have been evolved, especially for use in technological and other long-term forms of forecasting.

REFERENCES

Ferber, R. and Verdoorn, P. *Research Methods in Economics and Business*, Macmillan, 1962.

Moser, C. A. and Kalton, G. *Survey Methods in Social Investigation*, 2nd edn, Heinemann, 1971.

National Bureau of Economic Research, *The Quality and Significance of Anticipations Data*, Princeton University Press, 1960.

Reichhard, R. S. *Practical Techniques of Sales Forecasting*, McGraw-Hill, 1966.

9 Using forecasts for decision-making

9.1 The gap between information and decisions

Generally speaking, we make decisions on a basis of the information available at the time, conscious of the uncertainties of the situation, and more often than not the decision follows reasonably unambiguously from the information. Increasing numbers of cases are now coming to light, however, in which the decision does *not* follow clearly or unambiguously from the information in the system, and these cases are coming to light because of our growing ability to handle the phenomenon of uncertainty. The corollary of uncertainty is probability, and it is modern probability theory which is increasingly demonstrating its power either to cast some light on previously dark areas of speculation, or even to illuminate unambiguous courses of action which would hitherto have been unanalysable.

The general class of cases which appear to be susceptible to such analyses are those where considerable outlays are involved in decisions in the face of returns which are uncertain because of entirely unpredictable variations in nature, such as the weather, competitive behaviour, customer behaviour, or political events. Probability theory can offer guides to the best long-run strategy in the face of such uncertainties. Note that it does not obviate risk, but it focuses attention on the penalties involved under the worst sets of conditions, the rewards under the best, and normally suggests a strategy for maximizing long-run payoff.

We shall shortly discuss how probability analysis can accomplish these goals, but must first note that if these pieces of information are the outcomes of a decision analysis system the inputs must be in a form which the decision analysis system can handle. The required form is that the input information must be expressed in probabilistic terms. The input information to the decision analysis system is the output information from the forecasting system and other elements of the information system.

What we are doing at this point is to bring to a head a theme which has been trailed through all the preceding chapters, so that for the careful reader it will by now be quite explicit. Information for the decision-making system must be expressible in terms of *measurable uncertainty*, or alternatively, of probability.

There are several ways of obtaining measures of uncertainty. First, there are the classical statistical measures of standard deviation of the distribution of data expressed earlier. Perhaps more generally, decision analysis systems find it easier to digest information presented in the form of quintiles or deciles, bands each containing an equal number of observations. The decision analysis system also appreciates highest expected and lowest expected outcomes, as limits for the area of feasible investigation. It may sometimes appreciate a 'most likely' outcome, but only if this has a probability of occurrence attached to it.

Frequently, an effective decision analysis system will demand information about the probability of occurrence of outcomes which fall beyond certain control limits (e.g. losing money, negative cash flow and so on).

It is incumbent on forecasters to create a data collection and analysis system sufficiently flexible to respond to such demands. This can only be done by adopting a variety of approaches. As we saw in chapter 3 on time series analysis, it is possible to force output from a time series system in this form. Regression systems automatically offer measures of dispersion. Where basic economic or technological analysis is being employed, the provision of probability estimates is more difficult, and will depend as much on the analyst's intuition as on the statistical nature of the data.

At this point we must recognize the immense importance of survey techniques for providing information in this form, or for giving the analyst necessary guidelines to enable him to translate information into probabilistic form.

It is an established part of conventional market research methodology to include the standard measures of statistical dispersion of the data collected, which provides one analytical guidepost. In polling juries, panels, oracles, executives and so on, however, where the number of respondents is low and conventional statistical techniques are inapplicable, information can still be gathered in probabilistic form by asking questions in the form 'how likely do you consider it will be that . . .?' Certain controls are needed to ensure that the results conform to the basic laws of probability, but the technique is being applied increasingly commonly and successfully, as we shall see later in this chapter.

We must recognize that collecting, storing, and analysing information in probabilistic form is much more complex, cumbersome, time-consuming and expensive than handling simple 'best estimate' information. Decision analysts frequently complain that companies do not keep their information in the best form for decision purposes. Inevitably there must be a trade-off between the much increased information costs and the decisions which are subjected to fullblown analysis. Probabilistic information should probably be reserved for the critical and difficult decisions involving major investment and strategic planning. The analyst can usually inject some reasonable probability content into other information needed for decisions of intermediate scale and difficulty.

9.2 Probability

When we toss a coin we expect there will be the same chance that it will land heads as tails. The odds against a head are often expressed as 'fifty-fifty'. This implies the notion that if the toss were to be repeated 100 times, about half the results would be heads and about half tails. We should be a little surprised if the outcome were exactly 50 and 50, though it could happen. We would be even more surprised if the result showed a marked bias towards either heads or tails. This is, however, a possible outcome over one batch of 100 trials. If we repeat the batches we would expect *in the long run* that about half the results would be heads and half tails. The essential idea of probability as it is commonly conceptualized is that in a sufficiently large number of trials the results will tend to converge towards the figure expressed as the probability of outcome.

In the coin-tossing experiment we might express the probability of heads on any throw as one-half. This does not mean that in two given throws we expect one head and one tail, but that over a large number of throws about half will result in heads and half in tails.

The conventional development of probability theory depends on this idea of the limiting value of a large number of trials, and is extremely useful for many applications. Only recently, however, has a hitherto neglected approach to the subject, that of Bayesian statistics, been developed. This offers an alternative way of regarding probability, so that instead of probability being objectively based on the outcome of a large number of trials, the idea may also be applied to the outcome of a single trial, and probabilities of outcomes may legitimately be assigned to unrepeatable events by individuals with an interest in the outcomes. What is the probability that Labour will win the next British general election, that England will win the next Test series against Australia, or that in the coming baseball season a batter will beat Babe Ruth's record of sixty home runs?

On any of these issues, and many more, men of goodwill can generate arguments. In justifying their positions they will adduce many pieces of evidence — the number of times such an event has happened before would be one: the tendency in recent events to move one way or another would surely be brought in. Then analysis of current strengths and weaknesses of parties, team and players would be deployed and from it all people would make up their own minds on the chances: certainty, very good, fair, poor, impossible.

Economic events may be of the same kind. Will taxation be changed next year? Will competitors match our price changes? Will the economy be better or worse? The approach to such problems involves the same stages as before, scrutiny of past events, special attention to current patterns, and analysis of all the influences bearing on the situation at present. And then the manager who is concerned with the events may be able to commit himself: 'certainly, very likely, perhaps, unlikely, unthinkable'.

So far this book has been concerned with the first three stages, analysis of past events and current performance, and the means of getting at the less readily measured influences in current affairs. But the number of times a 'certainty' prediction will emerge is very small indeed. If the analysts are being honest, answers will generally take the form of 'perhaps'. Or in other words, 'very probable, probable, improbable' and as rarely as 'certainly', 'impossible'.

There is no great difficulty about assigning a number to a statement of the probability of occurrence of an event. If we assign the number 1 to certainty of an outcome, and 0 to certainty that an outcome will not occur, it is possible to assign some fraction between 1 and 0 to the probability of an outcome that is uncertain. Few single events are certain. The probability that the sun will rise tomorrow morning is for practical purposes 1. So is the probability that our tossed coin will come down *either heads or tails* on any given throw.

It is, however, impossible by conventional statistical analysis, to assign a probability of outcome to unique events involving uncertainty. We know that the probability of a pair of dice both showing 6 is $\frac{1}{36}$ because the throw may be repeated indefinitely. If, however, we ascribe a probability of $\frac{1}{36}$ to the likelihood that suppliers will increase their prices next year, we are *not* saying that in thirty-six years they will raise their prices once. What we are doing is to put a measurement on *the strength of our conviction* that next year, uniquely, supply prices will rise. In this case, since $\frac{1}{36}$ is really quite a small fraction of 1, we are saying that we regard it as highly unlikely that prices will rise.

The use of the idea of probability in this way involves subjective measures. A surgeon who has performed 100 operations with sixty cures expects from experience that the objectively measured probability of a cure with operation is $p = \frac{60}{100} = 0.6$. Given all the factors surrounding an individual patient's case, however, he may in a particular operation subjectively put the probability of a cure much higher or lower than than this — 0.995 or 0.05, highly probable or highly improbable. This is his subjective assessment based only partly on his knowledge of the long-term average. It is also heavily conditioned by his knowledge of the patient's general health and age, and detailed study of all facets of his condition.

He can use this type of assessment as a decision rule, whether to operate or not, much more effectively than the long-run average probability. Let us say that he puts the probability of a cure in this case at 0.95, he is saying with this particular set of circumstances he would expect a cure in 199 out of 200 operations. Even though his experience includes only 100 operations of all types, and very few of roughly the current type, he will no doubt go ahead with the operation confidently. At $p = 0.05$, he may decide not to operate, but to recommend alternative treatment.

Subjective probability assignments of the foregoing sort require to obey the fundamental laws of probability. The first of these is that mutually exclusive probabilities must be added to produce total probability. This is called the *Addition*

Law. The probability of a head on tossing a coin is $\frac{1}{2}$. The probability of a tail is $\frac{1}{2}$. The probability of either is $\frac{1}{2} + \frac{1}{2} = 1$ which is certainty. We have covered all possible outcomes. If we think that the probability of success in a test marketing operation is $\frac{3}{5}$, then the probability of failure is $\frac{2}{5}$. These are all the possible outcomes.

The second fundamental law of probability is that to obtain the joint probability of two independent items, each of whose probability of occurrence is known, we must *multiply* the two independent probabilities. This is the *Multiplication Law*. What is the probability that in two successive throws a penny will show a head? On the first throw $p = \frac{1}{2}$. If a tail shows, we are out already. Even if we get a head, however, the probability of a p on the second throw is $\frac{1}{2}$. The probability of the two occurrences then is $\frac{1}{2} \times \frac{1}{2} = \frac{1}{4}$. What is the probability that three dice will simultaneously show a 6. Answer, $\frac{1}{6} \times \frac{1}{6} \times \frac{1}{6} = \frac{1}{216}$.

If we think that the probability of our new plant coming on stream in time is $\frac{1}{5}$ and the probability of our raw materials being available at the prices ruling when we made the investment decision is $\frac{1}{4}$, then the probability of both these producing a satisfactory outcome is $\frac{1}{20}$. Pretty small.

The directors of Magnetized Torque Wrenches Ltd were planning a new plant. Its profitability depended on each of the following basic criteria being met, with the directors' evaluations of the likelihood of each. Remember the plant is basically unprofitable if any one condition fails to be met.

Commissioning date of project, not later than January 1974	0.90
Raw material prices not up by over 10 per cent	0.85
Wage inflation not greater than 5 per cent per annum	0.80
Reject level below 15 per cent	0.95
Market prices to rise by 4 per cent per annum	0.80
No serious strikes in first two years	0.90

All these look pretty fair bets, the sort of likelihood of trouble and difficulty management deals with all the time. They are 80 to 90 per cent sure that each will come out right. And so, no doubt, they go ahead. And they would be all right if our condition for a successful project was that *all* the things that had to go wrong were to go wrong simultaneously. The probability of each part going wrong is one minus the probability that it will go right, i.e. 0.10, 0.15, 0.20, 0.25, 0.15, 0.20, 0.10. Multiplying these probabilities we get 0.0000045 — an infinitesimal chance that every one of the conditions will *fail* to be met. But our directors need to know the probability that each and every one *will* be met. Failure on *any one* will render the project unprofitable. That is what the directors assessed, the level of badness on any one critical dimension that would render the total project unprofitable. That answer is got by multiplying the probability of success on each parameter.

0.9 x 0.85 x 0.80 x 0.95 x 0.85 x 0.8 x 0.9 = 0.355 888

For practical purposes this is nearly enough $\frac{1}{3}$. This means that in the directors' best estimate there is about one chance in three that the project will succeed, therefore two in three that it will fail.

Notice that as we extend the number of critical parameters, or if we have one which is not thought a reasonably safe bet, we may very quickly reduce the probability of overall success very low indeed. Thus if the probability of demand increasing were put as low as 0.4 to 0.5, the overall probability of success would come down to under 0.2, not much of a bet. It means that four out of five such projects will fail. And these are not necessarily what are generally called 'high risk' projects, meaning high uncertainty. The uncertainty on *any one* critical parameter was pretty low.

What can management do with this kind of reasoning? Essentially, it represents the results of a systematic search for the critical parameters of a decision. So the first step in deploying this kind of analysis is to specify the objectives of the exercise, for example, to isolate and measure those factors which would lead us to switch from a 'Go' to a 'No Go' decision or vice versa. This involves simplifying the critical parameters such as market share, price, costs and so on to a point where management can say 'well I'm 50 per cent certain that won't happen'. Once we are at that stage the rest of the analysis is as easy as the one outlined above.

There are two major difficulties in making this sort of analysis operational. The first is management's inclination to say 'we can't put any sort of measure on this', but this can be overcome in practice by phrasing the questions intelligently. The analyst who asks for the probability that a range of sales possibilities will be met is unlikely to get an intelligent answer. But if he asks 'would you say there's more or less than a 50 per cent chance that sales will reach a specified level?', a dialogue should develop from which intelligent assessments should emerge. The analyst needs to be armed *in advance* with the levels which matter — for example, sales over x mean full return on investment or discounted cash flow criteria will be met, x to y means profits but not as much as we would like, y to z means losses, worse than z means bankruptcy. In addition, the sum of the probabilities assigned to each of these bands should be 1. Also he must be content with answers in the form 50–50, or 1 in 10. It is pointless to speculate on minor differences. Going to subdivisions as fine as 1 in 20 normally represents a compromise of judgments, for example, between 3 and 4 in 10, coming out as 7 in 20, i.e. $p = 0.35$.

A second difficulty arises from a legitimate need to qualify statements. A sales level of x or a cost level of c, are meaningless in themselves for profit forecasting, and a manager asked to commit himself to the level of sales or costs that would turn a profit into a loss is bound to reply that it depends on prices. It is very difficult to isolate sales volume, prices and costs and pretend that two may be held constant, as they are all more or less mutually interdependent, but the extent to which they are tied together varies markedly from firm to firm, time to time, and product to product, so that general models cannot be constructed which will apply to all firms. One recently developed approach to decision-making under these conditions is described in the following section.

9.3 Loss boundary analysis

Where forecasts are being used to evaluate whether likely results of a decision will be profitable or unprofitable, and where the outcomes of the decision involve costs, prices and sales volume, with the three in an interactive situation, the recently developed technique of loss boundary analysis may be applied. The sort of decisions in which these conditions may apply are capital investment and marketing decisions involving product policy, price or sales promotional activity.

A traditional technique for dealing with such situations has been breakeven analysis; loss boundary analysis is an extension of this taking account of the full range of feasible prices, costs and sales likely to be encountered. To become operational the extended breakeven analysis has to be compared with forecasts of expected performance, including managerial assignments of their probability of attainment.

Loss boundary analysis starts from the same point as breakeven analysis. A project is under investigation which may affect costs and sales — let us say the addition of a widget line to the present range of magnetized torque wrenches. Management has only a broad idea of the likely demand for MTW's widgets, the prices at which they may be marketed, and indeed the total costs of getting them produced and on to the market.

To set up and man a widget line and sales force will account for annual fixed costs of £200 000. Direct costs of manufacturing and marketing amount to 50p per widget. The directors are contemplating marketing the widgets at about £1 each. The line under consideration will produce 600 000 widgets a year. If all the foregoing figures were certainties, it would be possible to relate profits to volume on the breakeven chart shown in Fig. 9.1, and the directors' decision would be to go ahead if they were confident of being able to sell 400 000 widgets a year at £1 each (given that the fixed cost line includes a margin for the real cost of capital and risk profits).

Four uncertainties in this situation limit the value of this type of analysis. First, can the firm sell the required volume at that price? Second, could they in fact make a larger profit at some other price involving probably a different volume? Third, are the cost estimates reliable? Fourth, would a different type of production facility, involving perhaps different product characteristics, cost structure and capacity perhaps be a more profitable or safer venture? It is those uncertainties that are the business of loss boundary analysis, which is designed to give management a clearer picture than can the simple breakeven chart of the risks and payoffs of a large number of alternative strategies.

The first stage is to produce a list of five or seven possible alternative prices for the product, and chart the sales revenue for each on the breakeven chart. Say 80, 85, 90, 95, 100 and 110 pence. This is done in Fig. 9.2. The seven breakeven points are now transferred to a new chart with sales volume on the vertical axis and price on the horizontal. The resultant curve, shown in Fig. 9.3 is the loss boundary curve for the project. This shows the combination of all sets of price and volume at which the project exactly breaks even. Management does not want anything to do with

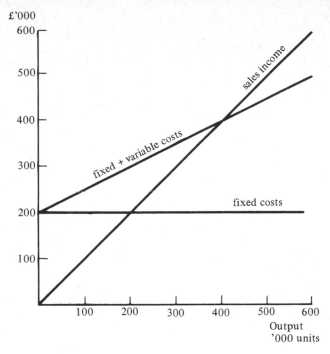

£'000

Fig. 9.1 Breakeven chart

This rudimentary decision analytical tool distinguishes powerfully the required sales level (given prices and costs) to make a project profitable, and enables the analyst to predict profits or losses at any given sales level. In this form, however, it cannot handle uncertainty over the prices/sales value relationship.

outcomes to the left of the curve. Uncertainty about whether cost estimates will be attained or not is easily taken care of by drawing a 'pessimistic estimates' curve, a fixed amount, or fixed percentage above the anticipated curve.

The loss boundary must always emerge as a curve of the shape shown when it is devised as we have done from a series of breakeven points. Some five to seven points are therefore required to enable the charter to draw a good, well fitting free-hand curve to the points.

The next stage is to obtain forecasts on managerial estimates of likely sales out-turns at the price levels previously plotted. These estimates should come from sources quite independent of the production of the loss boundary. If the same analyst or manager has to provide both, he should do the sales estimates first. Again most pessimistic (and most optimistic) estimates can be obtained. When these are entered on the loss boundary chart (Fig. 9.3) we have a widely based set of comparisons between a minimum acceptable and anticipated set of outcomes. It is clear that only a narrow range of all the feasible prices now in fact offers good security and profits prospects. It is prices, sales and costs within this range which can be used as a basis for subsequent discounted cash flow calculations.

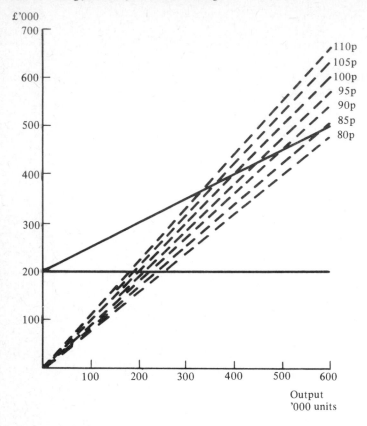

Fig. 9.2 Breakeven with a family of prices
This is an intermediate stage in evolving a loss boundary chart.

One of the four uncertainties outlined above has not yet been dealt with, namely comparison of different versions of the same project, for example, alternative plant with different capacity. Normally only two or three such alternatives exist in practice and it is no great burden to repeat the above analysis for each, and carry feasible outcomes only to further investigation.

This technique is applicable in all situations to which a breakeven analysis may be applied, and does one job which is at the root of much forecasting activity, the elimination of the unacceptable, in a neat and simply operated manner.

9.4 Decision trees

Where management is uncertain about outcomes in the face of a proposed decision, but can say that each of the likely outcomes will result in a particular gain or loss, it is possible to use decision trees as an aid to analysis.

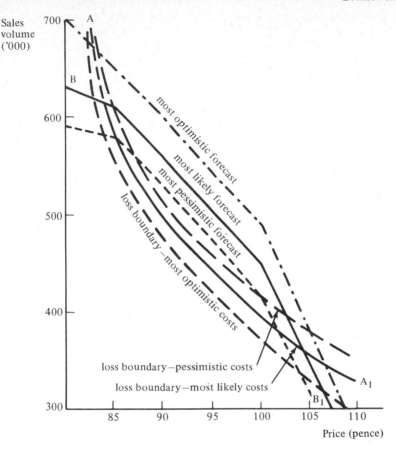

Fig. 9.3 The loss boundary chart complete

The curve AA₁ is the loss boundary curve derived from Fig. 9.2. The more or less parallel curves take into account management's views of optimistic and pessimistic outturns for costs for the project under review. The curve BB₁ gives us management's estimate of likely sales at the range of prices under consideration. A quick reading of this chart clearly suggests a price in the range 90 to 100. Profit on the project is maximized at the price where the vertical distance between the loss boundary and the sales forecast is greatest. This may differ under various conditions of optimism and pessimism about sales and cost outturns, so all nine (or more) cases should be investigated and the anticipated payoff weighted according to management's estimate of the probability that the outcome in question will be achieved.

For example, suppose Magnetized Torque Wrenches is proposing an advertising campaign to promote sales from 500 000 to the capacity 600 000 a year. Without considering the advertising costs, a sales increase of this magnitude would result in an increased contribution to profits and overheads of £50 000 a year (Fig. 9.1).

The agency has proposed two possible campaigns, one costing £10 000 and one costing £20 000, but they are not certain what the sales response to each will be. There are three possible decisions: not to advertise, to adopt the £10 000 campaign or to adopt the £20 000 campaign; each one is associated with a set of likely outcomes, shown in Fig. 9.4.

It is suggested in Fig. 9.4 that the decision not to advertise will result in a zero change in net cash flows, but advertising might produce a range of outcomes, reduced for simplicity's sake to three, full achievement of the target, achievement of half the target, or failure to influence sales at all. Each of these three outcomes is associated with its appropriate decision, and is called an 'event'. The event happens in due course, and management is bound to be uncertain about the likely occur-rence of events but using the methods discussed earlier it is possible to assign probabilities to those, from generalized knowledge and experience. Suggested probabilities are shown in Fig. 9.4; it is thought by management and/or the agency that if they spend £10 000 there are two chances in ten of selling 600 000 widgets, there are five chances in ten of selling 550 000 and three in ten of making no material difference to sales. Spending £20 000 results in the assigned probabilities being more optimistically distributed.

The next stage is to calculate the net cash flow which would result from each event. If we sell 600 000 widgets and we take the contribution per widget as 50p, then gross contribution from 100 000 sales is £50 000. When sales rise by only 50 000 net cash flow is £25 000. If sales do not change then our gross cash flow is zero. The same computation is repeated for each branch of the decision tree.

Thereafter each of the net cash flows is multiplied by the probability of its occurrence. On the decision to spend £10 000 this is £50 000 x 0.2; £25 000 x 0.5 and £0 x 0.3. The results are then added, £10 000 + 12 500 + 0 = 22 500. To obtain the *expected value* to be derived from the decision we must deduct the cost of implementing the decision, namely £10 000, so that the expected value of this decision is £12 500. We must then compare the expected value of the £10 000 advertisement with that of the £20 000 proposal, which turns out to be £50 000 x 0.5 + £25 000 x 0.4 − £20 000 = £15 000.

Does this mean we automatically adopt the £20 000 campaign? By no means. For a start the difference between £15 000 and £12 500 is very small, so although there is an indication here that the big campaign may be more profitable, it is far from overwhelming. However, both campaigns do offer a substantial positive expected value, and one probably better than not advertising (expected value, zero).

In deciding between the £10 000 and £20 000 campaigns, it is necessary first to reconsider the probabilities assigned and the various outcomes. Re-examining the decision tree we will see that of all the individual payoffs, the £10 000 offers the largest, £40 000 though with only a small chance of getting it. Some managers may feel this would be worth going for. Also the £20 000 decision offers the biggest negative cash flow, £20 000, again unlikely, but some managers may feel that this is worth avoiding. Furthermore, there is always an element of arbitrariness in the assignment of probabilities in this way. Suppose the probabilities on the £10 000 were 0.3, 0.5 and 0.2 instead of 0.2, 0.5 and 0.3. Then the expected value would be £17 500 and if the probabilities on the second leg were 0.4, 0.4 and 0.2 the

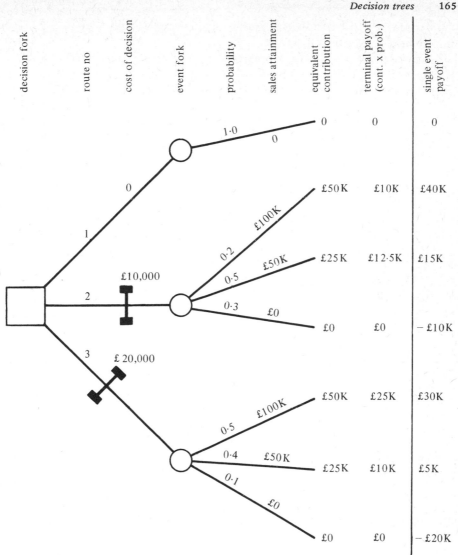

Route 1 Payoff = £0
Route 2 Payoff = £10 K + £12·5 K − £10 K = £12·5 K
Route 3 Payoff = £25 K + £10 K − £20 K = £15 K

Fig. 9.4   Simple decision tree

Trees of this sort incorporate into decisions probabilistic weighting of the (uncertain) outcomes of the decision, provided a measure of the uncertainty can be inputed in the form discussed frequently in this book. As well as showing the expected value of each of the alternatives (labelled 'payoff'), this diagram is laid out so as to highlight each of the individual outcomes which just might occur. Not all of us play the averages — there are those who have risk preference functions!

expected value would be £10 000. None of these changes involves changing a probability by more than one point.

In practice, many decision analyses produce this type of inconclusive result, but such conclusions are by no means useless. In the present case, the best conclusion that can be drawn is that it is difficult to distinguish between the £10 000 and £20 000 decision, but that either is better than not advertising. There is some chance of obtaining the largest net gain from the £10 000 decision, and the largest net loss from the £20 000 decision. Finally, £20 000 represents a much larger fixed commitment than £10 000. Most managements would, on these grounds, probably choose the £10 000 campaign. One can, however, still hear the sales manager exclaim that the big campaign gives him a fifty-fifty chance of selling capacity output, while the small one is unlikely to make it. Who is to say he is wrong?

Decision trees have greater power in handling future studies than are apparent from the discussion so far. This is because they can be used to handle the timing of postponeable decisions. Most decisions are not 'Go–No Go'. They are 'go now or postpone'.

Let us say the widget line is now at capacity and demand is nicely matched by the 600 000 annual throughput, but has been rising more or less steadily, and the underlying demand trend is upward. However, economic cycles have tended to make the demand pattern move in steps followed by plateaux. Right now we are on a plateau and considering an extension to the line. Our knowledge of business cycles suggests that the next jump in demand will be of about 200 000 and that it will occur some time in the next three years, with the following probabilities, next year 0.3, year two 0.5, and year three 0.2.

If we have the capacity to meet demand, it will be worth 50p contribution per unit to us. If we have the capacity but demand does not materialize, we must still meet fixed costs of £60 000 a year. If we do not have the capacity when demand is there the cost in terms of customer goodwill and losses of trade is imputed by sales management to be £20 000 applicable in each year in which we are short (including the discounted cost in the future of recreating the goodwill).

The decision tree for this situation is shown in Fig. 9.5.

From the data given, the best investment strategy is not obvious, but with the help of the possibilities carefully arrayed in tree form, it is not difficult to forecast which will be the best decision sequence. There are three possible strategies which we shall label, Go, No Go/Go, and No Go/No Go/Go. It is not sensible to consider not investing at all since for the purpose of this exercise we are taking it that demand is bound to rise sometime in our period.

The first step in solving our problem is to begin to grow our tree. We start with the square representing our first year's decision fork and draw two branches — the Go and No Go. The symbol ⚏ accompanied by the figure − 180 across the Go route signifies the cost of going this route, as it were a toll for using the road. To make this decision in year 1 means that we shall incur the annual cost of the plant of £60 000 a year. (For simplicity we have omitted the thousands and pounds from the decision tree.) For the moment, ignore the double stroke across this route.

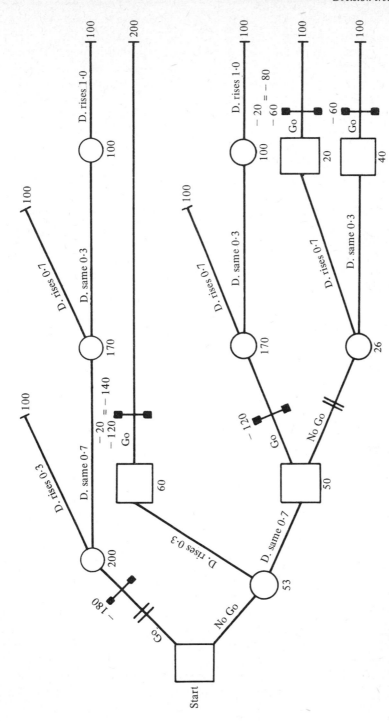

Fig. 9.5 A decision tree involving postponeable decisions

Proceeding on the Go route we come to the first chance fork. Demand rises or it does not and our ideas on the chances of those occurrences are represented by the labels 0.3 and 0.7. If demand does rise we shall get a payoff of £100 000 at the end of the year. If demand remains the same we incur the cost of −£60 000 already taken into account in our toll. We have no further decision to take and hope that next year demand will go up. Since we have already used up 0.3 of our original probability then the probability of a rise in year 2, given that it did not occur in year 1, comes down from five in ten to five in seven, which we take into our table at 0.7 for the sake of arithmetic simplicity. The interested reader can confirm that this makes no difference to the final outcome. Once again if demand does go up we get a payoff of £100. Failing this we know that demand must go up in year 3, so we are certain (p = 1.0) of our payoff of £100 then. We can now figure out how much the Go strategy is worth to us from our position at the start. (Again for simplicity's sake we are not discounting the value of later cash flows.)

In year 3 we are certain of £100K, so we write 100 under the third chance fork. In year 2 we have an 0.7 chance of £100K, which is worth £70K, added to the £100K gives us £170K at the second chance fork. The first year's payoff is worth £100K x 0.3 or £30K, so from the starting position the total payoff is worth £200K, from which we deduct the toll of £180K leaving us with an *expected monetary value* (EMV) (undiscounted) from the Go strategy of £20 000.

Now let's look more briefly at the other two strategies. From the start we go down the No Go route to the first chance fork. If demand has risen in year 1 then there are two consequences: we incur a penalty of £20K for not having had the capacity when it was needed (it's included in the toll), and second we don't have to concern ourselves with whether to invest or not. We go ahead with certainty of a payoff of £200K and tolls of £140K, so that decision fork gives us an expected monetary value of £60K. However, if demand doesn't rise we have to decide. The Go fork looks the same as the first one we did, while if we go down the No Go route for the second time we come to the same chance forks with a 20 penalty should demand have risen and in either case certainty of the need to invest in year 3.

When the tree is complete we should have all the logical routes, all the tolls, probabilities at chance forks, and terminal payoffs; then once again we can start working back. Consider the No Go/No Go route, and perch yourself at the year 3 decision nodes (it does not fork because we have got to invest anyway) and consider what the decisions are worth. In both the terminal payoff is a certain £100K but one toll is inflated by £20K as a penalty for not having had the capacity when demand rose, so our EMV on the first decision is £20K and on the second is £40K. Now hop back to the year 2 decision node. What is your EMV for the No Go route? It's 20 x 0.7 + 40 x 0.3 = 26. Now repeat the same exercise for the Go route from the second decision node. Here your EMV is 170 − the toll of 120 = 50. With the Go route worth £50K and the No Go route worth £26K, naturally you choose the Go route, so we can put a double slash mark across the No Go route to show that we are not interested in it any more.

Now we can hop back to the start and repeat the process. Satisfy yourself that the EMV for the No Go route is 53 and for the Go route is 20, so that we have done the right thing in slashing out the Go route. If we did everything right, then our best decision strategy is No Go/Go.

Of course the Market Research Manager of our mythical company, who is renowned for his original thinking, might well argue that none of these strategies makes much sense, because if we gave him a budget of £5 000 and a month to work in he could come up with a much firmer idea of whether demand were likely to go up this year or not. It is possible to incorporate the value of additional information into the sort of analysis we have just done, and decide whether it is worth while to get more information. This is less a matter of forecasting than of decision analysis, and involves somewhat more complex reasoning than is needed for the simple decision tree. (One of the best coverages of the whole of this fascinating field is to be found in Raiffa, *Decision Analysis* (1968). Professor Raiffa has also been developing a self-instructional package on decision theory, designed, among others, for managers, but at the time of writing this does not appear to have been published.)

9.5 Monte Carlo simulation

Monte Carlo simulation is designed to give managers a clear picture of operational outcomes under sets of circumstances in which many of the events deciding the outcomes are uncertain, and are not under management's control. For example, given particular stock control procedures, how often and for what durations are there liable to be stock outs? How often will stock be above some predetermined level? Another group of questions which can be answered by simulation is, given a particular number of counter clerks, or particular level of service facility, under conditions in which customers arrive at the facility at irregular times and requiring irregular amounts of service, how often and how long will customers have to queue and how often and for how long will service clerks be standing idle? Given the irregularities of the weather, what is the least cost programme for manufacturing and warehousing a weather-dependent article? Given uncertainty over future sales, and hence unpredictable irregularities in cash flow, what is the optimal investment strategy for a company using discounted cash flow procedures for evaluation?

The basic approach to each of these problems is the same, and relies for its success on the idea of a probability distribution of the uncertain future events. We have already handled this idea in a number of ways; using decision trees involves it, dealing with uncertain timings of trade cycle turning points involves it, loss boundary analysis involves it. What we are really saying is that although the specific incidence of any one event cannot be predicted, we can use the range, or distribution, of events to provide very useful information for decision-making.

The only trick in simulation is specifying the probability distribution of events, and a common field of discussion is whether to use equiprobable distributions, or distributions of unequal likelihood of occurrence. For instance, if we refer back to time series regression in chapter 3; there we argued for expressing the range or band of uncertainty of outcomes in quintiles or deciles — five or ten bands each of equal probability of occurrence.

Thus if we take sales in year Y for any product to be at a steady weekly rate of 101 to 110 and assume each outturn 101, 102, 103 . . . 110 to have an equal probability of occurrence, it would be possible to ask a computer to print out a series of numbers between 101 and 110 drawn in random order. We might for instance be concerned with the possibility that 101 might occur three times in succession. The computer would print out a long series of outcomes, and if required would also tell us how often the undesired outcome had occurred. In fact the foregoing example is so trivial that armed with ability to do the maths of probability it is not necessary to use a computer to find the answer.

The service provision example is much more demanding. Here there are two uncertain events: the timing of arrivals of customers and the length of time they require for servicing. Here the analyst requires probability distributions of both, which have to be obtained from direct investigation in accordance with a *pro forma. Thus:*

Customer No.	Arrival time	Departure time	Length of service (minutes)
1	9.03	9.06	3
2	9.03	9.08	5
3	9.05	9.15	10
4	9.06	9.08	2
and so on.			

From such records it is possible to derive the observed distribution of number of arrivals per minute and the length of time in service in the following form.

No. of arrivals per minute	Frequency of occurrence
0	23
1	28
2	16
3	9
4	2
>4	0

Length of service (minutes)	Frequency of occurrence
1	1
2	2
3	8
4	13
.	.
.	.
.	.
14	2
N	= 100

As a result of a number of such sampling operations it is possible to obtain computer simulation input data in a usable form related to the above.

Arrivals per minute	Probability of occurrence
0	0.30
1	0.35
2	0.21
3	0.11
4	0.03
>4	0.0

Service length (minutes)	Probability
1	0.01
2	0.02
3	0.08
4	0.13
.	.
.	.
.	.
14	0.02
	1.00

The computer can now be programmed to print out, minute by minute, the number of customers waiting to be served, and the number of sales people standing idle, under conditions controlled by management such as, varying the number of sales people from one to four, modifying meal break arrangements, arranging to have goods issue handled separately from cash collection or paperwork, and so on.

Visual scanning of such a printout can, of course, provide a mass of useful information to a manager responsible for such decisions. The computer is, however, a more versatile calculator than this, and can cope easily with an instruction only to print out the frequency and duration of outcomes which exceed certain previously determined control limits, and can provide a summary information such as the total idle time of the clerks and the total waiting time of the customers.

From here it is but a short step to programming the computer to search for and print out only the combinations of facilities which do not contravene specific control limits, or even that unique combination which, for example, minimizes clerical idle time, or minimizes total waiting time subject to any imposed constraints.

A much larger step, and one not often taken, is to program the computer with a model relating cost and efficiency of the firm or the market system with measures such as customer waiting and idle capacity, and to instruct the computer to search for and deliver that combination of facilities which would maximize system efficiency.

When we make a probability distribution of expected sales as part of our sales forecast and link the distributed sales to cash flow and through that to investment decisions, cash forecasts and production plans, and ultimately to company profits, we are talking in terms of specifying complex models of complicated business systems. The only way in which any of the business control areas such as profits, contribution, cash flows, budgets and so on can be linked with stochastic* forecasts is through simulation, using a probability distribution of sales about a mean extrapolation as the independent events of the system. To succeed with this technique it is necessary to specify not only the probability distribution of sales, but also a

* Stochastic events are those for which we can produce a probability distribution.

model linking projected sales to the projected control centres. For example, given a model which will suggest the functional relationship between changes in sales levels and changes in the net cash balance, it is possible to simulate the sales outcomes in order to identify the probability of a liquidity crisis.

To summarize, simulation offers management a great deal of predictive power for decision-making provided that probability distributions can be obtained for the uncertain events, and that management has some kind of model relating these events to areas of their activity which they wish to predict and control. As so often in the forecasting business, the most appropriate use of this technique is to high-light the possibility of exceptional conditions against which management should be forewarned.

9.6 Towards business models

Two types of models are relevant to management in a forecasting context: models of markets and models of the functioning of the business. Economists have been creating models of markets for many years, of a form familiar to all who have even the most rudimentary appreciation of economics. Such models, unfortunately, lack predictive power in practice, chiefly because it is very difficult to specify their parameters.

A much more powerful modelling technique is regression analysis, which tries to explain one aspect of market behaviour with reference to a number of others. This model is in the form of a functional relationship, i.e. sales are a function of (say) income, price and advertising.

As we saw in chapter 3, however, there are a great many imperfections in the regression technique, and much attention has been concentrated by business analysts on attempts to create specific models of situations. For example, the field of game theory tries to get at questions of the sort; suppose two of us are com-peting, each facing a system of rewards and penalties in competition with each other, what would my best strategy be in the game? If we change the groundrules (e.g. I seek to maximize my gain rather than minimize my loss) what changes of strategy should I adopt? Conceptually this type of reasoning is now highly developed, and intuitively should be relevant to bidding situations. However, there appears to be no record of successful application to a forecasting problem.

One reason for the slow progress of game theory is undoubtedly its intellectual and methodological complexity, and most analysts seem to be content with much simpler models which specify functional relationships either in linear or log linear form, or in the form of matrices.

The former type is familiar through the regression chapter, but often in a more closely specified form, e.g. an increment of x per cent in advertising in a given medium should produce y per cent change in sales, assuming other advertising in the market is constant. Normally, indeed, even such a conceptually simple model is qualified by recognition of diminishing returns to increasing inputs of advertising, the effects of competitive advertising and the lagged effects of previous advertisements. Such models, then, normally incorporate lag factors and saturation factors, which are covered by using some form of S-shaped curve formula.

More complex still are models which seek to identify optimal conditions given a number of conflicting independent variables, for example, the lowest cost location for a warehouse given inward goods haulage costs, outward distribution haulage costs, variable handling costs and varying requirements for customer service. So far, such models appear to have shown no valid forecasting applications.

The final model type we should mention is the matrix model, of which the input-output table is one. Another form which has had some marketing applications, with some forecasting content is the brand switching matrix, sometimes called a Markov chain. The idea behind this model is that if we can say that a market is divided among competing brands in certain proportions, and if from market research we can determine the probability that in a given period the user of any one brand will switch to another, then by setting up the probabilities of each interbrand switch in a matrix, it is possible to program the computer to print out expected brand shares in all subsequent weeks. The underlying assumption of this technique is that the brand-switching coefficient will remain constant over time. The use of the technique is, of course, to enable marketing managers to spot vulnerable brands on which to exercise their predatory instincts, and to take action to repair any vulnerability detected in their own brand.

The purpose of this section, however, is not to discuss models whose application is specific in any detail, so much as to suggest to managers the value as a mental apparatus of thinking in terms of modelling, and for this purpose the systems model is perhaps the best type to start with. Viewing the operations of the firm and its markets in systems terms is an interesting intellectual exercise, which may well have specific payoffs in the recognition of the interaction of components which depend on each other. The many techniques of forecasting discussed in this book in the end boil down to different ways of trying to get at and analyse relationships between different components of the economic system. Market demand for our products depends on a host of social and economic changes, and evolution of market institutions: our ability to respond to demand changes rests on the management of the system components within our own firm: men, machines, materials and money. The objects of the whole forecasting exercise can be stated in two simple systems propositions. Forecasting involves understanding first, the nature of the economic interactions between our resources, our firm, our markets and the total economy; and second, the directions in which each of these is evolving, no doubt often expressed in probabilistic terms, so that management can judge the degree of consistency between their decisions and the probable evolutions of the relevant systems.

9.7 Summary

All forecasting activity must take account of uncertainty about future events. Uncertainty is immutably lodged in nature, and any decision-making system, or related information system which does not take account of it is extremely deficient. Uncertainty can be handled, albeit crudely, by making a discipline of assessing the probabilities of various relevant potential outturns. A number of techniques are being developed which enable uncertainty to be handled in the decision-making system, notably decision trees and simulation. The costs of probabilistic information inputs to the decision-making system are very much higher than those of 'best estimate' information, and the analytic techniques are more complex. The analyses can be easily handled by computer, especially using interactive systems so that a major hurdle is removed. Nevertheless, probabilistic information is probably worth providing on a routine basis only for the more complex and important decisions.

Beyond the standard and now generally applicable techniques for analysing probabilistic data there is a large number of specific models designed to elucidate a particular aspect of some analyst's relevant system problem: the most relevant approach to evaluating an analyst's modelling proposals is to set them in a framework of an intellectual model of the system for which management is responsible. The question is, will building this model so increase knowledge of the operation of the system that decisions will be better to a degree that makes the cost of model building worth while?

REFERENCE

Raiffa, H. *Decision Analysis: introductory lectures on choices under uncertainty*, Addison-Wesley, 1968.

10 Managing forecasting

10.1 Forecasting and management systems

If this book has tried to convey any one central idea, it is that forecasting is a fundamental aspect of the manager's craft. Leading commentators on management, when classifying the functions of management usually produce a list along the following lines: planning, organizing, controlling and staffing, with a few variations. Invariably the first function listed is planning, whose dictionary definition is along the lines of 'arranging beforehand'. This book has not been about the arranging, but about the beforehand.

Management is only interested in a *relevant* beforehand, and the test of relevance must be in the context of a specific set of decisions giving rise to a specific set of information requirements. Information with a relevance to the future is the product of some sort of information system. The most highly developed management systems available today (normally mounted on computers) are just beginning to break through to an area in which the companies can claim to have the rudiments of an integrated planning and control system covering the key facets of the company's activities — sales budgeting; production scheduling; stock control; cash analysis and so on.

The nature of such systems is that there must be a number of entry points — for example, existing cash, or raw materials inflow. The crucial entry point, however, is that concerning the finished goods or services marketplace. Practically all firms are dependent on sales for the bulk of their revenue. The market is, however, only one aspect of the business environment, which embraces also labour and financial markets, relevant legislation and so on.

One thing which with crystal clarity distinguishes successful from unsuccessful management teams is their quality of awareness of important and relevant environmental changes. Some companies have systems for scanning the business environment and reporting relevant developments. Those in the author's experience are crude in the extreme.

The reason why such awareness is of such overwhelming importance is, of course, that it is the necessary condition for a flexible and adaptable company posture — or at an extreme, the basis for opportunism which may produce temporary windfalls or entry to new markets at the most opportune moments. At the other extreme it can warn of potentially damaging imminent developments. This is the context in which the whole business of forecasting, with its statistics and econometrics and surveys and all should be viewed. As an exercise in applied statistics *per se* forecasting will fail to help produce better decisions. As a development of a system designed to serve the company's needs for information concerning relevant developments in the business environment it can do for any company a job whose cash value will far outreach its cost.

Such a system needs four components — gathering relevant information; storing, retrieving and processing the information in response to specific task requirements; performing such calculations as are necessary to make the information yield its maximum value; reporting findings. It becomes very hard to distinguish the notion of a forecasting system from that of a general environmental scanning system, and there is little need to do so.

What has to be recognized is that, in the present state of the art, the power of statistics helped by a computer to perform the calculations necessary to get the best available answers from the data far outstrips the capacity of most companies' environmental information systems to provide relevant data for calculation. If bricks need straw, forecasts need data, and data is a costly commodity in terms of money and brains.

The problem of evaluating how much environmental data ought to be kept in an information system is that the costs of not having the data are immeasurable. They can theoretically be imputed in terms of wrong decisions, or decisions not made for lack of information: but how many companies try to record the costs of such failures of management foresightedness?

All of this excursion into the realms of theoretical management may alienate the practical reader, who may ask what it all has to do with managing forecasting. In fact it involves a central concept of management without which the chances of any managerially inspired activity going wrong cannot be measured. It involves the classic distinction between hunch and foresight. Management by hunch may work — sometimes. Management by foresight may work more often, more regularly and more predictably.

Of course it is not necessary to have elaborate formal systems of data collection, analysis, storage, retrieval and all the rest in order to have a well managed forecasting system which will measurably contribute to foresighted decisions — these are only appropriate to large organisations where the planning function has become highly devolved to disintegrated functional departments. The critical point is the attitude of mind of the chief executive team towards environmental information with relevance to the future.

Is it coming into the company?

Is it being stored (inside or outside the company) in a readily retrievable form?

Is it being held so that it is available for central analysis irrespective of its source — e.g. market research, sales force, business newspapers, technical periodicals, trade associations, corresponding companies overseas and so on?

Is there a developed network of personal contacts available to those who have to collect and analyse data in response to specific executive questions?

In the well managed company the answers to these questions will be known reasonably unambiguously by all the relevant personnel.

Given that planning is a primary function of the chief executive team, some organizational difficulties emerge if it is decided to delegate that part of planning we call forecasting. If the whole planning process is delegated, up to the point of actual decision, the chief executive is liable to be swamped by a welter of paper as his planning staff work through innumerable variations of many themes. If the task called forecasting is specially delegated, the chap who gets the job is likely to be a young mobile economist/statistician who has been in the company a short time, will leave shortly, and will be unable to communicate with management. If forecasting goes to the sales or marketing functions, it may have the luck to find itself under the market research wing, but the problem is that, at least for some purposes, forecasting needs higher level backing than can normally be given by a desk functionary in market research. Perhaps its happiest home would be in information systems, provided the company's concept of information systems was very much more enlightened than that of conventional financial accounting systems. This, of course, is a very large qualification, and a couple of forecasting chaps grappling with the uncertainties of ten years hence are unlikely to make congenial workmates for accountants striving to balance the records of a year ago.

In the smaller company things are probably easier. The chief executive team probably will not want to delegate planning and forecasting, and can centrally direct and control their own strategic information system, which generally will not be committed to paper. So long as they can readily retrieve the relevant data sources when formal elaboration is needed, then such a straightforward system will save a lot of shedding of sweat; the essential data and the decision parameters all in the head of a single decision taker is the most effective system there is.

Where calculation and processing are needed beyond the most rudimentary level, the processes outlined in this book are well within the scope of any manager; if he wants more elaborate help, there are two sources, both inexpensive and normally anxious to help. One is a computer bureau, of which there are several competing in every large town. They are in business to solve problems which have been framed in numerical terms. The other is the statistics or economics staff of the nearest university, business school or college, who normally welcome the chance to work on real problems and charge very little for their time. This last resource can often help also by providing knowledge of data sources not normally kept in the firm, and may allow access to their libraries. Such libraries form an invaluable back-up data store which companies simply do not try to use. This is little short of criminal negligence.

The foregoing relates particularly to the case where a company has a fully-fledged forecasting department. But the essence of this book has been that while such organizational appendages are no doubt a highly desirable luxury, for most firms they are not a basic necessity.

Anyone with a little practice can extrapolate lines on paper, or conduct complex regression calculations on an on-line terminal. Any manager with strategic responsibilities can and should master enough economics and statistics to enable him to interpret relevant data from the environment. The crux of this book has been to emphasize that a systematic scanning process, a mastery of the elementary tools of evaluation, and a consciousness of how decision problems can be broken down into specifically answerable questions, provide a powerful weaponry for the chief executive not only of the giant corporation, but also of the smaller and medium-sized companies whose survival depends upon flexible response to a changing business environment.

10.2 Criteria for forecast evaluation

The choice of forecasting method, it has been argued, should be determined principally by the uses to which the forecast results are to be put. Every forecasting project proposal should be prefaced by the questions 'Why is this forecast being constructed?' and 'How will the results be used?'

The first criterion by which one evaluates a forecast, or set of forecasts, and the methodology employed, is in terms of relevance to the project in hand. For many purposes a very rough and ready sort of projection is fully adequate, offering no more than a feel for which way some trends are moving, and whether market or capacity saturations are being reached. There is no point in producing refined estimates in this sort of situation. At the other extreme, for example, are the problems facing electricity planners, where the national cost of having idle capacity in terms of vastly expensive generating sets is matched only by the national cost in terms of power cuts of having insufficient capacity. Almost any amount of sophistication is justified if it can produce even a fraction of 1 per cent improvement in the accuracy or reliability of such a forecast.

If a simple projection on a piece of graph paper produces results as accurate and reliable as those of a complex computer model or an extensive piece of market research, then it is to be preferred, first because it is simpler to sell to the decision-makers (who have to believe in the forecasts), second, because it is cheap, third because it is quick. If, on the other hand, results cannot be obtained by simple means within the required limits of accuracy and confidence, then recourse is needed to the more expensive and time-consuming methods.

After relevance, the second criterion for valid forecasting is *accuracy*. Curiously, however, one does not mean entirely accuracy of final result, so much as accuracy of reasoning. It is easy to assert that Britain's GNP (gross national product) is

£'000 m

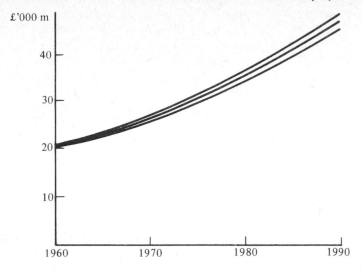

Fig. 10.1 Gross national product projected at rates of growth of 2.6, 2.7, and 2.8 per cent per annum. In terms of aggregate national income, and hence of any variable which we feel may be tied to GNP, it does not make a lot of difference which rate we choose.

£'000 m

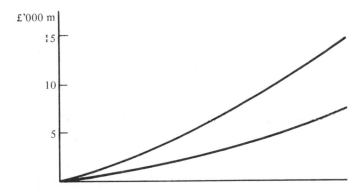

Fig. 10.2 Marginal discretionary consumers' income generated by GNP growth rates of 2.6 and 2.8 per cent. If we have a product (say a consumers' durable innovation or leisure item) which is competing for a share of the new growth income, then it makes a lot of difference which aggregate growth rate we pick.

growing, say, at 2.7 per cent per annum compound. On this basis one can go ahead to project GNP to the millennium if desired, and for some time at least the projections are likely to be fairly accurate. The fact that GNP is actually moving at 2.6 or 2.8 per cent would hardly be noticed at first. But a new luxury product which was trying to obtain a slice out of the new income wedge opening up could be significantly affected by the difference. Compare Figs. 10.1 and 10.2. Figure 10.1 might be relevant for planning basic utilities supply where there may be taken to be an existing match between services and demand but if, as an air conditioning producer, one has a target of say 2 per cent of all new discretionary income to be generated between 1970 and 1990, it matters very much which target one picks.

Whether 2.7 per cent is right or wrong matters, but what matters much more, particularly in the Fig. 10.2 case, is that the premises on which the 2.7 per cent are arrived at are stated, that the indicators to watch to obtain early warning of a deviation from 2.7 per cent are clearly shown, and that the implications for the overall forecast of such deviations are explicit. Having stressed that inaccurate results matter less than inaccuracies or faults in reasoning, it of course remains true that a forecasting method which consistently provides accurate predictions is invaluable — and many professional forecasters keep a small private menagerie of methods which work consistently and reliably but which are logically so spurious that they quail at the thought of ever publicizing them. Accuracy and error in forecasting are taken up in subsequent sections of this chapter.

The third criterion for a valid forecast is *plausibility*, both of result and of method. If decision-makers cannot be convinced of the validity of both the results and the method then the exercise is futile as the results will be unacceptable. This, incidentally, constitutes one of the barriers to the introduction of conceptually sophisticated forecasting methods in business; the executives have neither time nor inclination to master the explanations of what has been done.

Fourth is *durability*: once set up, the forecast should be capable of reasonably simple repetition and/or updating as necessary, and the validity of the methodology should not depend upon temporary phenomena in the economy.

Fifth, *flexibility*: the forecast should be capable of absorbing information from sources not originally available, and of being varied simply in response to changed circumstances through the forecast period. For example, if there is a forecast of steadily rising sales of a particular product over five years, and in the course of year two sales are observed to be falling rapidly, it is futile to maintain the original five-year forecast as if nothing had happened; new or amended information must be sought and taken into account to produce a revised forecast.

The sixth criterion is availability and *timeliness*. If the planning or decision-making executives cannot have their information by the required decision dates, for reasons of data non-availability or disorganization, the forecasting exercise is pointless. Better a simple forecast when needed than a superb job three months too late.

The seventh criterion on which a forecast may be judged is *precision*. It is conceptually possible to make a forecast absolutely precise, but few of us would ever care to undertake the exercise. Within the budget limits of the forecast operation, set by the degree to which errors in the final forecast will cost money, only a given degree of accuracy and precision can be achieved. These are not the same thing, although they both refer to possible errors in results. It is easier to ensure greater precision by devoting more resources and effort to constructing the forecast than it is to ensure greater accuracy.

A forecast which is 100 per cent accurate will give as the most probable outcome that which is realized in the event. A forecast which is supposed to be 100 per cent

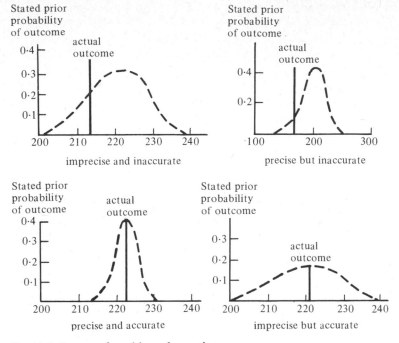

Fig. 10.3 Degrees of precision = forecasting

precise states that the predicted outcome is the only possible one. Figure 10.3 should make this clear.

The more imprecise the forecast, the easier it is to show an appearance of accuracy and vice versa. When evaluating forecasts, therefore, the degree of precision must be taken into account as well as the accuracy of the results.

Finally, we can turn to the *sensitivity* of forecasts. One of the principal determinants of the probability of error of a forecast is the confidence which can be placed in the relationship between the forecast dependent variable (e.g. sales) and the independent variables. Statistically there may be greater or less confidence in the relationship, but even where there is a high degree of confidence statistically, there remains the problem of how confident the forecaster is of the forecast which may have been adopted for an independent determining variable. If the forecaster is doubtful about either the stability of the relationship or the likely future performance of the underlying determinants of the forecast, the problem of sensitivity arises.

This involves us in a consideration of two further phenomena, the statistical significance and the commercial significance which may be attached to the forecaster's confidence limits. A close correlation with an independent variable in which little confidence can be placed may turn out to be statistically highly significant. This may or may not affect the sensitivity of the forecast, depending on whether unpredicted variations in the independent variable will so alter the forecast result as to push its decision-making implications from a Go to a No Go situation or vice versa. Such a forecast may be statistically stable, but highly sensitive to changes in the independent variables. However, if the spread of potential outcomes lies principally within either an acceptable or an unacceptable commercial range, then the forecast is not commercially sensitive. Precisely the same argument can be applied to the degree of confidence placed in the correlations among dependent and independent variables. The most desirable course of action, then, is to select independent determining variables (*a*) for the degree of confidence with which they may be projected, and (*b*) for the quality of the correlations which can be obtained between them and the dependent variables.

The problem of sensitivity goes beyond this, however, and also depends on the extent to which the forecast result leans on the behaviour expected of a particular variable. Even with a confident forecast of some chosen independent variable, and confident prediction that the future course of the relationship between the two will remain as it has been in the past, the forecast may be more or less sensitive to the behaviour of the independent variable or the relationship. This degree of sensitivity depends on the extent to which the final forecast result would vary as and when the behaviour of either of the two factors varies.

Thus, if the only forecast methodology adopted by a forecaster predicting sales of babies' nappies was to correlate nappy sales with crude birth rate, the forecast would be highly sensitive to changes in either the correlation coefficient through time or to changes in the Registrar General's predictions of crude birth rate. To reduce such sensitivity, the forecast method might also embrace regression of nappy sales on time, correlation of nappy sales with, say, promotional expenditure, and would utilize techniques not dependent on statistical production such as market research or opinion polling.

In summary, there are two stages in the control of sensitivity of forecasts: first, the reduction by the forecaster of uncertainty about the quality of his inputs, either factual or methodological, and second, the spreading of the 'burden of proof' of the forecast over as many 'witnesses' as possible.

The final aspect of sensitivity is that it may only be a relevant consideration in one direction. If the problem at issue is one of, say, planning the introduction of a new product, and if the breakeven point on the product is specified as *n* units throughout per annum, the forecaster may be required to specify only that sales will be greater than *n*. A forecast over *n* which is more sensitive upwards than downwards is good ground for proceeding, and a forecast of about *n* sensitive in the opposite direction is equally easy to interpret. This phenomenon is analogous to the phenomenon of skewed distributions in statistics, as illustrated in Fig. 10.4.

10.3 Getting at the data

Data are the inputs to the forecasting process. By data, we mean that body of information relating to past performance through the interpretation of which a forecast will be constructed. The information in the data base is of two types, numerical and

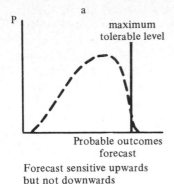

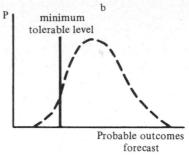

Fig. 10.4   Forecast sensitivity

interpretative. Numerical data are of a fairly familiar statistical type, either time series of, e.g. sales, or the results of census or sample surveys of some aspect of the situation under investigation. These may also be held in non-numerical form (e.g. opinions). Data such as, for example, production capacity frontiers are also held in this form.

The act of creating a forecast depends on interpreting the data contained in the base, attempting to ascribe reasons for observed changes over time, evaluating the extent to which these reasons will cause the data to change differently (and by how much) or remain the same over the future, and to ascribe numbers to the projected situation based on these interpretations.

The store of expertise, knowledge and experience used in these interpretations forms another part of the data base. Three types of training and skill are required fully to interpret the movements over time in data relating to business perform-ance: those of the manager, the economist and the statistician. The problems of interpretation are so complex that ideally it should be performed by a team including both training and experience in these three sets of skills. Only in this way is it possible to ensure that the interpretative base has sufficient width (in terms of spread of skills), length (in terms of experience), and depth or texture (in terms of imaginative and positive injection of original and systematic thinking into the fore-casting process) to ensure that as many as possible of the relevant aspects of the problem have been taken into account.

Interpretation of data is one cornerstone of valid forecasting, and valid forecast-ing depends largely on the art of interpretation. In many forecasting operations, much effort and expenditure on the collection of superb sets of past data is nulli-fied through lack of intelligence and imaginative interpretation.

Numerical data bases are normally tailored to fit the requirements of the fore-cast, and their dimensions depend on the time scale, complexity, and required precision and sensitivity of the forecast. Generally speaking, the length of the numerical data base should be at least as long as the forecast period as a rule of thumb. Many cases can be visualized in which much longer data bases may be required in order to ensure confidence in, say, the quality of regressions, but it will rarely be possible to shorten the data base without running into pretty severe risks of inadequacy.

If great expense and effort is involved in uncovering very early data or in their interpretation, this may not be justified as the gain in reliability of the results is likely to be rather low.

The width of the data base may have important repercussions on the sensitivity of the forecast, as discussed above. This concept of width implies first the range of data forming the different independent variables determining the forecast which may be used for forecasting by a common method, e.g. regression; and second, the range of different data classes, amenable to different methods. In most practical situations the range of relevant base data which can be made available is highly restricted, and the general problem is to find sufficient width to reduce the sensitivity of the forecast in relation to the obvious first choice determinants.

Summarizing, width may mean the uncovering of a number of series of independent variables all of which may be regarded as relevant determinants of the dependent variable, with all which the latter may be (say) correlated; alternatively it may mean the collection of a variety of types of data to be used independently by the best available methodologies, after which results will be compared. Generally speaking, the greater the width of the data base the lower the sensitivity of the forecast, and hence the greater the confidence that may be placed in the results.

The third dimension of the data base may be thought of as depth, implying such characteristics as reliability of accuracy of the raw data, relevance for the required application, the extent to which they may be transformed with a minimum of skulduggery into a forecastable form (one often has to stretch credibility of interpretation and manipulation quite far in transforming raw facts into usable data — a process often not unjustly referred to as cooking), and the degree to which they may be validated in terms of their consistency with related data already accepted as reliable, and data referring to deeper sectors of the economy.

Sources of data are as numerous as the data series themselves. Many of the better known ones are listed in the Appendix, but generally the most relevant and reliable data are to be found in the files of the forecasting organization. Frequently, however, such information does not exist in usable form for forecasting, having been collected for quite different applications; even after transformation much of the data may be of indifferent reliability. As with all information searches, the data search inside as well as outside the firm is a costly, time-consuming and frustrating business but it has to be undertaken with as much thoroughness as resources will allow. This problem can be mitigated by greater managerial attention to the relevance of the company information system to decision-making needs.

10.4 Specifying forecasting projects

In the light of earlier parts of this chapter, a reasonable question arises. In face of the fact that forecasting is an activity serving varied managerial ends, but involving specialized skills both in formulation and construction of forecasts and fitting them to specific management needs, who should specify the firm's forecast requirements?

The practical reason for posing this question is that not infrequently forecasting departments come into being under the wing of marketing, finance or operational research directors or managers, without any clear expectation of what forecasting is expected to do for the firm, and without any formal channels of communication with the executive parts of the business except at a fairly senior level. Frequently a new section has to perform ill-defined tasks on the corporate planning/fixed capital investment level, and these, as was indicated at the outset of this book, tend to be among the most complex of forecasting jobs. The new skills are only finding their feet in the firm, time constraints are likely to be severe, data files need to be created from raw facts, the essential trial and error process of refining forecasts cannot be fully carried out until much more experience is gained, and the result is that the new department chases its own tail for some time, answerable to a senior manager for whom it forms only a partial responsibility and lacking any serious opportunity to validate its potential contribution to the firm at all levels of management.

If the early results turn out to be indifferent, the chances are that the general reaction of the firm's managers to forecasting as a useful activity will range from indifference through disenchantment to outright hostility. The man in charge of a forecasting operation requires, therefore, to be first of all acceptable to a large segment of the management structure in personality, qualifications and experience as a useful specialist supporter of managerial effort. Managers in turn must be prepared to show him how they feel more reliable forecasts could help their decisions, with specific instances, and he must avail himself of every occasion to investigate such opportunities.

If this task is performed seriously and imaginatively the result will be an embarrassment of riches in terms of potential projects. These have to be ranked in order of priority by the forecasters, not only in terms of their importance to the firm but also at least initially, in terms of the speed with which valuable results may be got out, in order to establish forecasting as something which produces results. If the first two years of a unit's life are passed in refining estimates for hypothetical long-range plans most managers will wonder whether the unit is not simply a totally non-productive overhead. The many disappointed customers in the queue also have to know why they are required to wait, what can be done for them, and when they may expect some action. If the initial groundwork is properly laid the problem of the managers specifying the unforecastable, or the forecasters specifying the irrelevant need not occur.

The kernel of the thing is cooperative effort. This must be instituted by the senior forecaster putting his offerings in the shop window initially, promising to deliver only what he can expect to achieve, and then keeping his promises. He must make the approach. In response to intelligent approaches, managers are normally willing to be flexible in their requirements, especially as they begin to understand both the potential and the limitations of organized forecasting. They will learn what sort of projects they want specified and how to formulate their requests in such a way as to enable sensible forecasting to proceed.

While, therefore, the initial approach may come from the forecaster in search of projects, managers must define their project needs. Once a clear project definition has been evolved it is up to the forecaster again to specify objectives, method, time-table and budget, and to have these ratified by management as appropriate.

This vital aspect of the forecasting operation should not be left to chance, nor can it be conducted through interdepartmental memos or *pro formas*, at least in the early stages of the forecasting unit's life. If demand for services grows to such proportions that all project specifications cannot be economically handled on a face-to-face basis, then is the time for routinization of definition and specification procedures — but even then only as a means of sieving projects for acceptability. The forecaster who resorts to written contact as his main vehicle of communication with management before he is grossly overloaded with demands for forecasts has admitted total failure to get on a wavelength compatible with managers' ways of working. No forecast should ever be conducted without its objectives and uses having been thoroughly discussed in personal contact with the manager requesting the project.

10.5 What sort of forecasting systems?

In the whole field of management, important words tend to have multiple meanings: none more so than the word 'system'. In this book we have mentioned such ideas as forecasting systems, information systems, decision-making systems, analytical systems, management systems and no doubt some others. This section responds to the valid question 'what exactly do we mean by "systems"?'

It is clear that while the concept 'system' has central, unifying features, used as we have used the word, it may in practice mean a lot of quite different things, for the concept is highly abstract, and applicable in widely varying contexts.

The unifying features are these: a system is a vehicle, pattern or methodology designed to secure the achievement of some objective, or which, although not apparently designed to do so, has the effect of achieving some unitary end. Thus the solar system keeps the planets revolving round the sun, a navigation system keeps a ship on course, and an accounting system delivers proper accounts. The second essential facet of a system is that within itself it provides for automatic control of its own achievement towards its objective. Loss of control defines a condition of system disintegration. The third necessary condition for the existence of a system is that there should be some definable sequence of actions, processes and/or components which are interlinked or integrated in some way. Summarizing, in abstract we can say that a system is a set of processes or components, systematic-ally linked to each other so as to produce some outcome and in such a way that progress towards that outcome is internally controlled.

By this definition, the economy is a system, a firm is a system, a market is a system, or a business system is a system. At this point we must recognize a fourth aspect: that any given system is likely to be a component of another. Thus the solar system is a component of the galactic system and the earth and moon are gravitational systems within the solar system. It follows that whenever people are using techniques of any sort to produce specified results, then the people are part of the system designed to produce those results.

Thus markets are components of the economic system: firms are components of the market system: managements are components in the business system and forecasting is a component of the system of management. Within forecasting, one subsystem may be exponential smoothing systems; another may be a chief executive/chief forecaster interaction designed to generate an informed critical view of a series of statistical projections being fed into a long-range planning exercise.

In other words, a current fallacy, that systems are only to do with computers, is a pity. Systems are much more general. Another unfortunate fallacy is the notion that there exists 'a system' which exists only to be defeated by all right thinking humans. One must accept that many systems exist which deserve to be defeated by people with liberated minds, but the problem of delivering material things of human wellbeing is sufficiently awe-inspiring to require systems, and a systematic approach, to enable the task to be tackled. Since this is the task of business organizations, it is unquestionably proper that managements should take a systems view of the whole affair. This is not an Orwellian vision in which all our lives are to be run all the time in conformity with computer programmes: for most of us it is an essential precondition for minimization of the drudgery of unavoidable mechanistic work, and the ultimate release of every individual to seek after his personal gods, which presumably is the end towards which we would all aspire to shape our social system.

Clearly some systems occur naturally, but most of those with which management is concerned are manmade, and are designed to serve man's ends. Strictly in a context of forecasting it is necessary to recognize some constraints on system design. First, it is necessary for people to interact with data, and with data manipulation. processes, for a forecasting system to make any sort of sense. Therefore any system in which the design is so complex or the processes so intellectually sophisticated that their understanding is closed except to a select intellectual elite is unacceptable. The purpose of forecasting systems is better management decision-making. If understanding the essential elements of the system is beyond the specific intellectual skill (for example, in mathematics) or beyond the time available to the user manager for comprehension, the system is to that extent deficient.

Since forecasting is a process in management systems and management decisions are invariably time-constrained, we have another overriding reason for sticking pragmatically to simple systems which can be made to work.

The third overriding constraint is that not only must user management be able to understand the system output, and how it was obtained, they must also be in a position to contribute meaningfully and relevantly to the system inputs. It is here that a variety of human skills in interviewing and interacting between those responsible for the forecast creation process and those responsible for operating the management system must be given a great deal of attention. This is imperative. It is too often underdone, because it is too difficult for all the parties.

The final imperative in designing forecasting systems is that the system must fit the need. There must always be an element of '*ad hoc*-ery' about forecasting systems, founded on intrinsic variations in markets, organizations, management styles and objectives, data and the dispositions of the forecasters. This is not necessarily bad. It is probably essential in ensuring that the forecasting system remains relevant, flexible and up to date. To summarize, systems for forecasting must be, and be seen by management to be, relevant, simple, timely and flexible, and to give due weight to management and other expert human inputs.

10.6 What sort of management?

What can a mere author offer in the area of management style? Nothing, really, which has not been said innumerable times before: and yet, in a sense, all that has gone into this book has been about management style. The need for a book such as this, the sole motivation for writing it, has been a belief that in ever more crowded marketplaces, with ever more sophisticated products and services, and with ever increasing stake money before you can get into the marketplace at all, a very careful appraisal is required of what you will be able to achieve there. More and more management time will be needed for investigation and analysis, for planning and coordinating, to ensure that you will be able to stay in the marketplace and not lose your stake money.

Systematic appraisal is one of the keys without which you will be locked out of the game. If this book has helped a little in explicating some of the more important aspects of appraisal of the future, in terms which managers will find meaningful, then it will have achieved its objective. If it should turn out to help promote a systems view of management, this would be doubly gratifying.

10.7 Summary and conclusions

This concluding section attempts to synthesize the preceding discussions. It is an open question whether its most appropriate position is here, at the end, or at the beginning. This position has been chosen because it is easier to communicate once many basic propositions have been dealt with.

The book has been largely concerned with basic propositions: with attempting to state the fundamentals of management in respect of forecasting and the fundamentals of forecasting in respect of management. The unifying notion with which we have worked has been that of forecasting systems as contributors to management decision-making systems, and we have tried to work those notions pragmatically from the point of view of the manager towards a synthesis. We have not adopted a rigorous standpoint for the definition of systems, processes or objectives, because the management process is not amenable to full mathematical rigour. Management is about people, and so there can be no mathematically rigorous science of management. This is not to imply that there can be no disciplines, and no systems, and what we have tried to do in this book is to examine one by one the main disciplines and systems which have offered contributions towards the solution of the management problem of prediction, and to see whether they can be made to fit an overall view of the prediction and decision-making problem. We have not been able to come up with a central, unifying view of forecasting. We find that the disciplines still tend to live separately in economics, statistics, and market and other surveys. While this is so forecasting cannot be more than an aggregation of helpful, but limited, techniques.

But an aggregation of techniques without a central discipline does not make a system, any more than a collection of 1 000 men with rifles makes an army. We are allowed to talk about forecasting systems as such, only inasmuch as these are developed from the central point of information systems which form a wider theme than that of this book. Information systems of course, conceptually lock directly into planning, decision-making and control systems.

Some of the techniques of forecasting can be made to fit the techniques which are emerging to help decision-making. Classical time series analysis, long under a scholarly cloud, will probably be rehabilitated because its flexibility makes it uniquely adaptable to a wide range of decision situations. Exponentially smoothed time series will continue to develop as a basis for stock control and production scheduling systems, and although many improvements remain to be developed in the physical (hardware and software) systems, the basic principles will be in use for a long time.

The above two techniques represent the search for regularities in data, and their application to extrapolation in some direction or another. The third technique to contribute to the search for regularities is regression analysis, using time as the independent variable. In this, regression is probably being abused: our justification for retaining the technique, which amounts to no more than a sophisticated version of drawing our ruler through a set of points, is that it is a cheap and easily repeated method of getting rough snapshots of the situation.

More properly, regression lies in the field of the search for relationships amongst sets of data. Despite a number of formidable technical problems in the way of using regression on economic time series, the massive developments which have taken place in interactive computing in the past few years have brought this technique to a level where the manager can make his own analyses on a day-to-day basis, given only a few hours' training. It is hard to believe that ten years ago this was perhaps the most exotic technique in the armoury of the high-powered mathematical economists. Today it is actually useful. Still under development, but likely soon to become useful to practising managers on a day-to-day basis is input-output analysis, the other great set of economic regularities whose course the forecaster expects to pursue.

The third battery of techniques lies in the search for responses: market surveys, polls of executive opinion, sounding the oracles, making composites of sales force expectation, and all the rest. The great deficiency in these, as they are commonly practised, is failure to specify the objectives of the inquiry sufficiently clearly at the outset, and to stick to them. Especially, are the analysts clear on how they can quantify the responses on a meaningful scale, so that comparisons can be made among groups and through time?

This brings us to one of the fundamental points of this book, which cannot be overstressed. This is the absolute necessity of detailed statement and justification of the need for and objectives of any forecasting project, clear definition of what role it is to serve in the decision-making system, and the quality of the information it will be able to contribute to that system. To this end, forecasters have to rely very much on other people's work — Government and the United Nations, the Registrar General, Bank of England and Treasury: independent bodies such as the National Institute of Economic and Social Research, and the newspaper models, notably *The Sunday Times* and the *Sunday Telegraph*: industries and trade associations, large customers and any other relevant sources.

In the end, a forecast is the work of human ingenuity: it is to serve managerial ends, so that its production involves a synthesis of economic, social, mathematical and managerial inputs. Business forecasts cannot always be judged by the quality of their predictions, for it eventually becomes management's job to make them come true. The acid test is this. Does it work?

Appendix

Some principal British data and forecast sources
Publications of Her Majesty's Stationery Office
Abstract of Regional Statistics
Agricultural Statistics
Annual Abstract of Statistics
Annual Report of the Central Electricity Generating Board
Annual Report of Commissioners of HM Inland Revenue
Bankruptcy General Annual Report
Business Monitor
Census of England and Wales
Census of Scotland
Company Assets, Income and Finance
Companies General Annual Report
Digest of Scottish Statistics
Digest of Welsh Statistics
Economic Trends
Family Expenditure Survey
Financial Statistics
Highway Statistics/Housing Statistics
Input-Output Tables (see p. 33)
Insurance Business — Summary of Accounts and Statements
Life and other Long-Term Insurance Business — Full Accounts and Statements
List of Principal Statistical Services
Ministry of Agriculture Machinery Census

Ministry of Power Statistical Digest
Monthly Bulletin of Construction Statistics
National Food Survey
National Income and Expenditure
National Plan 1965
Overseas Trade Accounts of the United Kingdom
Overseas Trade Statistics
Registrar General Statistical Review of England and Wales — Population
Report of the Census of Distribution
Report of the Census of Production
Statistics on Income, Prices, Employment and Production
Summary of Activity at United Kingdom Aerodromes
Trade and Industry, Journal of the Department of Trade and Industry

Other publications

Bank of England Quarterly Bulletin: Bank of England Intelligence Department
Basic Marketing Statistics for the United Kingdom: Bureau of Commercial Research
Basic Road Statistics: British Road Federation
British Economy, Key Statistics, 1900—1964: London and Cambridge Economic
Service
Building Societies Statistics: Building Societies' Association
CBI *Industrial Trends Inquiry*: Confederation of British Industries
Co-operative Statistics: The Co-operative Union
Digest of Port Statistics: National Ports Council
Economic Forecast for Great Britain: Rediffusion Television Ltd.
Economic Review: National Institute of Economic and Social Research
Quarterly Economic Reviews: Economic Intelligence Unit
Iron and Steel Monthly Statistics: British Steel Corporation
Iron and Steel Annual Statistics: British Steel Corporation
Monthly Statistical Review: Society of Motor Manufacturers and Traders
Monthly Statistics of the Textile Council: Textile Council
Moodies' Industries and Commodities Service: Moodies Service Ltd.
Motor Industry of Great Britain: Society of Motor Manufacturers and Traders
Neilson Index Services: — Confectionery
                        Drugs
                        Food
                        Pharmaceuticals
Neilsen Farmers' Panel
Neilsen Specialist Sheep Panel, A. C. Neilsen Co.
Retail Business: Economic Intelligence Unit
SMMB Monthly Bulletin: Scottish Milk Marketing Board
Statistical Review: British Cycle and Motor Cycle Industries Association
United Kingdom Statistics: National Manufacturers Association
Year Book of Timber Statistics

Further reading

This short list, selected from the extensive literature on forecasting, consists of works which carry the arguments of the present book to a further level of sophistication, or which give more detail on selected aspects of forecasting.

General

Busch, Gerald A. 'Prudent manager forecasting', *Harvard Business Review*, May–June, 1961.

Butler, William F. and Kavesh, Robert A. *How Business Economists Forecast*, Prentice-Hall, 1966. An extensive series of readings in which business economists relate how they approach problems in forecasting.

National Industrial Conference Board, *Forecasting Sales*, Business Policy Study No. 106, 1964.

Reichard, Robert S. *Practical Techniques of Sales Forecasting*, Prentice-Hall, 1966. Discusses a large number of techniques, largely at appreciation level and attempts to relate them to management requirements. The approach is a little dated.

Robinson, Colin. 'Some principles of forecasting in business', *Journal of Industrial Economics*, **14**, No. 1, 1965.

Economic forecasting

Ball, R. J. and Burns, T. 'An econometric approach to short run analysis of the U.K. economy, 1955–56', *Operational Research Quarterly*, September 1968. Forecasts produced by Ball and Burns and published quarterly in *The Sunday Times*.

Beckerman, W. *The British Economy in 1975*, Cambridge University Press for National Institute of Economic and Social Research, 1965.

Brech, Ronald. *Planning Prosperity: a synoptic model for growth*, Darton, Longman & Todd, 1964

Brech, Ronald. *Britain in 1984*, Darton, Longman & Todd, 1963.

Department of Economic Affairs. *The Task Ahead*, HMSO, 1969.

National Economic Development Council. *Conditions Favourable to Faster Growth*, HMSO, 1963.

National Economic Development Council. *Growth of the U.K. Economy to 1966*, HMSO, 1963.

National Institute Economic Review, published quarterly by the National Institute of Economic and Social Research, contains carefully developed forecasts.

Roy, A. D. 'Short term forecasting for central economic management of the U.K. economy', in K. Hilton and D. F. Heathfield, eds, *The Econometric Study of the U.K.*, Macmillan, 1970.

Streissler, E. W. *Pitfalls in Econometric Forecasting*, Institute of Economic Affairs, 1970.

The National Plan, Cmnd 2764, HMSO, 1965.

Input-output analysis

Central Statistical Office. *Input Output Tables for the United Kingdom, 1954*, HMSO, 1961. Contains a general account of Input output.

Central Statistical Office. *Input Output Tables for the United Kingdom, 1963*, Studies in Official Statistics, No. 16, HMSO, 1970.

Chenery, H. B. and Clark, P. G. *Interindustry Economics*, Wiley, 1959.

'Provisional Input Output Tables for 1968', *Economic Trends*, No. 207, HMSO, 1971.

Leontieff, Wassily. *Input-Output Economics*, Oxford University Press, 1966.

Time trends

Battersby, Albert. *Sales Forecasting*, Cassell, 1968.

Croxton, F. E. and Cowden, D. J. *Practical Business Statistics*, Prentice-Hall, 1960.

Dyckman, T. R. and Stekler, H. O. 'Probabilistic Turning Point Forecast', *Review of Economics and Statistics*, **48**, No. 3, 1966.

Mathematical Trend Curves: an aid to forecasting, ICI Monograph No. 1, Oliver & Boyd, 1964.

Regression and econometric modelling

Carlson, J. A. 'Forecasting errors and business cycles', *American Economic Review*, **57**, No. 3, 1967.

International Business Machines Corporation. *Concepts and Applications of Regression Analysis*, IBM Data Processing Application, 1967.

Robinson, Colin. *Business Forecasting, an economic approach*, Nelson, 1971. Written primarily for students of economics, and concentrating particularly on regression methods, this is probably the best book with which to follow the present work.

Spencer, M. H., Clark, Colin and Hoguet, P. W. *Business and Economic Forecasting*, Irwin, 1961. Offers a non-technical approach to multiple regression and a number of detailed cases of forecasts using this method.

Theil, H. *Applied Economic Forecasting*, North Holland, 1966. Highly technical, for econometricians only.

Walters, A. A. *An Introduction to Econometrics*, Macmillan, 1968.

Adaptive forecasting

Imperial Chemical Industries. *Short-term Forecasting*, ICI Monograph No. 2, Oliver & Boyd, 1964.

International Business Machines Corporation. *Retail IMPACT: Inventory management program and control techniques*, IBM Application Program, IBM, 1967.

McLaughlin, R. L. 'The breakthrough in sales forecasting', *Journal of Marketing*, **27**, 1963, 46—54.

The economy

Cairncross, Sir A., ed. *Britain's Economic Prospects Reconsidered*, Allen & Unwin, 1970.

Caves, Richard E. and Associates. *Britain's Economic Prospects*, Brookings Institution, 1968.

Prest, A. R. *The U.K. Economy: a manual of applied economics*, Updated biennially.

Stonier, A. W. and Hague, D. C. *A Textbook of Economic Theory*, Longman, 1964.

Surveys

Adler, Max. *British Market Research Organisations and Services*, Crosby Lockwood, 1965.

Ferber, R. 'Anticipations Statistics of Consumer Behaviour', *American Statistician*, **20**, No. 4, 1966.

Heald, Gordon. 'The relationship of intentions to buy consumer durables with levels of purchase', *British Journal of Marketing*, Summer, 1970.

Juster, F. T. 'Consumer buying intentions and purchase probability, an experiment in survey design', *Journal of the American Statistical Association*, **61**, No. 315, 1966.

Moser, C. A. and Kalton, G. *Survey Methods in Social Investigation*, 2nd edn, Heinemann, 1971.

Parker, E. F. 'Forecasting future market profiles by the Delphi method', *The Business Economist*, 3, No. 1, 1971.

Technological forecasting

Jantsch, Eric. 'Forecasting the future', *Science Journal*, October 1967.
Quinn, J. B. 'Technological forecasting', *Harvard Business Review*, March/April 1967.

Models

Barclay, William D. 'Probability model for early prediction of new product market successes', *Journal of Marketing*, January 1963.
Barton, Samuel G. 'A marketing model for short-term prediction of consumer sales', *Journal of Marketing*, July 1965, pp. 19–29.
Bass, F. M. and Parsons, L. J. 'Simultaneous equation regression analysis of sales and advertising', *Applied Economics*, May 1969.
Bass, F. M., *et al. Mathematical Models and Methods in Marketing*, Irwin, 1961.
Duckworth, Eric. *A Guide to Operational Research*, Methuen, 1965.
Weiss, Doyle L. 'An analysis of the demand structure for branded consumer products', *Applied Economics*, January 1969.

Decision analysis and business systems

Kelley, William T. *Marketing Intelligence: the management of marketing information*, Staples Press, 1968.
Lindley, D. Y. *Making Decisions*, Wiley, 1971.
O'Brien, James J. *Management Information Systems*, Van Nostrand, 1970.
Raiffa, Howard. *Decision Analysis: introductory lectures on choices under uncertainty*, Addison-Wesley, 1970. An outstandingly clear introduction.

Index